Aman Ullah (Editor)

Semiparametric and Nonparametric Econometrics

With 12 Figures

Physica-Verlag Heidelberg

First published in "Empirical Economics"
Vol. 13, No. 3 and 4, 1988

ISBN 3-7908-0418-5 Physica-Verlag Heidelberg
ISBN 0-387-91350-5 Springer-Verlag New York

CIP-Kurztitelaufnahme der Deutschen Bibliothek

Semiparametric and nonparametric econometrics / Aman Ullah (ed.) - Heidelberg : Physica-Verl. ;
New York : Springer, 1989
(Studies in empirical economics)
ISBN 3-7908-0418-5 Physica-Verl.) Gb.
ISBN 0-387-91350-5 (Springer) Gb.
NE: Ullah, Aman [Hrsg.]

Printing: Kiliandruck, Grünstadt
Bookbinding: T. Gansert GmbH, Weinheim-Sulzbach
7100/7130-543210

Introduction

Over the last three decades much research in empirical and theoretical economics has been carried on under various assumptions. For example a parametric functional form of the regression model, the heteroskedasticity, and the autocorrelation is always assumed, usually linear. Also, the errors are assumed to follow certain parametric distributions, often normal. A disadvantage of parametric econometrics based on these assumptions is that it may not be robust to the slight data inconsistency with the particular parametric specification. Indeed any misspecification in the functional form may lead to erroneous conclusions. In view of these problems, recently there has been significant interest in the semiparametric/nonparametric approaches to econometrics.

The semiparametric approach considers econometric models where one component has a parametric and the other, which is unknown, a nonparametric specification (Manski 1984 and Horowitz and Neumann 1987, among others). The purely nonparametric approach, on the other hand, does not specify any component of the model a priori. The main ingredient of this approach is the data based estimation of the unknown joint density due to Rosenblatt (1956). Since then, especially in the last decade, a vast amount of literature has appeared on nonparametric estimation in statistics journals. However, this literature is mostly highly technical and this may partly be the reason why very little is known about it in econometrics, although see Bierens (1987) and Ullah (1988).

The focus of research in this volume is to develop the ways of making semiparametric and nonparametric techniques accessible to applied economists. With this in view the paper by Hartog and Bierens explore a nonparametric technique for estimating and testing an earning function with discrete explanatory variables. Raj and Siklos analyse the role of fiscal policy in St. Louis model using parametric and nonparametric techniques. Then there are papers on the nonparametric kernel estimators and their applications. For example, Hong and Pagan look into the performances of nonparametric kernel estimators for regression coefficient and heteroskedasticity. They also compare the behaviour of nonparametric estimators with the Fourier Series estimators. Another interesting application is the forecasting of U.S. Hog supply. This is by Moschini et al.

A systematic development of nonparametric procedure for estimation and testing is given in Ullah's paper. The important issue in the applications of nonparametric techniques is the selection of window-width. The Survey by Marron in this regard is extremely useful for the practioners as well as theoretical researchers. Scott also discusses this issue in his paper which deals with the analysis of income distribution by the histogram method.

Finally there are two papers on semiparametric econometrics. The paper by Horowitz studies various semiparametric estimators for censored regression models, and the paper by Tiwari et al. provides the Bayesian flavour to the semiparametric prediction problems.

The work on this volume was initiated after the first conference on semiparametric and nonparametric econometrics was held at the University of Western Ontario in May, 1987. Most of the contributors of this volume are the participants of this conference, though the papers contributed here are not necessarily the papers presented at the conference. I take this opportunity to thank all the contributors, discussants and reviewers without whose help this volume would not have taken the present form.

I am also thankful to M. Parkin for his enthusiastic support to the conference and other activities related to nonparametric econometrics. It was also a pleasure to coordinate the work on this volume with B. Raj, co-editor of *Empirical Economics*.

Aman Ullah
University of Western Ontario

References

Bierens H (1987) Kernel estimation of regression function. In Bewley TF (ed) Advances in econometrics. Cambridge University Press, New York, pp 99–144

Horowitz J, Newmann GR (1987) Semiparametric estimation of employment duration models. Econometric Reviews 5–40

Manski CF (1984) Adoptive estimation of nonlinear regression models. Econometric Reviews 3(2):149–194

Rosenblatt M (1956) Remarks on some nonparametric estimates of density function. Annals of Mathematical Statistics 27:832–837

Ullah A (1988) Nonparametric estimation of econometric functions. Canadian Journal of Economics 21:625–658

Contents

The Asymptotic Efficiency of Semiparametric Estimators for Censored Linear Regression Models[1]

By J. L. Horowitz[2]

Abstract: This paper presents numerical comparisons of the asymptotic mean square estimation errors of semiparametric generalized least squares (SGLS), quantile, symmetrically censored least squares (SCLS), and tobit maximum likelihood estimators of the slope parameters of censored linear regression models with one explanatory variable. The results indicate that the SCLS estimator is less efficient than the other two semiparametric estimators. The SGLS estimator is more efficient than quantile estimators when the tails of the distribution of the random component of the model are not too thick and the probability of censoring is not too large. The most efficient semiparametric estimators usually have smaller mean square estimation errors than does the tobit estimator when the random component of the model is not normally distributed and the sample size is $500-1,000$ or more.

1 Introduction

There are a variety of economic models in which data on the dependent variable is censored. For example, observations of the durations of spells of employment or the lifetimes of capital goods may be censored by the termination of data acquisition, in which case the dependent variables of models aimed at explaining these durations are censored. In models of labor supply, the quantity of labor supplied by an individual may be continuously distributed when positive but may have positive probability of being zero owing to the existence of corner-point solutions to the problem of choosing the quantity of labor that maximizes an individual's utility. Labor supply then follows a censored probability distribution.

---

[1] I thank Herman J. Bierens for comments on an earlier draft of this paper.
[2] Joel L. Horowitz, Department of Economics, University of Iowa, Iowa City, IA 52242, USA.

A typical model of the relation between a censored dependent variable y and a vector of explanatory variables x is

$$y = \max(0, \alpha + \beta x + u), \tag{1}$$

where α is a scalar constant, β is a vector of constant parameters, and u is random. The standard methods for estimating α and β, including maximum likelihood (Amemiya 1973) and two-stage methods (Heckman 1976, 1977) require the distribution of u to be specified *a priori* up to a finite set of constant parameters. Misspecification of this distribution causes the parameter estimates to be inconsistent. However, economic theory rarely gives guidance concerning the distribution of u, and the usual estimation techniques do not provide convenient methods for identifying the distribution from the data.

Recently, a variety of distribution-free or semiparametric methods for estimating β and, in some cases either α or the distribution of u, have been developed (Duncan 1986; Fernandez 1986; Horowitz 1986, 1988; Powell 1984, 1986a, b). These methods require the distribution of u to satisfy regularity conditions, but it need not be known otherwise. Among these methods, three – quantile estimation (Powell 1984, 1986b), symmetrically censored least squares (SCLS) estimation (Powell 1986a) and semiparametric M estimation (Horowitz 1988) – yield estimators of β that are $N^{1/2}$-consistent and asymptotically normal. These three methods permit the usual kinds of statistical inferences to be made while minimizing the possibility of obtaining inconsistent estimates of β due to misspecification of the distribution of u.

None of the known $N^{1/2}$-consistent semiparametric estimators achieves the asymptotic efficiency bound of Cosslett (1987). Intuition suggests that SCLS is likely to be less efficient than the other two, but precise information on the relative efficiencies of the different estimators is not available. In addition, limited empirical results (Horowitz and Neumann 1987) suggest that semiparametric estimation may entail a substantial loss of estimation efficiency relative to parametric maximum likelihood estimation. It is possible, therefore, that with samples of the sizes customarily encountered in applications, the use of semiparametric estimators causes a net increase in mean square estimation error relative to the use of a parametric estimator based on a misspecified model. However, precise information on the relative errors of parametric and semiparametric estimators is not available.

Expressions for the asymptotic mean square estimation errors of the various estimators are available, but their complexity precludes analytic comparisons of estimation errors, even for very simple models. Consequently, it is necessary to use numerical experiments to obtain insight into the relative efficiencies of the estimators. This paper reports the results of a group of such experiments. The experiments consist of evaluating numerically the asymptotic variances of three semiparametric estimators of the slope parameter β in a variety of censored linear regression models with one explanatory variable. The estimators considered are quantile estimators, semiparametric generalized least squares (SGLS) estimators (a special case of semiparametric M estimators), and SCLS estimators. The numerically determined variances of these estimators are compared with each other, with the Cosslett efficiency bound, and with an asymptotic approximation to the mean square estimation error of the maximum likelihood estimator of β based on correctly and erroneously specified distributions of the random error term u.

The next section describes the estimators used in the paper. Section 3 describes the models on which the numerical experiments were based and presents the results. Section 4 presents the conclusions of this research.

2 Description of the Estimators

It is assumed in the remainder of this paper that x and β are scalars, u is independent of x, and that estimation of α and β is based on a simple random sample $\{y_n, x_n : n = 1, ..., N\}$ of the variables (y, x) in equation (1).

a) Quantile Estimators

Let θ be any number such that $0 < \theta < 1$. Let $1(A)$ denote the indicator of the event A. That is, $1(A) = 1$ if A occurs and 0 otherwise. In quantile estimation based on the θ quantile, the estimators of α and β satisfy

$$[a_N(\theta), b_N(\theta)] = \arg\min N^{-1} \sum_{n=1}^{N} \rho_\theta[y_n - \max(0, a + bx_n)], \qquad (2)$$

where $a_N(\theta)$ and $b_N(\theta)$ are the estimators, and for any real z

$$\rho_\theta(z) \equiv [\theta - 1(z < 0)]z. \qquad (3)$$

This estimator can be understood intuitively as follows. Let u_θ denote the θ quantile of the distribution of u. Then $\max(0, u_\theta + \alpha + \beta x)$ is the θ quantile of y conditional on x. For any random variable z, $E\rho_\theta(z - \xi)$ is minimized over the parameter ξ by setting ξ equal to the θ quantile of the distribution of z. Therefore, $E\rho_\theta[y - \max(0,$

$u_\theta + a + bx)]$ is minimized with respect to (a, b) at $(a, b) = (\alpha, \beta)$. Quantile estimation consists of minimizing the sample analogue of $E\rho_\theta[y - \max(0, u_\theta + a + bx)]$.

Powell (1984, 1986b) has shown that subject to regularity conditions, $b_N(\theta)$ converges almost surely to β and $a_N(\theta)$ converges almost surely to $\alpha + u_\theta$. Moreover, $N^{1/2}[a_N(\theta) - \alpha - u_\theta, b_N(\theta) - \beta]'$ is asymptotically bivariate normally distributed with mean zero and covariance matrix $V_Q(\theta) = \omega(\theta)D^{-1}$, where

$$\omega(\theta) = \theta(1 - \theta)/[f(u_\theta)]^2, \tag{4}$$

f is the probability density function of u,

$$D(\theta) = E[1(\alpha + u_\theta + \beta x > 0)X'X], \tag{5}$$

and $X = (1, x)$. This paper is concerned exclusively with the (β, β) component of $V_Q(\theta)$ — that is, with the asymptotic variance of $N^{1/2}[b_N(\theta) - \beta]$.

b) The Semiparametric Generalized Least Squares Estimator

If the cumulative distribution function of u were known, β could be estimated by nonlinear generalized least squares (NGLS). Moreover, an asymptotically equivalent estimator could be obtained by taking one Newton step from any $N^{1/2}$-consistent estimator toward the NGLS estimator. When the cumulative distribution function of u is unknown, one might consider replacing it with a consistent estimator. The SGLS method consists, essentially, of carrying out one-step NGLS estimation after replacing the unknown distribution function with a consistent estimate.

To define the SGLS estimator precisely, let F denote the unknown cumulative distribution function of u, and let b_N be any $N^{1/2}$-consistent estimator of β. Given any scalar b, let $F_N(\cdot, b)$ denote the Kaplan-Meier (1958) estimator of F based on $y - bx$. In other words, $y_n - bx_n$ is treated as an estimate of the censored but unobservable random variable $y_n - \beta x_n$, and $F_N(\cdot, b)$ is the estimator of F that is obtained by applying the method of Kaplan and Meier (1958) to the sequence $\{y_n - bx_n\}$ $(n = 1, ..., N)$. Let $F(\cdot, b)$ denote the almost sure limit of $F_N(\cdot, b)$ as $N \to \infty$. It follows from the strong consistency of the Kaplan-Meier estimator based on $y - \beta x$ that $F(\cdot, \beta) = F(\cdot)$. For each b, let $F_b(\cdot, b) = \partial F(\cdot, b)/\partial b$, and let $F_{Nb}(\cdot, b)$ be the consistent estimator of $F_b(\cdot, b)$ defined by

$$F_{Nb}(u, b) = \frac{F_N(u, b + \delta b_N) - F(u, b)}{\delta b_N}, \tag{6}$$

where $\{\delta b_N\}$ is a sequence satisfying $\delta b_N \to 0$ and $|N^{1/2}\delta b_N| \to \infty$ as $N \to \infty$. For each y and x, define $\sigma_{y|x}^2$ as the variance of y conditional on x. That is

$$\sigma_{y|x}^2 = 2 \int_{-\beta x}^{\infty} u[1 - F(u)]du + 2\beta x \int_{-\beta x}^{\infty} [1 - F(u)]du$$

$$- \left\{ \int_{-\beta x}^{\infty} [1 - F(u)]du \right\}^2. \tag{7}$$

Let $s_{y|x}^2$ be the estimate of $\sigma_{y|x}^2$ that is obtained by substituting b_N and $F_N(\cdot, b_N)$ into equation (7) in place of β and F. For each y, x, and scalar b, define $\psi(y, x, b, F)$ by

$$\psi(y, x, b, F) = (1/\sigma_{y|x}^2) \left\{ y - \int_{-bx}^{\infty} [1 - F(u)]du \right\} [1 - F(-bx)]x. \tag{8}$$

Let ψ_N be the function obtained from ψ by replacing $F(\cdot)$ with $F_N(\cdot, b_N)$ and $\sigma_{y|x}^2$ with $s_{y|x}^2$. Let $H(\cdot)$ denote the cumulative distribution function of $y - \beta x$, and let $H_N(\cdot)$ denote the empirical distribution function of $y - b_N x$ based on the simple random sample $\{y_n, x_n\}$. For any $h > 0$, define the set X_h by

$$X_h = \{x : H(-\beta x) > h\}. \tag{9}$$

Let X_{Nh} denote the set obtained from X_h by replacing H with H_N and β with b_N. Finally, define λ by

$$\lambda = E\left\{ \frac{-x^2[1 - F(-\beta x)]^2 + x[1 - F(-\beta x)] \int_{-\beta x}^{\infty} F_b(u, \beta)du}{\sigma_{y|x}^2} \cdot 1(x \in X_h) \right\}, \tag{10}$$

where E denotes the expected value over the distribution of x. Let λ_N be the quantity obtained from (10) by replacing β with b_N, $F(\cdot)$ with $F_N(\cdot, b_N)$, $F_b(\cdot, \beta)$ with $F_{Nb}(\cdot, b_N)$, $\sigma_{y|x}^2$ with $s_{y|x}^2$, and the expected value with the sample average.

The SGLS estimator of β, β_N, is given by

$$\beta_N = b_N - \lambda_N^{-1} N^{-1} \sum_{n=1}^{N} \psi_N[y_n, x_n, b_N, F_N(\cdot, b_N)]1(x_n \in X_{Nh}). \tag{11}$$

The intercept α is not identified in SGLS estimation because no centering constraint is imposed on F. The estimate of α is subsumed in the location of the estimated distribution F_N. Accordingly, this paper is concerned exclusively with comparing the asymptotic variances of the quantile and SGLS estimators of β.

The SGLS estimator can be understood heuristically as follows. When $b = \beta$, the term in braces ({ }) in equation (8) is the expected value of y conditional on x. Therefore, if the functions $F(u, b)$ and $\sigma^2_{y|x}$ were known, the generalized least squares estimator of β would solve

$$N^{-1} \sum_{n=1}^{N} \psi[y_n, x_n, b, F(\cdot, b)] = 0. \tag{12}$$

Subject to regularity conditions, an asymptotically equivalent estimator could be obtained by taking one Newton step from any $N^{1/2}$-consistent estimator of β toward the solution of (12). The resulting estimator would be

$$\beta_N = b_N - (\lambda_N^*)^{-1} N^{-1} \sum_{n=1}^{N} \psi[y_n, x_n, b_N, F(\cdot, b_N)], \tag{13}$$

where λ_N^* is a consistent estimator of $\lambda^* = E_{yx} \partial \psi[y, x, \beta, F(\cdot, \beta)]/\partial b$. The SGLS estimator amounts to implementing this idea using consistent estimators for the unknown functions $F(u, b)$ and $\sigma^2_{y|x}$. Apart from the factor $1(x \in X_{Nh})$, λ_N is a consistent estimator of λ^*. $1(x \in X_{Nh})$ is included in λ_N and equation (11) because $N^{1/2}$-consistency of $F_N(u, b_N)$ as an estimator of $F(u)$ is guaranteed only if u is bounded away from $u_0 \equiv \inf \{u : H(u) > 0\}$ (Breslow and Crowley 1974). Inclusion of $1(x \in X_{Nh})$ in equation (11) and in λ_N implies that with probability 1, β_N does not depend on values of $F(u)$ or $F_N(u, b_N)$ for which u fails to satisfy this requirement.

Horowitz (1988) has shown that the SGLS estimator β_N converges almost surely to β. Moreover, $N^{1/2}(\beta_N - \beta)$ is asymptotically normally distributed with mean 0. The expression for the asymptotic variance of $N^{1/2}(\beta_N - \beta)$ is quite lengthy and requires additional notation. Let H^* denote the subdistribution function of uncensored values of $y - x\beta$:

$$H^*(u) = E[1(y - \beta x < u)1(y > 0)], \tag{14}$$

where the expectation is over the joint distribution of y and x. Given any y, x, and u, define $I_i(y, x, u)$ $(i = 1, ..., 4)$ by

$$I_1(y, x\ u) = F(u) \int_u^\infty \frac{1(y - \beta x < u') - H(u')}{[H(u')]^2} dH^*(u') \tag{15a}$$

$$I_2(y, x, u) = -F(u) \int_u^\infty \frac{1(y - \beta x < u')1(y > 0) - H^*(u')}{[H(u')]^2} dH(u') \tag{15b}$$

$$I_3(y, x, u) = F(u)\frac{1(y - \beta x < u)1(y > 0) - H^*(u)}{[H(u)]} \tag{15c}$$

$$I_4(y, x, u) = -F(u)[1(y > 0) - H^*(\infty)]. \tag{15d}$$

Let z be a random variable whose distribution is the same as that of x in equation (1), and define $D(y, x)$ by

$$D(y, x) = E_z \frac{z[1 - F(-\beta z)]1(z \in X_h)}{\sigma_{y|z}^2} \sum_{i=1}^4 \int_{-\beta z}^\infty I_i(y, x, u)du. \tag{16}$$

Let V_S denote the asymptotic variance of $N^{1/2}(\beta_N - \beta)$. It follows from Horowitz (1988) that

$$V_S = \lambda^{-2} E_{yx}[\psi(y, x, \beta, F)1(x \in X_h) + D(y, x)]^2, \tag{17}$$

where the expectation is over the joint distribution of y and x in equation (1). The ψ term in equation (17) represents the effects of sampling error in β_N when F is known, and the D term represents the effects of sampling error in F_N.

c) The Symmetrically Censored Least Squares Estimator

The SCLS estimator is given by

$$[a_N, b_N] = \arg\max \left[\sum_{n=1}^N [y_n - \max(y_n/2, a + bx)]^2 \right.$$

$$\left. + \sum_{n=1}^N 1[y_n > 2(a + bx_n)]\{(y_n/2)^2 - [\max(0, a + bx_n)]^2\} \right]. \tag{18}$$

Heuristically, this estimator amounts to applying ordinary least squares to a data set in which y_n is replaced by the "symmetrically censored" variable min $[y_n, 2(a + bx_n)]$ if $a + bx_n > 0$, and observation n is dropped otherwise. Powell (1986a) has shown that under regularity conditions, a_N and b_N converge almost surely to α and β. Moreover, $N^{1/2}(a_N - \alpha)$ and $N^{1/2}(b_N - \beta)$ are bivariate normally distributed with means of zero and covariance matrix $V_T = C^{-1}DC^{-1}$, where

$$C = E[1(-\alpha - \beta x < u < \alpha + \beta x)X'X], \tag{20}$$

and

$$D = E\{1(\alpha + \beta x > 0) \min [u^2, (\alpha + \beta x)^2]X'X\}. \tag{21}$$

d) Maximum Likelihood Estimation

Suppose u in equation (1) is distributed as $N(0, \sigma^2)$. Then the log-likelihood of the sample $\{y_n, x_n\}$ is

$$\log L(a, b, s^2) = \sum_{n=1}^{N} \log l(y_n, x_n; a, b, s^2), \tag{22}$$

where

$$l(y, x; a, b, s^2) = (1/s)\phi\left(\frac{y - a - bx}{s}\right)1(y > 0)$$

$$+ \Phi\left(\frac{y - a - bx}{s}\right)1(y = 0) \tag{23}$$

and ϕ and Φ, respectively, are the standard normal density and cumulative distribution functions. As is well known, the maximum likelihood estimators a_N, b_N and s_N^2 of α, β and σ^2 are strongly consistent, and $N^{1/2}(a_N - \alpha)$, $N^{1/2}(b_N - \beta)$ and $N^{1/2}(s_N^2 - \sigma^2)$ are asymptotically multivariate normally distributed with means of zero and a covariance matrix given by the inverse of the information matrix.

If u is not normally distributed, maximum likelihood estimation using the log likelihood function of (22) and (23) yields inconsistent parameter estimates. Therefore, $E[N(b_N - \beta)^2] \to \infty$ as $N \to \infty$. To obtain an asymptotic approximation to the mean square estimation error when the distribution of u is misspecified, suppose that the true cumulative distribution of u is $F(u; \sigma^2, v)$, where v is a (possibly vector-valued) parameter, F is a continuous function of v for each u and σ^2, and $F(u; \sigma^2, 0) = \Phi(u/\sigma)$. Let $\{v_N : N = 1, 2, ...\}$ be a sequence of v values such that $v_N \to 0$ and $N^{1/2} v_N = O(1)$ as $N \to \infty$. For each N, let $\{y_n, x_n\}$ be sampled from equation (1) with $u \sim F(u; \sigma^2, v_N)$. Define β_N^* as the value of b obtained by maximizing $E[\log l(y, x; a, b, s^2)]$, where l is as defined in (23) and the expectation is calculated under the assumption that u is distributed as $F(u; \sigma^2, v_N)$. Let $V_{\beta\beta}$ denote the (β, β) component of the inverse of the information matrix based on the log likelihood (22). Then it follows from Silvey (1959) that when b_N is obtained by maximizing (22), $N^{1/2}(b_N - \beta)$ is asymptotically normally distributed with mean $N^{1/2}(\beta_N^* - \beta)$ and variance $V_{\beta\beta}$. Thus, the asymptotic mean square estimation error is

$$\text{MSE} = N(\beta_N^* - \beta)^2 + V_{\beta\beta}. \tag{24}$$

3 The Experiments and Their Results

The experiments described in this section were carried out to compare $V_Q(\theta)$, V_S, V_T and MSE for various values of θ and specifications of the distribution of u. In computing MSE, it was assumed that β was estimated using the log likelihood function (23), even if the true distribution of u was not normal. This assumption reflects the situation in most applications, where the distribution of u is unknown and, therefore, the log likelihood function is misspecified unless, by accident, u has the assumed distribution. Thus, when the true distribution of u is non-normal, MSE indicates the error made by using a misspecified parametric model to estimate β. When the true distribution of u is normal, the differences between MSE and V_Q, V_S and V_T indicate the losses of asymptotic efficiency entailed in using estimators that are robust against misspecification of the distribution of u.

a) Design

The experiments are based on the model

$$y = \max(0, x + u). \tag{25}$$

This is the model of equation (1) with $\alpha = 0$ and $\beta = 1$. In each experiment, x has the beta $(3, 3)$ distribution on the interval $[-1 + \Delta, 1 + \Delta]$, where the real number Δ varies among experiments to achieve different probabilities that y is censored. The distribution of u is a mixture of symmetrically truncated normals. That is,

$$F = \gamma N_T(\mu_1, \sigma_1^2) + (1 - \gamma)N_T(\mu_2, \sigma_2^2), \tag{26}$$

where $N_T(\mu, \sigma^2)$ denote the cumulative distribution function obtained by symmetrically truncating the normal (μ, σ^2) distribution at $\mu \pm 4\sigma$, and γ is between 0 and 1. The values of the μ's, σ's and γ were selected to achieve different values of the variance, skewness, and kurtosis of the mixture. The mean of the distribution of u is 0 in all of the experiments. The normal distributions used in the mixtures are truncated to satisfy a regularity condition of Horowitz (1988) that requires the distribution of u to have bounded support.

Table 1 shows the parameters of the distributions used in the experiments. Experiments 1–12 involve varying the kurtosis of F while keeping the variance constant and the skewness equal to zero. For each value of the kurtosis, there are experiments with censoring probabilities of (roughly) 0.15, 0.50, and 0.85. Experiments 13–21 together with 1–3 involve varying the variance of F while holding the kurtosis and skewness constant at 0. At each value of the variance, there are experiments with censoring probabilities of approximately 0.15, 0.50, and 0.85. Experiments 22–24 involve a skewed distribution with nearly zero kurtosis. The number of experiments with skewed distributions is limited by the difficulty of creating skewed mixtures of normals with kurtosis close to 0.

In each experiment, the (β, β) components of $V_Q(\theta)$, V_S, V_T, and MSE were computed numerically. MSE was evaluated using the asymptotic approximation (24).

Table 1. Parameters of the Distributions of X and U*

Exp't	γ	Δ	μ_1	σ_1^2	μ_2	σ_2^2	σ^2	S	κ	P_c
1	1.0	0.0	0.0	0.25	0.0	0.25	0.25	0.0	0.0	0.50
2	1.0	0.65	0.0	0.25	0.0	0.25	0.25	0.0	0.0	0.15
3	1.0	-0.65	0.0	0.25	0.0	0.25	0.25	0.0	0.0	0.85
4	0.9615	0.0	0.0	0.20	0.0	1.50	0.25	0.0	3.0	0.50
5	0.9615	0.60	0.0	0.20	0.0	1.50	0.25	0.0	3.0	0.16
6	0.9615	-0.60	0.0	0.20	0.0	1.50	0.25	0.0	3.0	0.84
7	0.9260	0.0	0.0	0.15	0.0	1.50	0.25	0.0	6.0	0.50
8	0.9260	0.60	0.0	0.15	0.0	1.50	0.25	0.0	6.0	0.15
9	0.9260	-0.60	0.0	0.15	0.0	1.50	0.25	0.0	6.0	0.85
10	0.8621	0.0	0.0	0.05	0.0	1.50	0.25	0.0	12.0	0.50
11	0.8621	0.55	0.0	0.05	0.0	1.50	0.25	0.0	12.0	0.14
12	0.8621	-0.55	0.0	0.05	0.0	1.50	0.25	0.0	12.0	0.86
13	1.0	0.0	0.0	0.125	0.0	0.125	0.125	0.0	0.0	0.50
14	1.0	0.55	0.0	0.125	0.0	0.125	0.125	0.0	0.0	0.15
15	1.0	-0.55	0.0	0.125	0.0	0.125	0.125	0.0	0.0	0.95
16	1.0	0.0	0.0	0.41	0.0	0.41	0.41	0.0	0.0	0.50
17	1.0	0.80	0.0	0.41	0.0	0.41	0.41	0.0	0.0	0.14
18	1.0	-0.80	0.0	0.41	0.0	0.41	0.41	0.0	0.0	0.86
19	1.0	0.0	0.0	1.0	0.0	1.0	1.0	0.0	0.0	0.50
20	1.0	1.10	0.0	1.0	0.0	1.0	1.0	0.0	0.0	0.15
21	1.0	-1.10	0.0	1.0	0.0	1.0	1.0	0.0	0.0	0.85
22	0.70	-0.10	-0.12	0.05	1.08	0.25	0.41	1.12	0.02	0.49
23	0.70	0.48	-0.12	0.05	1.08	0.25	0.41	1.12	0.02	0.15
24	0.70	-1.10	-0.12	0.05	1.08	0.25	0.41	1.12	0.02	0.85

* Definitions of symbols: γ, Δ, μ_1, σ_1^2, μ_2, and σ_2^2 are as defined in Equation (26). σ^2, S, and κ, respectively, are the variance, skewness, and kurtosis of the distribution of u. P_c is the probability that y is censored.

b) The Relative Asymptotic Variances of the Three Semiparametric Estimators

The values of the (β, β) components of $V_Q(\theta)$, V_S and V_T obtained in the experiments are shown in Table 2. The table also shows the Cosslett asymptotic efficiency bound on the variance of $N^{1/2}(b_N - \beta)$ for each experiment. The asymptotic variances of the quantile estimators were computed for the $0.05, 0.10, ..., 0.90$, and 0.95 quantiles. However, only the variances corresponding to the 0.50 quantile (the least-absolute-deviations (LAD) estimator) and the most efficient quantile among those evaluated are reported.

The results show, not surprisingly, that the asymptotic variances of all the estimators increase as the censoring probability increases and as the variance of u increases, other parameters remaining constant. In all but two experiments, the most efficient quantile is above the median. This result, which has been observed in other numerical experiments (Horowitz 1986), occurs because with left-censoring, there are more data available for quantile estimation at high quantiles than at low ones.

None of the estimators achieves the Cosslett efficiency bound. The variance of the SGLS estimator is close to the bound when the distribution of u is normal or close to normal and there is little censoring. The asymptotic variances of the quantile and SCLS estimators are well above the Cosslett bound, as are those of the SGLS estimator when the distribution of u is far from normal or there is a high probability of censoring.

The SCLS estimator is less efficient than SGLS in every experiment, and SCLS is less efficient than the most efficient quantile estimator in all but three experiments. The variance of the SCLS estimator exceeds that of the SGLS estimator by a factor of roughly 1.10 to over 1,000, depending on the experiment. The relative efficiency of SCLS decreases as the probability of censoring increases. None of these results is surprising. The SCLS estimator discards information by artificially censoring low values of y so as to symmetrize the distribution of y conditional on x. The probability that an observation is artificially censored and, therefore, the severity of the information loss increases as the probability of true censoring increases. The other semiparametric estimators do not sacrifice information in this way.

The LAD estimator is either less efficient than the SGLS estimator or unidentified in 21 of the 24 experiments. Some of the differences between the variances of the two estimators are very large. For example, in experiment 3, the variance of the LAD estimator exceeds that of the SGLS estimator by approximately a factor of 79, and in experiment 18, the LAD variance exceeds the SGLS variance by more than a factor of 9,000. The efficiency of the LAD estimator in comparison with the SGLS estimator is lowest when the censoring probability is 0.85, but the efficiency of LAD also is low in several of the experiments with a censoring probability of 0.50. For example, in experiments 1, 16, and 19 the LAD variance is more than 5 times the SGLS variance.

Table 2. Asymptotic Variances of the Semiparametric Estimators of β

Exp't	GLS	LAD[1]	Most Eff. Quantile	θ[1]	SCLS	Cosslett Bound
1	3.23	17.37	5.97	0.85	18.26	3.02
2	1.96	3.29	2.97	0.65	2.81	1.93
3	25.26	1984.20	26.55	0.95	2727.3	9.52
4	3.91	14.66	5.68	0.85	15.38	2.78
5	1.86	2.95	2.61	0.65	2.66	1.71
6	135.96	894.44	28.02	0.95	1167.9	9.62
7	4.16	11.64	5.34	0.80	12.35	2.45
8	1.73	2.34	2.11	0.65	2.25	1.38
9	172.72	714.04	35.12	0.90	908.6	10.89
10	4.56	4.54	3.20	0.75	5.90	1.37
11	1.03	0.97	0.91	0.60	1.45	0.55
12	59.58	164.67	37.27	0.85	187.9	10.72
13	1.95	8.69	4.08	0.85	8.38	1.82
14	1.05	1.90	1.67	0.70	1.57	1.00
15	13.26	302.30	21.79	0.95	364.2	7.35
16	4.94	29.03	8.02	0.80	31.91	4.50
17	3.22	4.80	4.67	0.55	3.94	3.09
18	52.81	4.94×10^5	33.87	0.95	74659.	13.14
19	10.61	69.52	14.64	0.80	86.69	9.84
20	7.54	11.00	11.00	0.50	8.46	7.43
21	137.44	N.I.[2]	43.49	0.95	N.I[2]	22.57
22	9.76	14.00	13.23	0.90	N.A.[3]	3.01
23	4.58	2.25	2.00	0.40	N.A.[3]	0.84
24	26.04	N.I[2]	23.84	0.95	N.A.[3]	13.09

[1] LAD is the least absolute deviations (0.50 quantile) estimator. θ denotes the quantile corresponding to the most efficient quantile estimator.

[2] The estimator is not identified.

[3] The SCLS estimator is inconsistent and was not evaluated.

The LAD estimator performs best in comparison to SGLS when the censoring probability is 0.15. Among the experiments with this censoring probability, the LAD variance does not exceed the SGLS variance by more than a factor of 1.8.

The ratio of the LAD variance to the SGLS variance decreases as the kurtosis of F increases if the other parameters of F and the censoring probability are held constant. This is to be expected since SGLS is basically a method of moments estimator and, therefore, is likely to be sensitive to outliers in the data.

There are three experiments in which the variance of the LAD estimator is less than that of the SGLS estimator. In two of these (experiments 10 and 11), the kurtosis of F is 12, the highest kurtosis included in the experiments. In these experiments, however, the differences between the SGLS and LAD variances are less than 6 percent. The difference between the variances of the two estimators is more substantial in experiment 23, where F is skewed. In this experiment, the SGLS variance is approximately double the LAD variance.

Now consider the most efficient quantile (MEQ) estimator. There are 15 experiments in which the MEQ variance exceeds the SGLS variance and 9 experiments in which the opposite is the case. The ratio of the MEQ variance to the SGLS variance tends to be highest when the censoring probability is 0.50 and lowest when the censoring probability is 0.85, other parameters remaining constant, but this pattern does not hold in all of the experiments. There are two sets of experiments (10−12 and 19−21) in which the highest ratio occurs with a censoring probability of 0.15 and two (13−15 and 22−24) in which the lowest ratio occurs with this censoring probability.

There are 12 experiments (1−3 and 13−21) in which F is normal. In 10 of these, the SGLS estimator is more efficient than the MEQ estimator. The ratio of the MEQ variance to the SGLS variance varies from 1.05 to 2.09 in these experiments. In experiments 18 and 21 F is normal and the MEQ variance is less than the SGLS variance. In both of these experiments, the probability of censoring is 0.85. The SGLS variance exceeds the MEQ variance by 56 percent in experiment 18 and by a factor of 3.16 in experiment 21.

The ratio of the MEQ variance to the SGLS variance tends to decrease as the kurtosis of F increases, other parameters remaining constant. Experiment 12 is the only exception to this pattern. When the censoring probability is 0.15 or 0.50, the SGLS estimator is more efficient than the MEQ estimator through a kurtosis of 6 and less efficient at a kurtosis of 12. The SGLS estimator is less efficient than the MEQ estimator in all of the positive-kurtosis experiments with a censoring probability of 0.85. Depending on the experiment, the variance of the SGLS estimator exceeds the variance of the MEQ estimator by up to a factor of 5 when the censoring probability is 0.85.

In experiments 22−24, where F is skewed, the SGLS variance is less than the MEQ variance when the censoring probability is 0.49 and larger than the MEQ variance

Table 3. Mean Square Estimation Errors of Semiparametric and Maximum Likelihood Estimators

Exp't	MSE of Most Efficient Semiparametric Estimator	β_N^{*1}	MSE of Maximum Likelihood Estimator when		
			N=500	N=1000	N=1500
1	3.23	1.00	2.94	2.94	2.94
2	1.96	1.00	1.91	1.91	1.91
3	25.26	1.00	9.33	9.33	9.33
4	3.91	1.03	3.49	4.05	4.61
5	1.86	1.01	1.77	1.78	1.80
6	28.02	1.11	16.51	22.31	28.11
7	4.16	1.08	5.92	8.83	11.74
8	1.73	1.01	1.63	1.70	1.77
9	35.12	1.23	41.09	66.70	92.31
10	3.20	1.21	26.03	48.93	71.84
11	0.91	1.03	1.80	2.36	2.92
12	37.27	1.46	136.58	244.58	352.59
13	1.95	1.00	1.80	1.80	1.80
14	1.05	1.00	1.00	1.00	1.00
15	13.26	1.00	7.33	7.33	7.33
16	4.94	1.00	4.35	4.35	4.35
17	3.22	1.00	3.06	3.06	3.06
18	33.87	1.00	12.69	12.69	12.69
19	10.61	1.00	9.43	9.43	9.43
20	7.54	1.00	7.35	7.35	7.35
21	43.49	1.00	21.02	21.02	21.02
22	9.76	1.16	19.03	31.05	43.08
23	2.00	1.22	10.54	18.01	25.48
24	23.84	0.89	21.44	27.79	34.13

[1] β_N^* is the almost sure limit of the maximum likelihood estimator of β. The true value of β is 1.0.

when the censoring probability is 0.15 or 0.85. The ratio of the MEQ variance to the SGLS variance is 1.36 when the censoring probability is 0.50, 0.44 when the censoring probability is 0.15, and 0.92 when the censoring probability is 0.85.

c) The Relative Asymptotic Mean Square Estimation Errors of Semiparametric and Quasi Maximum Likelihood Estimators

Table 3 shows the mean square errors of the most efficient semiparametric estimator of β (that is, either SGLS or the most efficient quantile estimator) and the maximum likelihood estimator. The maximum likelihood estimator is based on the assumption that the distribution of u is normal, so it is inconsistent in experiments where u is not normally distributed. Accordingly, Table 3 includes the value of β_N^*, the almost sure limit of the maximum likelihood estimator, for each experiment.

In experiments 1–3 and 13–21 u is normally distributed, so the maximum likelihood estimator is more efficient than the most efficient semiparametric estimator. However, the differences between the mean square errors of the semiparametric and maximum likelihood estimators are very small (less than 15 percent) when the probability of censoring is 0.15 or 0.50. The mean square error of the most efficient semiparametric estimator exceeds that of the maximum likelihood estimator by roughly a factor of 2–3 when the probability of censoring is 0.85.

In experiments 4–12 and 22–24, the distribution of u is non-normal, so the maximum likelihood estimators are based on a misspecified model. In all of these experiments except 5, 6 and 8, the mean square error of the maximum likelihood estimator exceeds that of the most efficient semiparametric estimator when the sample size is in the range 500–1,000 or above. In experiments 5 and 8, the mean square error of the most efficient semiparametric estimator is only slightly larger than that of the maximum likelihood estimator with sample sizes of 500–1,000. Not surprisingly, the ratio of the mean square error of the maximum likelihood estimator to that of the most efficient semiparametric estimator increases as the departure of u from normality increases. Thus, for example, with a sample size of 1,000, the maximum likelihood estimator is either more accurate or only slightly less accurate than the most efficient semiparametric estimator in experiments 4–6, where the distribution of u has a kurtosis of 3. But in experiments 10–12, where the kurtosis is 12, the mean square error of the maximum likelihood estimator exceeds that of the most efficient semiparametric estimator by a factor of 2.6–15, depending on the probability of censoring.

4 Conclusions

As is always the case with numerical experiments, it is not clear how far the results presented here can be generalized. However, certain patterns that may have some generality are present.

First, the SCLS estimator is always less efficient than the SGLS estimator and usually is less efficient than the most efficient quantile estimator. The loss of efficiency by SCLS tends to be quite large unless the probability of censoring is low.

The SGLS estimator appears to be more efficient than the most efficient quantile estimator when the tails of the distribution of u are not too thick (that is, the kurtosis of the distribution of u is not too high) and the probability of censoring not too large. In the experiments with symmetric distributions of u, the variance of the SGLS estimator exceeds that of the most efficient quantile estimator only when the kurtosis of the distribution of u is 12 or the probability of censoring is 0.85. In the experiments with high kurtosis or high probability of censoring, however, the variance of the SGLS estimator can be several times the variance of the most efficient quantile estimator.

The variance of the LAD estimator is usually larger than that of the most efficient quantile estimator and is especially large when the probability of censoring is high. Consequently, SGLS tends to be more efficient than LAD, regardless of the probability of censoring, when the tails of the distribution of u are not too thick.

Only one skewed distribution of u is included in the experiments reported here, so it is not possible to reach conclusions concerning the effects of skewness on the relative efficiencies of SGLS and quantile estimators. With the skewed distribution, the most efficient quantile estimator is more efficient than the SGLS estimator when the censoring probability is 0.15 or 0.85, and the LAD estimator is more efficient than SGLS when the censoring probability is 0.15. These results suggest that skewness may have an important effect on the relative efficiencies of SGLS and quantile estimators. This effect might be a useful topic for future research.

Finally, the mean square estimation error of the most efficient semiparametric estimator (among those considered in this paper) tends to be less than that of the maximum likelihood estimator when the latter estimator is based on a misspecified distribution of u and the sample size is in the range 500–1,000 or more. Even if the maximum likelihood estimator is based on a correctly specified model, the loss of efficiency due to the use of the most efficient semiparametric estimator is small unless the probability of censoring is high. These results are based on asymptotic approximations whose accuracy in finite samples is unknown. Nonetheless, they suggest that the use of semiparametric estimation methods is likely to be advantageous with sample sizes in the range frequently encountered in applications.

References

Amemiya T (1973) Regression analysis when the dependent variable is truncated normal. Econometrica 41:997–1016

Breslow N, Crowley J (1974) A large sample study of the life table and product limit estimates under random censoring. The Annals of Statistics 2:437–453

Cosslett SR (1987) Efficiency bounds for distribution-free estimators of the binary choice and the censored models. Econometrica 55:559–585

Duncan GM (1986) A Semiparametric censored regression estimator. Journal of Econometrics 32:5–34

Fernandez L (1986) Nonparametric maximum likelihood estimation of censored regression models. Journal of Econometrics 32:35–57

Heckman J (1976) The common structure of statistical models of truncation, sample selection, and limited dependent variables and a simple estimator. Annals of Economic and Social Measurement 5:475–492

Heckman J (1979) Sample selection bias as a specification error. Econometrica 47:53–162

Horowitz JL (1986) A distribution-free least squares estimator for censored linear regression models. Journal of Econometrics 32:59–84

Horowitz JL (1988) Semiparametric M estimation of censored linear regression models. Advances in Econometrics: Robust and Nonparametric Statistical Inference 7 (forthcoming)

Horowitz JL, Neumann GR (1987) Semiparametric estimation of employment duration models. Econometric Reviews 6:5–40

Kaplan EL, Meier P (1958) Nonparametric estimation from incomplete observations. Journal of the American Statistical Association 53:457–481

Powell JL (1986a) Symmetrically trimmed least squares estimation for tobit models. Econometrica 54:1435–1460

Powell JL (1986b) Censored regression quantiles. Journal of Econometrics 32:143–155

Powell JL (1984) Least absolute deviations estimation for the censored regression model. Journal of Econometrics 25:303–325

Silvey SD (1959) The lagrangian multiplier test. Annals of Mathematical Statistics 30:389–407

Nonparametric Kernel Estimation Applied to Forecasting: An Evaluation Based on the Bootstrap

By G. Moschini[1], D. M. Prescott[2] and T. Stengos[2]

Abstract: The results reported in this paper lend support to the nonparametric approach to estimating regression functions. This conclusion is based on a comparison of two sets of eight quarterly forecasts of U.S. hog supply generated by a well specified parametric dynamic model and by non-parametric kernel estimation. Despite the relatively small sample size, the nonparametric point forecasts are found to be as accurate as the parametric forecasts according to the mean square error and mean absolute error criteria. Bootstrap resampling is used to estimate the distributions of the forecast errors. The results of this exercise favour the nonparametric forecasts, which are found to have a tighter distribution.

1 Introduction

In recent years, econometricians have shown increasing interest in nonparametric approaches to estimation and statistical testing. Traditionally, the estimation of economic models and the testing of hypotheses has been conducted in the context of parametric, and frequently linear parametric models. Many critical assumptions are embodied in parametric specifications of economic models. While these assumptions add structure to the model and typically reduce the variance of parameter estimates, there is always the risk that the parameterization is inappropriate with the result that estimators will be biased and inferences invalid. Over the years, considerable advances have been made in the development of more flexible parametric models that impose fewer restrictions on the data, see for example, Lau (1986). However, as White (1980) has pointed out, all of these parametric models suffer from a number of statistical drawbacks.

As Ullah (1987) has discussed, the nonparametric approach makes few assumptions about the structure of the data generating process under investigation. As such,

---

[1]   Giancarlo Moschini, Department of Economics, Iowa State University, USA.
[2]   David M. Prescott and Thanasis Stengos, Department of Economics, University of Guelph, Canada.

The authors are grateful to Aman Ullah for his very helpful comments on this paper. However, the authors remain responsible for any errors and limitations.

this approach to estimation and inference is less likely to suffer from specification error. In addition, nonparametric methods can focus directly on the issue at hand, obviating the need to estimate "nuisance" parameters. For example, it is not necessary to estimate derivatives in order to generate forecasts. Only direct estimates of the conditional mean are required. On the other hand, since less structure is supplied by the investigator, nonparametric methods place more emphasis on the information contained in the data themselves. Not surprisingly, for nonparametric methods to yield precise statistical inferences, larger data sets are typically required.

The purpose of the present paper is to apply the nonparametric approach to the problems of regression estimation and forecasting. The method is illustrated with an application to a dynamic model of U.S. hog supply. Out-of-sample nonparametric forecasts are compared to those obtained from a linear parametric model. By conventional standards, the linear model gives an excellent representation of the hog supply process and therefore it provides a realistic benchmark against which the nonparametric model can be evaluated. The nonparametric and parametric forecasts are evaluated on the basis of two criteria. First, eight quarterly out-of-sample point forecasts are compared to the actual levels of hog supply in the forecast period. Second, the distributions of the forecast errors are compared by bootstrapping the two alternative models.

In the next section we describe the nonparametric methods that we used to estimate the model of hog supply and to generate the out-of-sample point forecasts. In Section 3 we present the results of estimating a conventional linear parametric model of hog supply. In Section 4, we compare the parametric and nonparametric forecasts and their standard errors, as computed by the bootstrap technique. The details of the bootstrap resampling procedures that we use to simulate the distributions of the OLS and nonparametric forecast errors are presented in the Appendix.

2 Nonparametric Estimation

The notation in this section follows that of Ullah (1987). Let $(y_i, x_{i1}, ..., x_{ip})$, $i = 1, ..., n$ be the i-th independently and identically distributed observation from an absolutely continuous $p + 1$ variate distribution with density $f(y, x_1, ..., x_p) = f(y, x)$. The conditional mean of y given x can be written as $M(x) = E(y|x)$. In parametric estimation, $M(x)$ is typically assumed to be linear in x but, in the nonparametric approach, $M(x)$ remains a general functional form. The conditional mean of y can be expressed as

$$E(y|x) = M(x) = \int y \frac{f(y, x)}{f_1(x)} dy \qquad (1)$$

where $f_1(x)$ is the marginal density of x. Investigators are frequently interested in estimating the first derivatives of $M(x)$ with respect to x_j. This problem is considered by Ullah and Vinod (1987) and Rilstone and Ullah (1987). However, in the non-parametric framework it is not necessary to estimate these derivatives in order to compute forecasts. Forecasts are estimated directly by constructing an empirical counterpart to (1).

Silverman (1986) discusses the use of nonparametric methods to the estimation of density functions. Consider first the estimation of the univariate density function $f(z)$ using the random sample $z_1, ..., z_n$. Let $\hat{F}(z)$ be the empirical cumulative distribution function defined as the proportion of the sample values that are less than or equal to z. An estimate of the density function $f(z)$ can be obtained from

$$\hat{f}(z) = \frac{\hat{F}(z + h/2) - \hat{F}(z - h/2)}{h}$$

for small values of h, or

$$\hat{f}(z) = (hn)^{-1} \sum_{t=1}^{n} I\left(\frac{z - z_t}{h}\right) \tag{2}$$

where

$$I(\ ) = 1 \quad \text{if} \quad -\frac{1}{2} < \frac{z - z_t}{z} < \frac{1}{2}$$

$$= 0 \quad \text{otherwise}$$

The estimate $\hat{f}(z)$ described by (2) has the significant deficiency that it is not smooth; spikes and potholes are likely to characterize $\hat{f}(z)$, especially where the data are sparse. The family of kernel estimators, introduced by Rosenblatt (1956), attempts to correct this problem:

$$\hat{f}(z) = (nh)^{-1} \sum_{t=1}^{n} K\left(\frac{z - z_t}{h}\right) \tag{3}$$

where the kernel function K satisfies certain conditions, including:

$$K(z^*) \geq 0, \quad \int K(z^*)dz^* = 1, \quad \int z^* K(z^*)dz^* = 0, \quad \text{for } z^* = (z - z_t)/h \tag{4}$$

Since it is possible to choose the function K so that it is continuous, the resulting kernel estimator of the density function will also be continuous. In the present paper, the kernel is chosen to be the standard multivariate normal density function, which assigns a positive weight to every observation in the sample when estimating the point, $f(z)$. The largest weights are attached to the observations closest to the point z. Unlike the histogram estimator (2), the kernel estimator uses information on each side of a spike or a pothole to flatten spikes and fill in potholes. Clearly, the choice of the kernel and the window width h determine the degree of smoothness imposed on $\hat{f}(z)$. If the kernel function K is very flat, all data in the sample receive similar weights in the estimation of $f(z)$ and this imposes a high degree of smoothing. Similarly, if the window width h is large, the estimation of $f(z)$ draws in distant data points and this also has a smoothing effect.

Regarding statistical properties, Ullah (1987) has surveyed the extensive literature which provides results on the consistency and asymptotic normality of the kernel estimator. These conditions for asymptotic normality include the requirement that the window width, h, tend to zero as the sample size tends to infinity.

We now return to the multivariate case $f(y, x)$ where y is a scalar and x is $1xp$. The kernel estimator of the joint density is

$$\hat{f}(y, x) = n^{-1} h^{-(p+1)} \sum_{t=1}^{n} K\left(\frac{y - y_t}{h}, \frac{x - x_t}{h}\right)$$

Similarly, the estimator for the marginal distribution of x is

$$\hat{f}(x) = n^{-1} h^{-p} \sum_{t=1}^{n} K_2\left(\frac{x - x_t}{h}\right)$$

where $K_2(x^*) = \int K(y^*, x^*) dy^*$. Again, the asterisk denotes the transformation $y^* = (y - y_t)/h$, in which y_t is considered fixed. Similar transformations apply to the elements of x. Using equation (1), which defines the conditional expectation of y given x, it is natural to define the nonparametric estimator of the regression function to be

$$\hat{E}(y \mid x) = \int y \hat{f}(y \mid x) dy$$

$$= \frac{h^{-1}}{\sum K_2\left(\frac{x - x_t}{h}\right)} \int \left\{ y \sum K\left(\frac{y - y_t}{h}, \frac{x - x_t}{h}\right) \right\} dy$$

$$= \frac{h^{-1}}{\sum K_2\left(\frac{x - x_t}{h}\right)} \sum \int (y_t + hy^*) K(y^*, x^*) h dy^*$$

After evaluating the integral and assuming that $\int y^* K(y^*, x^*) dy^* = 0$, the nonparametric estimator of the regression function can be written as

$$\hat{E}(y|x) = \frac{1}{\Sigma K_2\left(\dfrac{x-x_t}{h}\right)} \; \Sigma y_t K_2\left(\frac{x-x_t}{h}\right)$$

$$\hat{E}(y|x) = \Sigma y_t r_t \tag{5}$$

where

$$r_t = K_2\left(\frac{x-x_t}{h}\right) / \Sigma K_2\left(\frac{x-x_t}{h}\right)$$

Expression (5) can be evaluated at any value of x to yield the nonparametric estimator of the regression function. Clearly, out-of-sample forecasts, conditional on a set of known x values, can be calculated using (5).

In applications, the investigator must choose the window width h as well as the kernel function. The choice of the window width is important since bias is an increasing function of h while variance is a decreasing function of h. Ullah (1987) points out that the mean square error optimal value of h is proportional to $n^{-1/(4+p)}$. In the case of the multivariate normal, the factor of proportionality is a function of the standard deviations of the elements of x, see Singh and Ullah (1985). Since our explanatory variables do not have the same variances, we choose a separate window width for each explanatory variable:

$$h_i = c_i n^{-1/(p+4)}, \quad \text{for } i = 1, \ldots, p$$

where c_i is the standard deviation of x_i.

Another issue is the treatment of seasonality. In the present paper all series are deseasonalized by least squares methods. To construct quarterly forecasts that are comparable to the original series of hog supply, the quarterly adjustment factors are added to the OLS and nonparametric forecasts. Thus, both forecasting methods employ the same seasonal factors.

3 A Model of U.S. Hog Supply

To illustrate the use of nonparametric estimation to forecasting we present a relatively simple model of U.S. hog supply using quarterly data over the period 1961 to 1984. Studies of the hog sector have shown that hog supply depends on expectations of hog prices, feedgrain prices and seasonality, see for example Martin and Zwart (1975). A linear parametric model that is consistent with this general hypothesis is the following:

$$S_t = \beta_1 PRC_{t-4} + \beta_2 PRH_{t-4} + \beta_3 S_{t-1} + \epsilon_t \tag{6}$$

where S_t is hog production in quarter t, PRC_{t-4} is the relative price of corn in quarter $t-4$ and PRH_{t-4} is the relative price of hogs in quarter $t-4$. These series are published by the U.S. Department of Agriculture. Relative prices are calculated by deflating nominal prices by the consumer price index (U.S. Department of Commerce). The lagged dependent variable allows for the possibility that current supply depends on a long history of corn and hog prices. The final term, ϵ_t, is the random disturbance term for quarter t. The disturbance terms are assumed to be identically and independently distributed with a zero mean and a finite variance. Note that no intercept or quarterly dummy variables are included in equation (6), which reflects the fact that all data series were deseasonalized by a least squares procedure before (6) was fitted.

The supply equation was estimated by OLS using ninety-six quarterly observations spanning the period 1961 to 1984. The results of the OLS estimation are reported in Table 1. The linear parametric model apparently explains the supply of hogs

Table 1. OLS Estimates and Bootstrap Results. The Supply of Hogs, 1961–1984

Variable	OLS Estimates		Bootstrap Results	
	Estimated Coefficient	Standard Error	Mean Coefficient	Standard Error
PRH(−4)	1.760	0.373	1.800	0.377
PRC(−4)	−6.971	1.609	−7.069	1.581
S(−1)	0.884	0.036	0.871	0.037

$\bar{R}^2 = 0.888$, $F(2,93) = 376.0$, Durbin h: −0.331, SSR $= 1.96 \times 10^6$

Breusch-Godfrey Test (4th. order)   2.145
Breusch-Pagan Test   2.040
ARCH test (4th. order)   2.621

reasonably well. All of the interesting coefficients are of the expected sign and are significantly different from zero. A crucial assumption for OLS parameter estimates to be consistent is that the disturbances be independent. In addition, the bootstrapping method that we use to construct confidence intervals for the estimated coefficients and point forecasts also relies on the independence assumption. The Durbin-Watson statistic is not appropriate for testing for first order autocorrelation when the lagged dependent variable appears on the right-hand side. However, the Durbin h-statistic, which is appropriate in this case, takes the value -0.33 and this is consistent with independent disturbances at the five percent level of significance. To check further, we also used the Breusch-Godfrey test (see Breusch 1978 and Godfrey 1978) for higher orders of autoregressive structure in the disturbances. The tests did not reject the null hypothesis of no autocorrelation against the alternative of autocorrelation up to order four. We also used the Breusch-Pagan test to examine the possibility that the disturbances are heteroscedastic, but this too was rejected. Finally, the ARCH test of Engle (1982) for fourth order autoregressive conditional heteroscedasticity also fell well below the critical value. In light of these tests, we can be reasonably confident that the disturbances are identically and independently distributed.

In the last two columns of Table 1 we report the results of bootstrapping the OLS equation. Consider first the estimated coefficients. Asymptotically, the OLS and bootstrap means will converge to the true parameter values, provided the necessary assumptions are valid. In particular, the random disturbances must be i.i.d. Thus, if the model is well specified, the means calculated from the resampling procedure will be close to the OLS coefficients. In the present example, the mean slope coefficients calculated over one thousand resamplings are indeed remarkably close to the OLS coefficient estimates. The bootstrap results confirm the earlier specification tests, all of which indicated that the underlying disturbances are i.i.d. Second, consider the estimated standard errors. Again, both the OLS and bootstrap procedures are asymptotically valid. In the present example the two methods give very similar estimates of the coefficients' standard errors. Overall, these results can be thought of as mutually supportive. The linear parametric model seems to be a good representation of the data generating process. Similarly, in the present model the bootstrap method produces results that are plausible. This gives us confidence that the bootstrap procedure is a valid approach to calculating forecast intervals for the present model.

4 A Comparison of Forecasts

In this section we compare the parametric and nonparametric point forecasts and the distributions of these point forecasts. Although the nonparametric forecasts do not require us to calculate the regression function at points within the estimation-period

Table 2. OLS and Nonparametric Forecasts

		Forecasts*			
Quarter	Actual	OLS	S.E.	NP	S.E.
1985 1	3618	3667	164	3668	214
2	3743	3530	162	3543	226
3	3554	3296	164	3298	191
4	3814	3764	164	3738	191
1986 1	3565	3547	167	3515	176
2	3567	3456	170	3446	165
3	3237	3245	176	3249	204
4	3614	3735	171	3727	174
Means	3589	3530		3523	
Mean Absolute Error		104		110	
Mean Square Error		18030		17989	

* The deficiencies of the reported standard errors are discussed in the text.

sample, it is interesting to note that the sum of squared residuals (SSR) of the non-parametric fit is 1.72×10^6. As reported in Table 1, the SSR for the linear parametric model is 1.96×10^6. Thus within the estimation-period sample the nonparametric approach provides a better overall fit.

Table 2 presents the point forecasts and standard errors generated by the linear parametric model and the nonparametric approach, as well as the actual values of hog supply. The eight quarterly out-of-sample forecasts are constructed conditionally on the observed values of the explanatory variables. Thus, the forecast-period data were not used in the estimation of the linear model. Similarly, the nonparametric forecasts are independent of the actual values of the dependent variable in the forecast period. Given the structure of the model, the 1986 forecasts are conditional on the actual values of the exogenous variables in 1985. However, in both the parametric and non-parametric cases, the lagged dependent variable is set equal to the previous forecast, not the observed value. Interestingly, the OLS and nonparametric forecasts are very close to each other, which again confirms that in the present case the linear parametric model provides a good representation of the hog supply process. Over the eight quarters, the OLS and nonparametric forecasts tend to under predict hog supply by 1.6% and 1.8% respectively. According to the criterion of mean absolute error, the OLS forecasts are slightly superior, but the nonparametric forecasts are preferred according to mean square error. On the basis of the accuracy of the eight quarterly forecasts, the two methods perform equally well.

The standard errors that are reported in Table 2 must be treated with considerable caution. The OLS standard errors treat all explanatory variables, including the lagged dependent variable, as fixed numbers. This assumption is valid for the first prediction only. Beyond that, the sequential forecasts of hog supply are dependent on the previous forecast, which is obviously a random variable. Consequently, the true variance of the forecast errors increases as the forecast period extends beyond the estimation sample. By treating the dependent variable as fixed, this effect is ignored in the reported standard errors. The slight upward trend in the reported standard errors is due entirely to the changes in the explanatory variables and not to the dynamic nature of the model.

The standard errors of the nonparametric forecasts are derived from the variance of the forecast error, which can be expressed as

$$V(u|x) = V(y|x) + V(\hat{E}(y|x)) \tag{7}$$

where $u \equiv y - \hat{E}(y|x)$ is the forecast error. Using results reported in Singh and Ullah (1985), an estimate of the variance of the forecast error is therefore:

$$\hat{V}(u|x) = \hat{V}(y|x) + \frac{(2\sqrt{\pi})^{-p}\,\hat{V}(y|x)}{\Sigma K_2\left(\dfrac{x-x_t}{h}\right)} \tag{8}$$

where the conditional variance of y is estimated by

$$\hat{V}(y|x) = \sum_{t=1}^{n} y_t^2 r_t - [\hat{E}(y|x)]^2 \tag{9}$$

and $\hat{E}(y|x)$ and r_t are defined in (5). As in the case of the parametric model, the conditional variances in (8) are not strictly valid because the sequential forecasts cannot be treated as fixed numbers. Thus, the estimator of the variance assumes that in the forecast period the lagged dependent variable is an actual realization when in fact it is recursively generated by the model. The nonparametric standard errors reported in Table 2 are therefore unreliable.

In order to compare the distributions of the parametric and nonparametric forecast errors, the two models were bootstrapped. The use of the resampling technique known as bootstrapping in the regression context is discussed in Freedman (1981) and Freedman and Peters (1984). Veall (1987) and Prescott and Stengos (1987) apply bootstrapping to the construction of forecast intervals. An advantage of this approach

Table 3. Bootstrapped Distributions[1] of Forecast Errors

OLS Results

Quarter		Mean Error	MAE	MSE (x10³)	SDV	95% Prediction Interval	
1985	1	18.4	112.6	20.6	142.2	-271.2	305.1
	2	29.7	153.4	37.4	191.1	-367.7	392.8
	3	47.4	182.2	52.3	223.7	-405.8	475.9
	4	55.5	202.9	65.6	250.0	-447.1	553.2
1986	1	59.1	215.6	72.1	262.0	-442.9	562.6
	2	61.5	227.3	79.1	274.6	-438.2	601.5
	3	70.7	248.8	95.2	300.3	-514.1	633.4
	4	71.8	261.1	104.0	314.4	-501.3	682.1
Average		51.8	200.5	65.8	244.8		

Nonparametric Results

Quarter		Mean Error	MAE	MSE (x10³)	SDV	95% Prediction Interval	
1985	1	60.8	130.4	28.8	158.6	-245.5	405.7
	2	71.9	172.3	46.1	202.3	-309.2	467.5
	3	56.3	170.6	46.7	208.7	-330.8	476.6
	4	42.8	163.6	44.6	206.8	-393.5	464.9
1986	1	34.4	160.8	42.9	204.2	-370.6	438.9
	2	32.7	165.8	44.6	208.7	-357.8	478.2
	3	29.6	172.3	47.3	215.5	-407.4	456.2
	4	33.5	165.3	44.4	208.1	-364.8	457.2
Average		45.3	162.6	43.2	201.6		

[1]   Based on 1,000 bootstrap resamplings.

is that the stochastic nature of the lagged dependent variable can be accounted for in a straightforward fashion. Moreover, such comparisons are based on a common approach and there is no a priori reason to expect the bootstrapping method to favour either of the two forecasting techniques. The details of how the bootstrap resampling strategy is applied to the nonparametric forecasts is described in the Appendix. Table 3 presents the bootstrap estimates of the distributions of forecasts errors. The OLS results appear in the first block of Table 3.

The first column of Table 3 reports the mean forecast errors calculated over 1,000 bootstrap samples. Each of the bootstrap resamplings generates a simulated "actual" dependent variable and a simulated forecast. The difference between the two is a simulated forecast error. To the extent that the disturbances are i.i.d. and that the models produce unbiased forecasts, one would expect the mean forecast errors to be zero. While the numbers in the first column do not appear to be randomly distributed around zero, nevertheless the mean errors are small in comparison to the point forecasts.

Our main interest focuses on the other columns. The second and third columns present the mean absolute and mean square errors respectively, while the fourth column reports the standard deviations of the forecast errors as estimated by the bootstrap procedure. All three measures provide qualitatively similar results. Consider first the pattern through time. All three measures increase abruptly after the first forecast period. This reflects the fact that the lagged dependent variable is known only in the case of the first forecast. After that, the lagged dependent variable is itself forecast. In the case of the OLS model, all measures of forecast error continue to increase as the forecast period moves into the future. This is presumably due to the fact that the lagged dependent variable, which is sequentially forecast, has an increasing variances as the forecast period moves into the future. The nonparametric forecasts are considerably less sensitive to this effect. The lower panel of Table 3 shows that there is an abrupt increase after the first forecast period, but thereafter the measures of forecast error show only a modest increase through time. Of course the forecasts are conditional on the actual values of the explanatory variables that were realized in this two year period. The distribution of forecast errors depends on the values of the exogenous variables as well as the distribution of the (forecast) lagged dependent variable. In the case of the nonparametric forecasts, these effects appear to counteract each other, leaving the distribution of forecast errors largely unchanged through time. This suggests that the effects of (a) the conditional values of the exogenous variables and (b) the stochastic nature of the lagged dependent variable on the distribution of forecast errors are different between the two models.

The results reported in Table 3 also suggest that in the context of this particular study, the nonparametric multi-period forecasts are generally superior to the linear model's multi-period forecasts. This conclusion is essentially based on the quality of the nonparametric forecasts for "further-ahead" forecasts.

The conclusions that we have drawn in this paper have recently been confirmed and even strengthened by further experiments that are reported in Moschini et al. (1988). In these later experiments a more parsimonious model that uses the ratio of corn and hog prices as an explanatory variable has been estimated with quarterly data over the period 1961–1985. Two-year forecasts were made over the period 1986–1987. The results of these updated experiments are essentially the same as those reported here but are, in fact, somewhat more favourable to the nonparametric approach.

Summary

The results reported in this paper lend support to the nonparametric approach to estimating regression functions. A well specified parametric dynamic model of hog supply was used to generate eight out-of-sample quarterly forecasts. The distribution of these forecasts was compared to forecasts computed from a nonparametric model of hog supply. Despite the fact that the estimation sample was limited to 96 quarterly observations, the nonparametric point forecasts were found to be as accurate as the parametric forecasts according to mean square error and mean absolute error criteria. The bootstrap resampling technique was used to estimate the distributions of the forecast errors. The results of this exercise favoured the nonparametric forecasts, which were found to have a tighter distribution.

Appendix

This appendix describes the bootstrap resampling procedure used to estimate the sampling distribution of the nonparametric forecasts. A similar procedure was used in the case of the parametric forecasts.

1. Estimated model:

$$y_t = \hat{M}(y_{t-1}, x_t) + e_t \quad \text{for } t = 1, 2, \ldots n$$

2. Bootstrap Sample ($j = 1, 2, \ldots, 1,000$)

$$y_1^j = \hat{M}(y_0, x_1) + e_1^j$$

$$y_t^j = \hat{M}(y_{t-1}^j, x_t) + e_t^j \quad \text{for } t = 2, \ldots n$$

where the symbol e_t^j refers to the randomly selected nonparametric residual in period t.

$$y_{n+1}^j = \hat{M}(y_n, x_{n+1}) + e_{n+1}^j$$

$$y_{n+i}^{j} = \hat{M}(y_{n+i-1}^{j}, x_{n+i}) + e_{n+i}^{j} \quad \text{for } i = 2, \ldots m$$

where m is the number of forecasts.

3. Bootstrap Forecast (j-th sample)

$$y_{n+1}^{fj} = \hat{M}^{j}(y_n, x_{n+1})$$

$$y_{n+i}^{fj} = \hat{M}^{j}(y_{n+i-1}^{fj}, x_{n+i}) \quad \text{for } i = 2, \ldots m$$

4. Bootstrap Forecast Error (j-th sample)

$$u_{n+i}^{j} = y_{n+i}^{j} - y_{n+i}^{fj} \quad \text{for } i = 1, 2, \ldots m$$

References

Breusch TS (1978) Testing for autocorrelation in dynamic linear models. Australian Economic Papers 17:334–355

Breusch TS, Pagan AR (1979) A simple test for heteroscedasticity and random coefficient variation. Econometrica 47:1287–1294

Engle RF (1982) Autoregressive conditional heteroscedasticity with estimates of the variance of United Kingdom inflations. Econometrica 50:987–1007

Freedman DA (1981) Bootstrapping regression models. Annals of Statistics 9:1218–1928

Freedman DA, Peters SC (1984) Bootstrapping a regression equation: Some empirical results. Journal of the American Statistical Association 79:97–106

Godfrey GL (1978) Testing for higher-order serial correlation in regression equations when the regressors include lagged dependent variables. Econometrica 46:1303–1310

Lau LJ (1986) Functional forms in econometric model building. In: Griliches Z, Intriligator MD (eds) Handbook of econometrics, vol III. Elsevier Science Publishers, New York

Martin L, Zwart A (1975) A spatial and temporal model of the North American pork sector for the evaluation of policy alternatives. American Journal of Agricultural Economics 57:55–66

Moschini G, Prescott DM, Stengos T (1988) Nonparametric forecasting: An application to the US hog supply. Unpublished manuscript, Department of Economics, Iowa State University

Prescott DM, Stengos T (1987) Bootstrapping confidence intervals: An application to forecasting the supply of pork. American Journal of Agricultural Economics 69:266–273

Rilstone P, Ullah A (1987) Nonparametric estimation of response coefficients. Unpublished Paper, Dept. of Economics, University of Western Ontario

Rosenblatt M (1956) Remarks on some nonparametric estimates of a density function. Annals of Mathematical Statistics 27:832–837

Silverman BW (1986) Density estimation for statistics and data analysis. Chapman and Hall, London

Singh RS, Ullah A (1985) Nonparametric time series estimation of joint DGP, conditional DGP and vector autoregression. Econometric Theory 1:27–52

Ullah A (1987) Nonparametric estimation of econometric functionals. Canadian Journal of Economics (forthcoming)

Ullah A, Vinod HD (1987) Nonparametric kernel estimation of econometric parameters. Journal of Quantitative Economics (forthcoming)

Veal M (1987) Bootstrapping the probability distribution of peak electricity demand, International Economic Review 28:302–312

White H (1980) Using least squares to approximate unknown regression functions. International Economic Review 21:149–170

Calibrating Histograms with Application to Economic Data

By D. W. Scott[1,2,3] and H.-P. Schmitz[1,4]

Summary: In this paper the problem of automatic calibration of histograms by cross-validation is considered, assuming the true underlying density is continuous with continuous first derivative. The histogram is one of the simplest semiparametric estimators used by economists, but it is surprisingly difficult to construct histograms with small estimation errors. Cross-validation algorithms attempt to automatically determine histogram bin widths that are nearly optimal with respect to mean integrated squared error. Alternative philosophies and approaches of cross-validation for histograms are presented. It is shown that the classical Sturges' rule performs poorly and that cross-validation is a relatively difficult task. Understanding the performance of cross-validation algorithms in this simple setting should prove valuable when cross-validating other more complex semiparametric procedures.

Key words: Histogram; Bin width; Cross-validation; Automatic bin width selection.

1 Introduction

Semiparametric methods in economics have provided a novel and powerful tool for modeling real economic data that are not easily fit by usual parametric models. The simplest semiparametric tool is the classical histogram. A practical consideration to successful semiparametric modeling is choosing calibration or smoothing parameters

[1,2] Acknowledgments: This research was begun while the first author was a visiting scholar at the University of Bonn and he would like thank Dr. Wolfgang Härdle for the invitation and to acknowledge the excellent research atmosphere that exists in the institute. The authors would also like to thank a referee for some helpful comments. The research was supported in part by 1) Deutsche Forschungsgemeinschaft (SFB 303), Universität Bonn, W. Germany and 2) the Office of Naval Research grant number N00014-85-K-0100. Deutsche Forschungsgemeinschaft (SFB 303), Universität Bonn, W. Germany. The replace with programs are available by e-mail at scottw@rice.edu.
[3] David W. Scott, Department of Statistics, Rice University, P.O. Box 1892, Houston, TX 77251-1892, USA.
[4] Heinz-Peter Schmitz, Universität Bonn, 5300 Bonn, FRG.

that essentially determine the optimal noise suppression level. The smoothing parameter for the histogram is the bin width. While experienced economists and statisticians can often twiddle these parameters close to optimal values, automatic or data-based algorithms are of extreme practical value. With large micro-data sets often encountered in economics, twiddling may not be successful since alternative choices of smoothing parameters may give pictures that "look good" while supporting opposing hypotheses. Automatic procedures hold the most promise in this situation. Cross-validated histograms have a wide array of applications including testing goodness-of-fit (McDonald (1984), estimating modes and other distributional shape features, and estimating quantities useful, for example, in inequality of income analysis such as quantiles and Lorenz curves (see Sendler 1979 and Beach and Davidson 1983).

In Fig. 1, four histograms of the 1983 German gross-income sample (DIW 1983) are presented with 13, 51, 95, and 150 bins, respectively, on the interval (4, 15). The income of 5,625 households was transformed by the natural logarithm to reduce skewness. The first histogram was constructed using the rule of Sturges (1926):

$$\text{number of bins} = 1 + \log_2 n$$

where n is the sample size. This density is skewed slightly to the left. However it would appear that the original income data might be adequately fitted by the lognormal distribution, which has been the standard approach in economics since Gibrat (1930). The second histogram with 51 bins gives a more detailed view of the data with a similar interpretation. The remaining two histograms suggest the data might come from a multimodal distribution. In fact, the last histogram looks very noisy and complex. If one is interested in analyzing "the form of the income densities as carefully as possible" to solve an economic problem like K. Hildenbrand and W. Hildenbrand (1986, p. 252) it is natural to ask the statisticians for a good choice of the bin width. Some have argued the histogram simply presents the data, but we prefer to view the histogram as a bona fide estimator of a true underlying smooth probability density function.

As the number of bins increases, less grouping or averaging occurs and the histogram displays more high frequency noise. Thus the bin width serves as a control on the amount of detail and noise allowed to appear in the histogram. The noise is always assumed to be high frequency superimposed upon the true density curve, which is assumed to be primarily low frequency with some medium-to-high frequency portion. For a finite sample, distinguishing true wiggles in the underlying density from local features only in the noise is the problem. The bimodal feature may be real or an artifact of the noise in the realization of this data set. Or the underlying density may be much more complex, as suggested by the fourth histogram. We shall generally assume that our sample size is sufficiently large that the true density is well-represented by a histogram constructed using an optimal bin width. For a complex density, this sample size may be quite large.

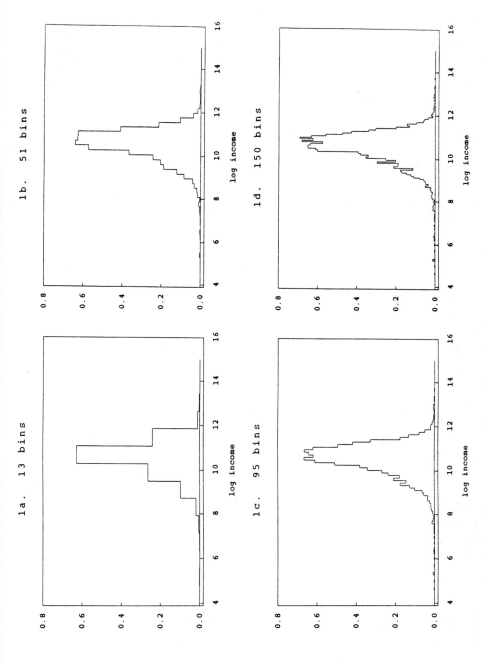

Fig. 1. Four histograms of the 1983 sample of 5,625 German households' income

In the following sections, two cross-validation algorithms for automatically choosing the bin width are presented. To study the algorithms' performance with normal data, a Monte Carlo simulation study is presented. Finally, the algorithms are applied to the German income data. From the mathematical point of view, it is more convenient to focus on specifying the bin width rather than the number of bins in a histogram. For example, in Fig. 1a, it is difficult to correctly count the number of bins without reference to Fig. 1d.

2 Cross-Validation of Histograms

2.1 Introduction

Rather than relying upon subjective measures of the effect of bin width choice, a particular squared error criterion to be minimized is introduced. Let $\{X_i\}$ denote a sample of size n from a probability density function f, which has a smooth first derivative. Given a choice of bin width h, cover the entire real line by bins $I_k(h) = [kh, (k + 1)h)$, for $-\infty < k < \infty$. Here zero has been arbitrarily taken to be a bin edge. Let the number of points in bin $I_k(h)$ be denoted by $v_k(h)$; of course, $\sum_k v_k(h) = n$ for all h. Then the histogram density estimator is defined by

$$\hat{f}(x|h, n) = \frac{v_k(h)}{nh} \quad \text{for } x \text{ in } I_k(h).$$

The histogram defined in this manner is nonnegative and integrates to one.

The measure of error between $\hat{f}(x|h, n)$ and f focused upon is the integrated squared error (ISE), defined as

$$\text{ISE}(h, n) = \int [\hat{f}(x|h, n) - f(x)]^2 dx. \tag{1}$$

The more ambitious goal is to choose the bin width h to minimize the integrated squared error. Such a bin width would depend not only on the sample size but also on the particular realization. Alternatively, the error criterion chosen could be the average or mean integrated squared error (MISE), defined as

$$\text{MISE}(h, n) = E[\text{ISE}(h, n)].$$

Following the usual decomposition of mean squared error, the MISE may be separated into integrated variance and integrated squared bias. Scott (1979) showed that the respective sum of these two error components can be approximated as

$$\text{MISE}(h, n) = \frac{1}{nh} + \frac{1}{12} h^2 \int f'(x)^2 dx + O\left(\frac{1}{n}\right). \tag{2}$$

From this remarkably simple expression, several important facts may be deduced. First, for large samples the optimal bin width will decrease at a rate inversely proportional to the third root of the sample size. Precisely,

$$h_n^* = \left[\frac{6}{n \int f'(x)^2 dx}\right]^{1/3}. \tag{3}$$

Thus the optimal number of bins grows at a rate $O(n^{1/3})$, a much faster growth than Sturges' rule of $O(\log_2 n)$. Clearly Sturges' rule, which is widely given in introductory textbooks and used in computer packages, is suboptimal and wastes data by using too few bins. If the data are $N(\mu, \sigma^2)$, then

$$h_n^* = 3.49 \, \sigma n^{-1/3}. \tag{4}$$

Scott (1979) suggested as a first approximation constructing a histogram using formula (4) substituting the sample standard deviation for σ. This simple rule performs surprisingly well. When applied to the German income data, this rule gives a bin width of 0.150 or 74 bins.

Second, if h is too small the MISE is dominated by integrated variance error, corresponding to a rough histogram. However, the integrated squared bias is small. On the other hand, if h is too large, the variance is small and the MISE is dominated by bias errors, corresponding to an oversmoothed histogram with too few bins. Sturges' rule falls into this latter category.

Finally, for large samples, the only fact about the density f relevant to constructing optmal histograms is a particular measure summarizing the "roughness" of its first derivative,

$$R(f') = \int f'(x)^2 dx. \tag{5}$$

Formula (3) indicates that the optimal bin width decreases with increasing roughness. The normal density is not very rough and almost provides an upper bound on the optimal bin width (Terrell and Scott (1985).

2.2 Least-Squares or Unbiased Cross-Validation

Rudemo (1982) and Bowman (1984) independently proposed an unbiased cross-validation estimate of the integrated squared error for fixed values of the bin width. Stone (1985) considered some of its asymptotic optimality properties. Expanding equation (1).

$$\text{ISE}(h, n) = \int \hat{f}(x|h, n)^2 dx - 2 \int \hat{f}(x|h, n)f(x)dx + \int f(x)^2 dx. \tag{6}$$

The third term amounts to a fixed constant that does not depend upon the bin width and may be ignored. The first term may be computed directly from a histogram estimate. Rudemo showed that the second term and the following random variable have exactly the same expectation:

$$-\frac{2}{n} \sum_{i=1}^{n} \hat{f}_{-i}(x_i|h, n),$$

where $\hat{f}_{-i}(x_i|h, n)$ is a histogram estimate of the $n - 1$ points excluding x_i and evaluated at $x = x_i$. It is straightforward to show that the unbiased cross-validation (UCV) estimate is

$$\text{UCV}(h, n) = \frac{2}{(n-1)h} - \frac{(n+1)}{n^2(n-1)h} \sum_k v_k(h)^2. \tag{7}$$

The unbiased cross-validation bin width is obtained by finding the minimum of (7) over h. Aside from the constant third term in (6), UCV(h, n) provides precisely unbiased estimates of MISE(h, n) for each h; hence the unbiased label. In some situations, the search for the minimum away must exclude the region near zero because UCV(h, n) is unbounded below for h near zero; this can occur if there are many empty bins (Silverman 1986). An example of this estimate may be found in Section 3; see also Scott (1986) and Scott and Terrell (1987).

2.3 Biased Cross-Validation

An alternative cross-validation algorithm may be constructed based upon an estimate of $R(f')$ in equation (5), in which, $\nu_k(h)$ is abbreviated as ν_k:

$$\hat{R}_h(f') = \frac{1}{n^2 h^3} \sum_k (\nu_{k+1} - \nu_k)^2 - \frac{2}{nh^3}. \tag{8}$$

This estimate employs a first difference approximation to the first derivative and removes a fixed asymptotic bias (see Scott and Terrell 1987). Substituting (8) into the first two terms of (2), the biased cross-validation estimate of the MISE(h, n) becomes:

$$BCV(h, n) = \frac{5}{6nh} + \frac{1}{12n^2 h} \sum_k (\nu_{k+1} - \nu_k)^2. \tag{9}$$

The biased cross-validation bin width is obtained by finding the minimizer of (9). To be precise, the BCV bin width corresponds to a local minimum since for extremely large bin widths, BCV $(h, n) \rightarrow 0$. The use of the normal rule (4) provides an indication of the appropriate search interval. For small samples, there may not be any discernible local minimum, reflecting poor estimates of $R(f')$. Since equation (2) is only approximate, the biased label is appropriate, although asymptotically unbiased would be more accurate. Finally, notice the remarkable algebraic similarities of the UCV and BCV formulae.

3 Examples and Simulations with Normal Data

3.1 An Example with 1,000 Normal Points

Using the S system (Beckers and Chambers 1984), a $N(0, 1)$ sample of size 1,000 was generated using the function *rnorm*. The two resulting cross-validation functions are plotted in Fig. 2. Since proportional rather than absolute errors in the bin width are important, these figures are plotted using a log(h) scale. The vertical axes have the same length and are directly comparable, since the UCV curve is shifted by a fixed constant. When computing the cross-validation functions, the histogram bins covered the interval $(-5,5)$ and always began at the point -5. The minima of these two curves

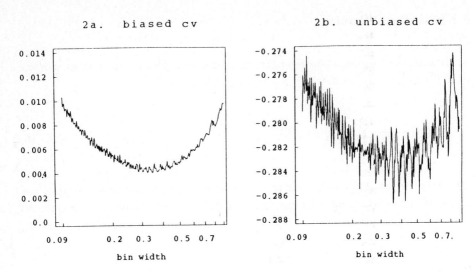

Fig. 2. An example of the biased and unbiased cross-validation functions for a sample of 1,000 standard normal points

are 0.324 and 0.356, respectively, and the corresponding histograms (not shown) are visually indistinguishable in any interesting manner.

The unbiased cross-validation curve displays much more vertical variability than the biased cross-validation curve. This variability may partially be explained as a bin edge effect. However, because adjacent bin counts are almost uncorrelated, this noise accurately reflects vertical noise in these cross-validation functions observed *across samples* for fixed bin widths. Such excess variability suggests the location of the minimum of the unbiased cross-validation function will also be more variable. This idea was examined in the following Monte Carlo simulation study.

3.2 Monte Carlo Simulation Study of Cross-Validation Bin Widths

The previous example was repeated 1,000 times with sample sizes of 100 and 1,000. The cross-validation bin widths were converted into fractions of the values 0.752 and 0.349, the respective optimal values for normal samples of size 100 and 1,000 predicted by formula (3). The simulation results are summarized in Fig. 3 by four histograms on a fixed scale. The consistency of each procedure is apparent as the histograms increasingly cluster around the value of 1.0 as the sample size increases. The variability of the UCV estimates is greater than that of the BCV procedures. However, it should be noted that the variability of the bin widths actually minimizing ISE is about the same

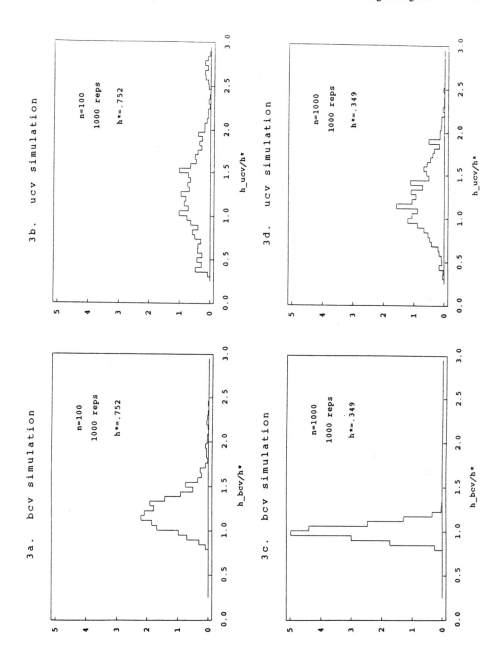

Fig. 3. Histograms summarizing a simulation of the bin widths obtained by cross-validation. A 1,000 samples of size 100 and 1,000 each were cross-validated by both techniques. The resulting bin widths have been normalized by the fixed bin width minimizing the MISE. The optimal MISE bandwidth, denoted by h^*, is given by equation (4). The minimizers of the unbiased and biased cross-validation functions in equations (7) and (9) are denoted by h_{ucv} and h_{bcv}, respectively

as that of the UCV procedure. The BCV procedure, on the other hand, is clustering around the optimal MISE bin width. Based upon the work of Scott and Terrell (1987), the UCV bin width is most likely negatively correlated with the bin width actually minimizing the ISE. The reasons for this behavior are well beyond the scope of this article, but are a fascinating feature inherent in many cross-validation problems.

Scott and Terrell (1987) present theorems estimating the variability of these cross-validation bin widths. For normal data, the vertical standard deviation of the UCV curve is 8.9 times that of the BCV curve. The ratio of the (horizontal) standard deviations of the bin widths in Fig. 3c and 3d is 4.55, and the average bin width ratios are 0.999 and 1.243, respectively. Thus the horizontal variability is about half of the vertical variability. It should be clear from our discussion below that we believe both cross-validation functions are important and they should be used in careful conjunction.

4 Application to the German Income Data

The two cross-validation functions for the logarithmically transformed German income data sample are plotted in Fig. 4. The biased cross-validation bin width is 0.115 or 95 bins; see Fig. 1c. The unbiased cross-validation function requires more careful examination. It clearly excludes bin widths greater than 0.2, but the sharp minimum near zero is likely an artifact of the procedure; see the discussion in Section 2.2. The curve is actually remarkably flat in the region of interest. After magnifying the scale, there are

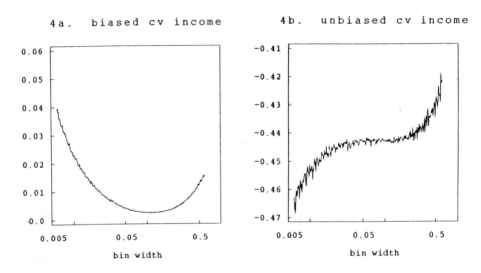

Fig. 4. Cross-validation functions applied to the German income data

hints of interesting local minima at several bin widths corresponding to between 150 and 300 bins, but not a clear choice. Given the large sample size, the differences in these graphs are interesting and remarkable.

Hence from the point of view of mean integrated squared error, the optimal histogram most likely has several modes, although the histogram with as many as 51 bins is only unimodal. In experiments carried out informally by the first author, expert statisticians preferred histograms that were quite rough by the MISE criteria. This is reasonable, since a rough histogram can be smoothed by eye, whereas a histogram with too few bins has information lost that cannot be recovered.

Before drawing a few conclusions, consider the question, have we done the right thing with these data? The histogram with 95 bins seems to be a good visual summary of these data. Included in that analysis is the decision to transform from the original data scale, providing much more detail. As a result the histogram has a bin width derived from statistical theory. Cross-validated histograms are an important tool for data representation and density estimation. However in our economic surrounding (K. Hildenbrand and W. Hildenbrand 1986) derivatives of densities play an important role. How well are modes treated by the MISE criterion? In fact, it may be shown that the first differences of a histogram are not consistent with the first derivative, and that an optimal histogram asymptotically has numerous bumps, many only a bin or two wide (recall the estimator of $R(f')$ in equation (8) has a negative sign on the second term). It may be shown that the frequency polygon, a density estimator constructed by linear interpolation of the midpoints of a histogram, is consistent for both the density and its derivative when optimized with respect to MISE (Scott 1985a). The biased cross-validation estimate of the MISE of a frequency polygon is

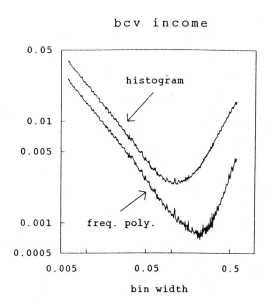

Fig. 5. Biased cross-validation functions applied to the German income data for both the histogram and frequency polygon density estimators

$$\mathrm{BCV_{FP}}(h, n) = \frac{271}{480nh} + \frac{49}{2880n^2 h} \sum_k (\nu_{k+1} - 2\nu_k + \nu_{k-1})^2 .$$

In Fig. 5 this function is plotted on a *log-log* scale together with the histogram BCV function. The 51-bin histogram in Fig. 1b is the one from which the BCV-optimal frequency polygon is constructed. This histogram has only one mode in the main part of the distribution.

Of course, it is possible that a more statistically powerful density estimator such as the averaged shifted histogram (Scott 1985b) could in fact reveal the presence of a second mode, but at this point the work of the statisticians has to be completed by economic interpretation. So one possibility is to divide the sample into subsamples motivated by an economic theory of income distribution. Investigating these groups with calibrated histograms may give an answer on the existence of a second mode.

5 Discussion and Conclusions

Statisticians have often found reason to consider biased rather than unbiased procedures, for example, in ridge regression and Stein estimation. Here the comparison is between an unbiased estimate of mean integrated squared error and an estimate based upon an asymptotic expansion of the MISE. Given the fairly large variability inherent in cross-validation procedures, we believe it is wise to consider more than one automatic estimate. Here, the procedures tend to produce too few bins for small samples, but in other situations such as kernel density estimation the opposite occurs. Simulations with fairly large samples are apparently necessary for a complete understanding of the small-sample and asymptotic behavior of cross-validation algorithms. Most researchers have been performing experiments with simulated data sets with perhaps a hundred points. We have shown that generalizing that experience towards asymptotic behavior can be misleading.

For very large datasets, we suspect that unbiased cross-validation is too sensitive to the data, whereas biased cross-validation takes a much broader view of the data. The UCV sensitivity is reminiscent of chi-squared goodness-of-fit tests problems with very large data sets, where the null hypothesis is always rejected with real data. Thus these transformed German income data are nearly normal, but unbiased cross-validation cannot decide what is really plausible (how non-normal). That is, the unimodal estimates have about the same estimated risk or MISE as the multimodal estimates. One possible interpretation is that unbiased cross-validation believes that f is indeed quite complex but does not have enough data to definitively display that hypothesis. Indeed, an important application of these cross-validation histograms is providing goodness-of-fit evidence that functional forms fit poorly (see McDonald 1984).

Many semiparametric economic procedures require cross-validation of more demanding functions, such as derivatives. This is of course a more difficult problem, and we urge caution about placing too much faith in any automatic procedure. In many situations the conclusions are really robust towards a poor choice of smoothing parameter, but not always. It may be desirable to use derivative information to construct variable or adaptive bin histograms. Unfortunately, this tasks seems quite difficult since the number of cross-validation parameters (bin widths) grows rapidly.

Finally, we would like to echo a referee's observation concerning the relationship between this work and economic analysis.

Economists have certain reasons for being interested in the problem of estimating the density for the distribution of income and these reasons may influence the type of statistical analysis required, and vice versa, the type of statistical analysis available (or possible) should influence objectives set forth by the economist.

For some examples of novel applications of nonparametric statistical models, see Härdle and Scott (1988).

7 References

Beach CM, Davidson R (1983) Distribution-free statistical inference with Lorenz curves and income shares. Review of Economic Studies L 723–735

Becker RA, Chambers JM (1984) S: an interactive environment for data analysis and graphics. Wadsworth, Belmont, California

Bowman AW (1984) An alternative method of cross-validation for the smoothing of density estimates. Biometrika 71:353–360

DIW (1983) "Das Sozio-Ökonomische Panel". Deutsches Institut für Wirtschaftsforschung, Berlin

Gibrat R (1930) Une loi des répartitions économiques: t'effet proportionnel. Bulletin Statistique Géneral Francais 19

Härdle W, Scott DW (1988) Economic application of WARP: weighted average of rounded points. Technical Report 88-5, Dept. of Statistics, Rice University

Hildenbrand K, Hildenbrand W (1986) On the mean income effect: a data analysis of the U.K. family expenditure survey. In: Hildenbrand W, Mas-Colell A (eds) Contributions to mathematical economics. In honor of Gérard Debreu. North-Holland, Amsterdam, pp 247–268

McDonald JB (1984) Some generalized functions for the size distribution of income. Econometrica 52:647–663

Rudemo M (1982) Empirical choice of histogram and kernel density estimators. Scandinavian Journal of Statistics 9:65–78

Scott DW (1979) On optimal and data-based histograms. Biometrika 66:604–610

Scott DW (1985a) Frequency polygons: theory and application. J American Statistical Association 80:348–354

Scott DW (1985b) Averaged shifted histograms: effective nonparametric density estimators in several dimensions. Ann Statist 13:1024–1040

Scott DW (1986) Choosing smoothing parameters for density estimators. Computer Science and Statistics: Proceedings of the 17th Symposium on the Interface. North-Holland, pp 225–230

Scott DW, Terrell GR (1987) Biased and unbiased cross-validation in density estimation. J American Statistical Association 82:1131–1146

Sendler W (1979) On statistical inference in concentration measurement. Metrika 26:109–122

Silverman BW (1986) Density estimation for statistics and data analysis. Chapman and Hall, London

Stone CJ (1985) An asymptotically optimal histogram selection rule. In: Olshen R (ed) Proceedings of Berkeley Symp. in Honor of Jerzy Neyman and Jack Kiefer, vol 2. Wadsworth, CA, pp 513–520

Sturges HA (1926) The choice of a class interval. J American Statistical Association 21:65–66

Terrell GR, Scott DW (1985) Oversmoothed nonparametric density estimates. J American Statistical Association 80:209–214

The Role of Fiscal Policy in the St. Louis Model: Nonparametric Estimates for a Small Open Economy

By B. Raj and P. L. Siklos[1]

Abstract: This paper reevaluates the efficacy of monetary and fiscal policies and bidirectional causality between income and each of the policy instruments used in the St. Louis model for aggregate demand using nonparametric (or infinite parametric) spectral methods. We proceed by estimating the strength of the correlations (or partial coherences) between income and each of the policy instruments over various frequencies. Then we obtain the corresponding band regression and Hannan's efficient estimates of both the lead and lag coefficients in the St. Louis model. The analysis is carried out with seasonally adjusted quarterly data and is divided into the flexible, fixed, and managed flexible exchange rate regimes.

   We find that while estimates from parametric regressions yield the standard conclusions for the St. Louis model, results from the nonparametric analysis are quite different. Specifically, the results of our analysis reveal that (i) both monetary and fiscal instruments are strongly correlated with income over cycles of 10 quarters or longer for the most recent period of the managed flexible exchange rate regime, and (ii) bidirectional causality exists between income and the fiscal policy instrument. These results suggest that both monetary and fiscal policy have a long-lasting effect on aggregate demand and that bidirectional causality exists between income and policy instruments. An explanation for the existence of bidirectional causality might be that the Canadian government generally pursued a purposeful discretionary fiscal policy during the post-World War II period. Furthermore, it appears that discretionary policy action may have been anticipated by rational, farsighted, and forward-looking economic agents. Finally, our results for the flexible exchange rate and fixed rate regimes are in agreement with the Mundell-Fleming view of the role of monetary fiscal policy in an open economy.

---

[1] The authors are, respectively, Professor and Assistant Professor of Economics. Financial support from the Social Sciences and Humanities Research Council of Canada and the Research Office of Wilfrid Laurier University is gratefully acknowledged. Earlier versions of this paper were presented at the Fourth International Symposium on Forecasting, London, England, July 1984, and at the Economics Department, University of Waterloo, Waterloo, Ontario, Canada, January 1988. The authors are indebted to Stan Winer and William Frazer for helpful comments. Tim Kuehn provided computational assistance.

Baldev Raj and Pierre L. Siklos, School of Business and Economics, Wilfrid Laurier and University, Waterloo, Ontario, Canada N2L 3C5.

1 Introduction

There is renewed interest in analyzing the efficacy of monetary and fiscal policy in Andersen-Jordan's reduced form "St. Louis" equation (hereafter AJ) as evidenced by the publication of a collection of original papers in a book edited by Hafer (1986), and the "special issue" (October 1986) of the Review of the Federal Bank of St. Louis. A brief summary of the debate is given below along with a justification for using a non-parametric methodology in testing the efficacy of monetary and fiscal policy in the St. Louis model.

1.1 An Overview of the Debate

The original version of the AJ equation featured least squares estimates of a regression model for the United States, which explained the change in aggregate demand (nominal GNP) using such variables as the current and lagged values of changes in the money stock (M1 or base), full employment fiscal expenditures, and full employment tax receipts for U.S. quarterly data from 1952Q1 to 1968Q4. A striking result from the AJ equation was that the monetary variable has a significant and lasting effect on aggregate demand[2] (as indicated by the sum of current and lagged coefficients), whereas the fiscal variables have no lasting effect on aggregate demand.[3]

The result of the AJ equation conflicted sharply not only with results from large econometric models of the time but also with conventional wisdom. As such, the AJ work has been the subject of intense controversy and criticism. Three major criticisms are that: (i) the equation is misspecified because important exogenous variables were excluded, (ii) the AJ equation did not use relevant exogenous variables, and (iii) use of an ordinary least squares regression had resulted in simultaneous equation bias.

---

[2]   The result that increases in money stock has a sizeable stimulative effect on aggregate demand is supported by an empirical result from a St. Louis type model. This result is also consistent with theoretical analysis including non-Ricardian and Ricardian assumptions (McCallum 1986, Section 3).

[3]   Friedman (1977) later showed that effects of fiscal variables in the AJ equation also became lasting when the period 1970Q1–1976Q2 was added to the original sample. It was, pointed out by Carlson (1978), however, that the absolute change specification for the AJ equation was invalid for the sample set used because of heteroskedastic residuals. He showed that the AJ result continues to hold when variables in the reduced form model are entered in relative rather than absolute changes.

These criticisms were recently reviewed by McCallum (1986) and Batten and Thornton (1986). Batten and Thornton applied the "RESET" misspecification test of Ramsey and Schmidt (1976) to the original AJ equation and found no support for the claim that the equation is misspecified. McCallum (1986) reviewed earlier evidence published by Modigliani and Ando (1976) from a Monte Carlo experiment which suggested misspecification problems but found that the Modigliani-Ando study had failed to distinguish between the reduced form and final form multipliers in the AJ equation. He argued that AJ's estimates reflect all the direct and indirect effects via lagged values of change in nominal GNP. Earlier, Darby (1976) had contended that the reduced form equation captured direct and indirect effects via excluded exogenous variables (Batten and Thorton 1968 also note this; see their footnote 9).

McCallum (1986, p. 4) summarized his review of the evidence regarding the inappropriate use of indicators of policy in the AJ equation when he wrote that, "... if there is a fiscal policy measure that carries a strongly significant sum of coefficients in an equation of the St. Louis form, its existence has not been well publicized." Finally, Batten and Thornton (1986) applied Wu's chi-square test for exogeneity to the original AJ equation and found it to be statistically insignificant at the 5 percent level. This suggests that the AJ results were not questionable on grounds of simultaneity. However, Elliot (1975) had earlier performed the Wiener-Granger-Sims (hereafter WGS) causality test between money and income and government expenditures and income. He found that bidirectional causality existed between government expenditures and income while unidirectional causality existed from money to income.[4] Batten and Thornton (1986) also tested Sims' (1980, 1982) contention that monetary policy actions would be small if the interest rate variable were added to the equation. Batten and Thornton added the change in interest rate variable to the AJ equation and found the qualitative conclusions of the AJ model were not altered.

Questions regarding the endogeneity of policy actions were investigated earlier by Goldfeld and Blinder (1972) in some detail (also Blinder 1986). McCallum (1986, p. 15) summarized his review of their argument by noting that, "... the point is important enough to warrant continued discussion." He also compared least squares and instrumental variables (IV) estimates of the AJ equation for U.S. quarterly data from 1954–1980 and found that the IV estimates show a larger initial effect of government expenditures and a small initial effect of money on income. He concluded that "... the effects stressed by Goldfeld and Blinder may indeed be of quantitative importance." The IV estimates are, however, imprecise due to an extreme multicollinearity problem.

---

[4] Unidirectional causality in the WGS sense is a necessary though not sufficient condition for exogeneity in the statistical sense.

1.2 Objectives of the Analysis

In this paper we adopt a different methodology to evaluate relative monetary-fiscal effects described by the AJ equation in the relative change form. The degree of partial coherence between income and each of the policy instruments will be examined in the frequency domain by applying a nonparametric (or infinite parametric) spectral method. The existence of bidirectional causality between policy instruments and income in the WGS sense will also be tested for by obtaining Hannan's efficient and the band regression estimates of the AJ equation with both lead and lag coefficients of policy instruments in the AJ equation. These results are easily obtained as a by-product of the spectral estimates and require only a fairly weak set of assumptions about the error term.

Our investigation strategy is to start with a more general model with a view to testing whether restrictions imposed a priori by the AJ equation are supported by the data. This strategy is in direct contrast to the more commonly used approach of starting with a restrictive model and empirically testing if a more general specification is supported by the data.

Using this strategy we can accommodate a longer lag structure for policy instruments in the AJ equation than is feasible under the commonly used parametric approach. We find evidence that the correlation between the fiscal instruments and income is almost as strong as the correlation between money and income over cycles of 10 quarters or longer for the mixed flexible exchange rate period from 1954Q2 to 1984Q4. Further, band regression estimates of the sum of both lead and lag coefficients in the St. Louis model show that the issue of bidirectional causality between income and fiscal policy instruments is quantitatively important. We also find substantial evidence that fiscal policy's influence on income persists while money's effect on income does not persist under the fixed exchange rate regime. (Some of these results are partly reminiscent of earlier work on monetary-fiscal policy influence on income in the reduced form framework for Canada by Prachowny 1977 and Winer 1979.) For the flexible exchange rate regime these results are also consistent with predictions from the Mundell—Fleming model and provide an important confirmation of their modeling approach for the role of monetary-fiscal policy in an open economy.

This paper could be seen as a follow-up study to an earlier one done of the United States (Raj and Siklos 1986), which reached similar conclusions. However, it has a number of features which distinguishes it from the earlier Raj-Siklos study. First, our analysis focuses on Canada, covering the period 1954Q1 to 1984Q4, and distinguishes between three different exchange rate regimes consisting of a flexible exchange (FLE), fixed exchange (FXE), and managed flexible exchange (MFLE) rate periods. Second, we compute band regression estimates of the lead and lag coefficients in the St. Louis model in addition to Hannan's efficient estimates. Third, we allow for the openness of the Canadian economy by including nominal exports as an additional policy instrument in the model.

1.3 Organization of the Paper

The rest of the Paper is organized as follows: Data and method of inquiry are presented in Section 2. The BSR and spectral estimates, along with their interpretations,
are presented and contrasted with results from earlier related studies in Section 3. The
paper concludes with some summary remarks.

2 Data and Estimation Methods

2.1 Variable Definitions and Source of Data

We use Canadian seasonally adjusted quarterly[5] data covering the period 1954Q1 to
1984Q4. The period includes three distinct exchange rate régimes: (i) a FLE rate
period (31 observations, 1954Q2 to 1962Q1); (ii) a FXE rate period (31 observations,
1962Q1 to 1970Q1), and (iii) a MFLE rate period (58 observations, 1970Q2 to
1984Q3).[6] Our analysis considers each period separately in assessing causal links
between income and alternative policy instruments in the AJ expenditure equation.
We also use nominal exports (hereafter exports) as a regressor in the AJ equation, in
addition to the usual monetary and fiscal policy variables. (The use of exports in the
AJ equation is in keeping with its modern formulation [Batten and Thornton 1986]
and serves to account for the interdependencies of a country's economy with the rest
of the world.)

  We distinguish between exchange-rate regimes in order to assess whether possible
differences exist in the causal links between income and policy instruments in the AJ
equation for the different regimes. Subdividing the sample in this fashion is in line
with the traditional theoretical approach to modeling open economy macroeconomics
as developed by Meade, Mundell, and Fleming, and is ably summarized by Frankel and
Mussa (1981). Distinct exchange rate regimes have been utilized in the past by other
researchers who have analyzed the Canadian economy using both structural and reduced form models (Winer 1986a, 1986b and references therein).

---

[5] We are aware that the use of seasonally adjusted data generally confounds the analysis and may
even bias the results. However, we use the data and framework of the AJ equation to focus on the
issues relevant to this paper.

[6] This was roughly the sample division used by Winer (1986a, p. 70) except that we included
the period 1970Q2 to 1972Q4 as part of the managed float regime. We analyzed the combined
sample period as a managed float period mainly to add valuable observations to an already small
sample.

The price of subdividing a sample according to the exchange rate regime in place is that the number of observations available are relatively few for a spectral analysis. Despite this shortcoming, we felt additional insights are gained through such an analysis, although the results require the usual caution and need careful interpretation.

All variables in the AJ equation are expressed in log-change form to account for heteroskedasticity (Carlson 1978) and also to remove the unit roots usually found in macroeconomic variables (Nelson and Plosser 1982). This specification has the desirable feature of relating relative rather than absolute changes in variables in the AJ equation. Income (Y) is measured by nominal Gross National Product, the monetary policy instrument (M) is defined as $M1$, the fiscal policy instrument (G) represents full employment federal government budget expenditures, and exports (X) are defined as nominal merchandise exports of goods and services. Except for G, all data were taken from a Canadian Socioeconomic Information Management System (CANSIM) data tape. The data for G were supplied by the Ministry of Finance.[7] The definitions of variables conform as closely as possible to those used in the current version of the AJ equation.

2.2 Band Spectrum Regression and Spectral Analysis

Spectral methods used in this paper involve a weaker set of assumptions as compared to the distributed lag method and may be suitable in modeling situations where little a priori knowledge is available (Howrey 1980). We also use the BSR method to supplement estimates in the frequency domain framework for ease of interpretation and to provide additional insights into the relationship between income and various policy instruments in the AJ equation. An advantage of the BSR method, which is a frequency domain regression, it that is possesses standard small sample properties (Engle 1974, p. 1). In obtaining the BSR results we have zeroed out cycles of one year or less in duration. The choice of the one year cutoff is motivated by the AJ result that fiscal policy has no lasting effect (Batten and Thornton 1986) as measured by the magnitude and statistical significance of the sum of current and lagged coefficients up to four quarters. BSR for the two-sided regressions were undertaken under a fairly weak set of assumptions for the error term. (For instance, the error term is allowed to have an ARMA structure.) This might be an important consideration as the variables in the AJ model are specified in the rate of change form and it is generally believed that moving average terms are present in many macroeconomic variables when they are expressed

---

[7] For a description of the construction of this series, see Ministry of Finance, Annual Report (1985).

in first-difference form (Nelson and Plosser 1982). These estimates will also enable us to determine whether any "feedback" between income and fiscal policy, in the WGS sense, is sensitive to the zeroing out of high frequencies. Hannan's (1965, 1970) efficient estimates of the two-sided distributed lag model are also presented.

2.3 Model Specification

The model used for testing the null hypothesis that G has a zero long-run effect on Y, conditional on M and X, is of the form:

$$y = a + b(L)m + c(L)g + d(L)x + e(L)u \tag{2.1}$$

where all variables in lower case (except u) represent the log-change of the level of the corresponding upper-case variables, while u is an independently and identically distributed random variable. We multiply the dependent variable and regressors in log-change form by 400 to convert them to approximately annualized growth rates. The lag polynomials $b(L)$, $c(L)$ and $d(L)$ are two-sided and, in theory, of infinite order. The lag polynomial $e(L)$ is one-sided. If the influence of excluded variables is combined with a hypothesized white noise disturbance term in the AJ equation, the composite error term follows an infinite autoregressive process (McCallum 1986, and Batten and Thornton 1986, footnote 9). In our application of the BSR method we chose to limit the regressor lag length to 4, partly in keeping with the choice made in most earlier studies of the St. Louis model, and partly to conserve degrees of freedom.

The BSR method is a special case of Hannan's efficient[8] procedure to obtain estimates of a two-sided distributed lag model. A "filtering" procedure is used to zero out certain bands by weighting each observation by the reciprocal of the square root of diagonalized covariance matrix of the error terms. Hence, the effective degrees of freedom are smaller for the BSR procedure since the exclusion of frequencies requires an appropriate degrees of freedom correction.

An implementation of this procedure, therefore, amounts to obtaining the generalized least squares (GLS) estimates of the two-sided distributed lag model in the frequency domain.[9] The BSR procedure starts out by computing the least squares

---

[8] A regression analogue of Hannan's estimator can be developed as in Amemiya and Fuller (1967).

[9] The BSR procedure is allowed to have an arbitrary pattern of serial correlation so long as the error term is covariance stationary. In our application, we believe this assumption is satisfied since the variables in the model are in log-change form and the sample periods considered involve short chronological periods.

residuals regression for model (2.1) corresponding to the assumed number of lead/lag terms. The Fourier transform of these residuals along with all variables in the model are obtained and used to compute consistent (i.e., smoothed) estimates of the spectrum and cross-spectrum of the variables in the model. Consistent estimates are then generated through the application of an inverse Fourier transform to obtain the GLS estimates of the model in the time domain.

In spectral analysis the choice of a truncation point is important. We chose an appropriate truncation point based on the advice outlined in Jenkins and Watts (1968, chs 9, 11). The truncation point of eight quarters is considered optimal for our problem. Further, since the choice of an appropriate window is also important for spectral analysis, we use the Parzen window to smooth the periodograms. (These two choices were also utilized in Raj and Siklos's earlier study (1986) on United States data.) Summary statistics for spectral estimates to be presented later on also include the measure of partial coherence which shows the strength of a relationship (squared coefficient) between the dependent variable and a regressor at corresponding frequencies, conditional on the remaining regressors. The partial coherences are obtained for aligned series to correct for bias (Jenkins and Watts 1968, p. 399– 404).[10] Other spectral summary measures, such as phase and gain, are obtained from the unaligned series since they are not subject to bias due to misalignment. The BSR and Hannan's efficient estimates of the two sided distributed model are also obtained for the unaligned series. It is well known that the interpretation of the phase summary measure introduces some ambiguity, which suggests that care needs to be exercised in its interpretation (Hause 1971).

3   Spectral, Band Spectrum Regression Estimates, and their Interpretations

3.1 The OLS Estimates of the Standard AJ Equation

The least squares estimates of the standard AJ model (obtained by regressing the m, g, and e variables on y for the three exchange rate periods), are presented in Table 1. These results generally conform to the standard predictions of the closed economy version of the AJ model. Thus, the cumulative impact of monetary policy lagged four quarters is statistically significant at 10 percent while fiscal policy has a zero long run

---

[10] Suppose that the sample cross covariance function (ccv) of two unaligned series has a peak at lag S, where S may be positive or negative. The aligned series are obtained by lagging or leading one of the series so that the ccv has its peak at the zero lag.

Table 1. The OLS estimates of the AJ equation for one-sided distributed lags for Alternative Exchange Rate Regimes

Variable	FLE Coeff. (t-stat)	FXE Coeff. (t-stat)	MFLE Coeff. (t-stat)
Constant	3.044 (1.370)	9.904 (2.235)*	5.962 (2.746)*
m_t	-.130 (-.704)	.054 (.173)	.062 (.742)
m_{t-1}	.264 (1.607)	.092 (.539)	.233 (2.697)*
m_{t-2}	.296 (1.716)	.086 (.511)	.237 (2.794)*
m_{t-3}	-.368 (-1.975)*	-.192 (-1.106)	.047 (.510)
m_{t-4}	.415 (2.102)*	.176 (.689)	.057 (.622)
$\sum_{i=0}^{4} m_{t-i}$	.477 (1.833)*	.215 (.291)	.635 (4.390)*
g_t	-.013 (-.105)	.121 (1.367)	.049 (.868)
g_{t-1}	.058 (.562)	-.016 (-.139)	-.032 (-.572)
g_{t-2}	-.039 (-.366)	-.032 (-.236)	.071 (1.259)
g_{t-3}	-.065 (-.613)	-.146 (-1.546)	-.023 (-.415)
g_{t-4}	-.101 (-.916)	-.055 (-.593)	-.053 (-.963)
$\sum_{i=0}^{4} g_{t-i}$	-.160 (-.517)	-.128 (-.491)	.011 (.089)
e_t	.099 (2.772)*	-.001 (-.019)	-.006 (-1.067)
e_{t-1}	.087 (2.167)*	.000 (.010)	.002 (.301)
e_{t-2}	.074 (1.769)*	.003 (.095)	-.005 (-.929)
e_{t-3}	.130 (3.030)*	-.040 (-.895)	.001 (.148)
e_{t-4}	.012 (.323)	-.056 (-1.271)	.014 (1.070)
$\sum_{i=0}^{4} e_{t-i}$	.403 (2.660)*	-.092 (-.616)	.006 (.348)
OBS:	28	28	55
DF:	12	12	39
R^2	.810	.614	.511
SEE	3.879	3.326	4.101
D.W.	1.839	1.908	1.251

* signifies statistically significant at the 10% level of significance.
The t-statistic is shown in parenthesis.

obs = number of observations
DF = degrees of freedom
R^2 = coefficient of multiple determination
SEE = stantard error of estimate
D.W.= Durbin-Watson statistic.

effect on nominal GNP growth for the same lag length. There is, however, one important exception. Monetary policy has no significant long-run impact for the FXE rate period.[11]

Such a result need not, however, be inconsistent with the AJ approach, which has mainly emphasized estimates for a closed economy. The insignificance of lagged monetary policy under fixed exchange rates is consistent with the Mundell-Fleming model of an open economy. A caveat to the above interpretation is that the reduced form AJ equation is consistent with several structural models and any structural interpretation assigned to it requires the usual caution. Finally, the exports variable displays a long-run influence on income for the FLE period only. The conventional summary measures R^2 and the Durbin-Watson statistic do not show any cause for alarm, except that the latter statistic lies in the indeterminate range.

On the basis of these results the following tentative conclusions might be drawn. First, monetary policy effectiveness in the AJ equation does not hold for the FXE rate period. Second, exports may be an important policy instrument in the AJ equation during the FLE rate period, in addition to the monetary and fiscal policy instruments. This suggests that an AJ type equation may be misspecified in an open economy setting, as was recognized in the few attempts to estimate the St. Louis model for open economies (Winer 1979). Third, errors in the AJ equation are not necessarily uncorrelated, as evidenced by the less than flat spectrum of the residuals (not shown here) under the MFLE rate period (Ashley and Granger 1979 came to a similar conclusion). The evidence in favor of correlated errors in the AJ equation suggests that its estimation should be obtained under a more general error structure.

3.2 Spectral Estimates

The partial coherence estimates of alternative policy instruments with income in each of the three exchange periods are given in Fig. 1. These estimates are obtained under a more liberal lag structure as well as a fairly weak set of conditions for the error term in the AJ model. Also, no a priori one-way causality restrictions (in the WGS sense) are imposed to income from each of these instruments. Another feature of these estimates is that they provide the conditional linear relationship of each of these instruments on income over different frequencies; hence, they represent partial correlation estimates at individual frequencies. The plots in Fig. 1 show the strength of the partial coherences

---

[11] The t-test is a two-tailed test. Since a number of alternative hypotheses are begin tested, the actual significance level is perhaps much higher (i.e., the 10 percent significance level times the number of independent hypotheses being tested).

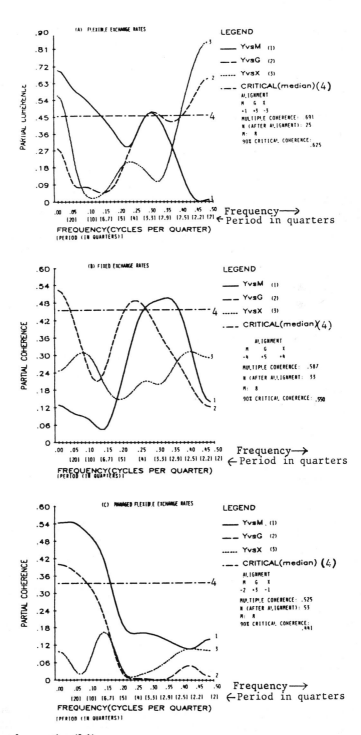

Fig. 1. Partial coherences for equation (2.1)

(or correlations) between income and each policy instrument for the St. Louis equation (2.1) in the frequency domain. The frequencies reported cover a range from 0 to 0.5 cycles per quarter. The corresponding time period for these frequencies are listed inside the square brackets along the horizontal axis.

Moving from left to right on the horizontal axis the time period decreases from an upper bound of "infinite" period to a period of two quarters. (The lower bound time period corresponds to the highest frequency for which one can obtain a partial coherence from the spectral analysis.) The partial coherence between income and each policy instrument can be read directly from the graph for a given frequency or time period. For instance in Fig. 1(c) the partial correlations between income and money are about 0.54 and 0.14, respectively, for the time period of 20 quarters and two quarters. The critical value of partial coherence is marked as line "4" on the respective graphs above which a given partial coherence is statistically significant. The time period for which the correlation between income and each policy instrument is statistically significant can easily be read from these graphs. Some considerations pertaining to the derivation of the respective partial coherences, the partial coherence critical value, and an interpretation of these graphs follows.

As noted in Section 2, alignment of the series was found to be necessary to reduce bias in the estimation of partial coherences. The number of quarters required to lag (+) or (−) a series in order to produce a peak at the zero lag in the cross-correlations of the series (as required by the alignment procedure), is shown in Fig. 1. Also shown is the truncation point (m) used to generate the cross-spectral estimates. The statistic n/m, where n is the number of observations, is used to find the critical level for zero coherence (Granger and Hatanaka 1964, p. 79 and Granger and Hughes 1968). The statistically significant partial coherences are, therefore, those which exceed the critical value shown. These are, of course, sensitive to the choice of the significance level. Where appropriate, however, we shall indicate the sensitivity of the results to a significance level of 90 percent. The critical coherence at this level of significance is also indicated in Fig. 1.

The results show that estimates of equation (2.1) have the following characteristics: (i) A degree of partial coherence that varies over frequencies as well as over exchange rate regimes, and (ii) in several cases, significant partial coherences exist over cycles of longer than four quarters. For example, while money and income have significant partial coherences over cycles of seven quarters' duration and longer in the FLE and MFLE rate periods, money is significantly related to income only over cycles of less than four quarters' duration for the FXE rate period. This conclusion holds even when the 90 percent level of significance is used, except that in the FXE sample, monetary policy ceases to be significantly related to nominal GNP, even for cycles of short duration.

Similarly, while fiscal policy and income shows significant partial coherences over cycles of duration longer than one year in the FXE and MFLE rate periods, fiscal policy is significantly related to income only over cycles of duration shorter than 3.3

quarters in the FLE rate period. These results hold when the 90 percent level of critical coherence is taken, except for the FXE period.

Finally, exports show statistically significant partial coherences with income over cycles of 40 quarters and longer only in the FLE exchange (at the median level only) rate period. Thus, long-run influences, as measured by the sum of lagged coefficients of policy instruments in the standard AJ model, might be underestimating the policy lag length.[12]

Two other conclusions from the estimates of Fig. 1 are worthy of mention. First, the low frequency significance of monetary actions on GNP growth for the flexible and managed float regimes suggest that the latter period may be treated as if it were an episode of purely flexible exchange rates. Yet, the partial coherences between fiscal policy and income differ markedly between the same two regimes. It appears, therefore, that in estimating AJ type equations, distinctions between exchange rate regimes should not be overlooked for the sake of convenience. Second, while the significance of the exports variable is also sample sensitive, this need not necessarily be viewed as evidence of omitted variables bias since this criticism has, so far, been directed at closed economy U.S. studies while the present empirical exercise consists of data for a small open economy.

The fiscal policy ineffectiveness results in Table 1 appear to be the result of a one-sided lag structure imposed a priori on the regression model without any strong theoretical arguments. The significant partial coherences of fiscal policy with income over cycles with long periodicities (i.e. low frequencies) in the FXE and MFLE rate periods could also be due to the fact that fiscal policy lags income instead of leading it. (Such a result may be due to the discretionary stance of this policy adopted by fiscal authorities over the years, even though causality runs from fiscal policy to income.) Indeed, the sign of the phase angle (not shown),[13] corresponding to a spectral analysis of model (2.1) for the unaligned data, reveals the fact that fiscal policy lags while monetary policy leads income,[14] especially over the long cycles. An interpretation of fiscal policy lagging income might be that rational economic agents had anticipated the actual policy stance taken by the authorities and incoporated it into their decision

---

[12] In contrast, the AJ result for the United States is that estimates are insensitive to the choice of lag length. See the October 1986 issue of the *St. Louis Review,* and Batten and Thornton (1984).

[13] There is an indeterminacy of $2\pi k$ radians in estimating the phase. We note that the two-sided lag results support our interpretation of the phase results as a future lag. Following Hause 1971, p. 216), we use the unmodified word "lag" to describe phase, whereas the translation of phase in the time domain is expressed as pure delay or pure lag. These timing estimates can be viewed as the discrete lag estimates (between stimulus and response variables) from the frequency response function of the distributed lag model.

[14] The Mundell-Fleming model predicts that monetary policy will lead income during the FXE period (see Sarlo 1979).

making.[15] An alternative interpretation of the results in Fig. 1 might be that fiscal policy is in fact endogenous to income in the WGS sense. The plausibility of this interpretation is explored by calculating the BSR results corresponding to the spectral analysis of the unaligned series in model (2.1).

3.3 Band Spectrum Regression Estimates

The BSR estimates for a two-sided lag structure are presented in Table 2 for the MFLE rate period only. Practical considerations precluded reporting the BSR estimates for the FLE and FXE period. The chosen lag length is four, corresponding to the one-sided distributed lag version of the AJ model. The lead length is also specified as four since the cross-correlations (not shown) of some of the policy variables with income were found to peak at the three-period lead. As a result, for a four period lead/lag length, the degrees of freedom would be negative in the BSR estimates for the FLE and FXE rate periods. This can also be seen by estimating degrees of freedom from information about sample sizes given in Table 1.

In calculating the BSR results in Table 2 for the MFLE rate period, we dropped the exports variable from model (2.1) since it was found to have an insignificant partial coherence with income.[16]

The results in Table 2 show that monetary policy has a cumulative impact on income for both lag and lead terms, thereby casting doubt on the "strong exogeneity" of money in the AJ equation for Canada during the MFLE period at a significance level of about 10 percent. The negative sign for the cumulative effect of lead terms suggests that past expansionary montary policy may set up expectations for a future contraction.

A scenario such as this one also appears consistent with the monetary policy stance taken by the Bank of Canada in recent years and extensively documented by Courchene (1977, 1981, 1983) and, more recently, by Howitt (1986). They pointed out that the Bank of Canada has been manipulating exchange rates and the domestic

---

[15] McCallum (1984) and Barsky (1987) point out that low frequencies may not necessarily be the equivalent of the long-run concept in economics. Viewing the low frequencies as consistent with fully anticipated policies may result in a misspecification. Strictly speaking, since the monetary and fiscal variables in (2.1) are not used to proxy expectations, the problem raised above does not apply. Insofar as the interpretation of the results is dependent on the assumption that the series utilized are a kind of proxy for expectations, misspecification is possible. We note, however, that the errors-in-variables issue is likely to be empirically small for post-World War II data (Barsky 1987).

[16] In effect we assume that the influence of exports is subsumed in the error term of model (2.1). Such a practice may be acceptable under the circumstances (Raj and Siklos 1986).

Table 2. Band Spectral Regression and Hannan Efficient Estimates of Two-sided Distributed Lag Version of Equation: (2.1).

Summary Results

Variable	BSR Estimates		Hannan Efficient Estimates	
	coefficient [significance	(t-value) level]	coefficient [significance	(t-value) level]
$\sum_{i=0}^{4} m_{t-i}$	.564 [0.005]	(3.289)	.567 [0.001x10^{-1}]	(4.676)
$\sum_{i=-1}^{-4} m_{t-j}$	-.255 [0.102]	(-1.732)	-.256 [0.0200]	(-2.458)
$\sum_{i=0}^{4} g_{t-i}$	.018 [0.898]	(.130)	.017 [0.867]	(.169)
$\sum_{i=-1}^{-4} g_{t-j}$	.363 [0.009]	(2.959)	.362 [0.002x10^{-1}]	(4.174)
Observations	51		51	
Degrees of freedom	16		32	
R^2	.732		.732	
S.E.E	.109		.154	
D.W.	1.694		1.702	
Q_{21} (sig. level)[3]	6.946 (0.998)		6.868 (0.998)	

Note: 1. t-statistic in parenthesis. Null hypothesis is that all coefficients are cumulatively zero.

2. Significance level in square brackets

3. Box-Pierce Unadjusted Q statistic test for serial correlation in the residuals.

R^2 = coefficient of multiple determination
D.W. = Durbin-Watson Statistic
SEE = Standard Error of Regression

interest rate in conducting monetary policy since 1970. Hence, it would appear that recent Canadian macroeconomic experience has elements of both flexible and fixed exchange rates. This could explain why monetary policy may not be strongly exogenous.

Unlike monetary policy, only the cumulative effect of future fiscal policy has a statistically significant impact on nominal GNP growth. This is also true when cycles of four quarters or longer are estimated, thereby reaffirming the evidence in Fig. 1. In fact, a comparison of the BSR and Hannan efficient estimates in Table 2 suggests that fiscal policy has a primarily long-run effect on income.

Finally, it is interesting to note that nominal GNP responds to future (expected) fiscal policy alone. On interpretation for such a result is that individuals, having discounted the role of past fiscal policies, base their calculations of the future course of the combined impact of real GNP and inflation on their best guess about the future course of government discretionary actions. This is precisely the kind of evidence that led Lucas (1976) to formulate his critique of econometric policy evaluation.

4 Concluding Remarks

The AJ equation assumes a priori that fiscal and monetary instruments are "strongly exogenous" (Engle, Hendry, and Richard (1983). Some empirical evidence that fiscal policy may not be strongly exogenous was provided by Raj and Siklos (1986) for the United States. In this paper we utilized a similar nonparametric approach for analyzing the reduced form AJ equation for an open economy and obtained some interesting new results. First, we found that fiscal policy is significant with income in the FXE and MFLE rate periods over cycles of significantly longer than one year, with fiscal policy lagging income over low frequencies. Thus, the efficacy of fiscal policy, even in the reduced form framework, cannot be ruled out. These results are not necessarily inconsistent with theoretical analysis involving Ricardian and non-Ricardian assumptions (McCallum 1986, Sections 3 and 4). Second, long-run efficacy of monetary policy under the FXE regime is questionable since money and income are not significantly related to income over cycles of one year duration and longer. Third, fiscal policy does not appear to be "strongly exogenous" in the WGS sense as assumed in conventional St. Louis equation specifications. Our results suggest that the reduced-form model is not likely to yield good predictions for income over the MFLE period. These results might also suggest that the conventional AJ model does not fully capture the complex relation between income and the fiscal policy instrument.

Appendix

Data from CANSIM — Canadian Socio-Economic Information Management System. Note that, as of 1987, CANSIM no longer provides the Nominal GNP series separately, though it can be reconstruceted from available series in CANSIM. All series were seasonally adjusted at the source.

Series (notation)	Series number
Nominal GNP (Y)	D40552
Nominal Merchandise Esports of Goods and Services (X)	D399524
Money Supply — $M1$ (M)	131627

Data from other source: Full Employment Federal Government Budget Expenditures (G). Series obtained from Finance Department (Ottawa). A description of the series and the methodology used to construct it can be found in *Economic Review*, April 1978, p. 85–86, Otawa: Department of Finance.

References

Amemiya T, Fuller WA (1967) A comparative study of alternative estimators in a distributed lag model. Econometrica 35:509–529

Ashley RA, Granger CWJ (1979) Time series analysis of residuals from the St. Louis model. Journal of Macroeconomics 15:305–327

Barsky RB (1987) The fisher hypothesis and the forecastibility and persistence of inflation Journal of Monetary Economics 19:3–24

Batten DD, Thornton DL (1984) How robust are the policy conclusions of the St. Louis model? Some further evidence. St Louis Review 66:26–32

Batten DD, Thornton DL (1986) The monetary-fiscal policy debate and the Anderson-Jordan equation. St Louis Review 68:9–17

Blinder AS (1986) Ruminations on Karl Brunner's reflections. Chapter 4 in Hafer RW (ed) referenced below

Carlson KM (1978) Does the St. Louis equation now believe in fiscal policy? St Louis Review 60: 13–19

Courchene TJ (1977) The strategy of gradualism: an analysis of Bank of Canada policy from mid 1975. CD Howe Research Institute, Montreal

Courchene TJ (1981) Money, inflation, and the Bank of Canada volume II: an analysis of monetary gradualism, 1975–80. CD Howe Research Institute, Montreal

Courchene TJ (1983) No placd to stand? Abandoning monetary targets: an evaluation. CD Howe Research Institute, Montreal

Darby MR (1976) Comments on Modigliani and Ando. In: Stein JL (ed) Monetarism. North-Holland. Amsterdam, pp 67–58

Elliot JW (1975) The influence of monetary and fiscal actions on spending. Journal of Money, Credit, and Banking (May 1975), pp 181–192

Engle RF (1974) Band spectrum regression. International Economic Review 15:1–11

Engle RF, Hendry DF, Richard JF (1983) Exogeneity. Econometrica 51:277–304

Federal Reserve Bank of St Louis Review "Special Issue" (1986) 68:1–71

Frankel JA, Mussa ML (1981) Monetary and fiscal policies in an open economy. American Economic Review 71:253–258

Friedman BM (1977) Even the St. Louis model now believes in fiscal policy. Journal of Money, Credit, and Banking (May 1977), pp 365–367

Goldfeld SM, Blinder AS (1972) Some implications of endogenous stabilization policy. Brookings Papers on Economic Activity 3:585–640

Granger CWJ, Hatanaka M (1964) Spectral analysis of economic time series. Princeton University Press, Princeton

Granger CWJ, Hughes AO (1968) Spectral analysis of short series – a simulation study. Journal of the Royal Statistical Society A131:83–99

Hafer RW (ed) (1986) The monetary versus fiscal policy debate: lesson from two decades. Rowman and Allanheld, New Jersey

Hannan EJ (1965) The estimation of relationships involving distribute lags. Econometrica 33:206–224

Hannan EJ (1970) Multiple time series. Wiley, New York

Hause JC (1971) Spectral analysis and the detection of lead-lag relationships. American Economic Review 61:213–217

Howitt P (1986) Monetary policy in transition: a study of Bank of Canada policy, 1982–85. CD Howe Institute, Montreal

Howrey EP (1980) The role of time series analysis in econometric model evaluation. In: Kmenta J, Ramsey JB (eds) Evaluation of economic models. Academic Press, New York

Jenkins GM, Watts DG (1968) Spectral analysis and its applications. Holden-Day, San Francisco

Lucas RE Jr (1976) Econometric policy evaluation: a critique. In: Brunner K, Meltzer AH (eds) The Phillips curve and labor markets. Carnegie – Rochester Conference Series on Public Policy 1:19–46

McCallum BT (1984) On low frequency estimates of long-run relationships in macroeconomics. Journal of Monetary Economics 14:3–14

McCallum BT (1986) Monetary versus fiscal policy effects: a review of the debate. Chapter 2 in Hafer RW (ed) referenced above

Ministry of Finance Annual Report (1985) Ministry of Finance, Government of Canada, Ottawa

Modigliani F, Ando A (1976) Impact of fiscal actions on aggregate income and the monetarist controversy: theory and evidence. In: Stein JL (ed) Monetarism. North-Holland, Amsterdam

Nelson CR, Plosser C (1982) Trends and random walks in macroeconomic time series: some evidence and implications. Journal of Monetary and Economics 10:139–162

Prachowny MFJ (1977) The effectiveness of fiscal and monetary policies under fixed and flexible exchange rates: some empirical evidence for Canada, 1950–1970. Weltwirtschaftliches Archiv 113:462–485

Raj B, Siklos PL (1986) The role of fiscal policy in the St. Louis model: an evaluation and some new evidence. Journal of Applied Econometrics 1:287–294

Ramsey JB, Schmidt P (1976) Some further results on the use of OLS and BLUS residuals in specification error tests. Journal of the American Statistical Association (June 1976), pp 389–390

Sarlo C (1979) The role of money in the Canadian economy: fixed vs flexible exchange rates. Canadian Journal of Economics 12:89–93

Sims C (1980) Macroeconomics and reality. Econometrica 48:1–48

Sims C (1982) Policy analsis with econometric models. Brookings Papers on Economic Activity 1:107–152

Winer SL (1979) Short-run monetary-influences in federal state: with application to the Canadian economy, 1947 to 1973. Public Finance Quarterly 7:395–424

Winer SL (1986a) The role of exchange rate flexibility in the international transmission of inflation in long and shorter runs: Canada, 1953 to 1981. Canadian Journal of Economics 19:662–686

Winer SL (1986b) Money and politics in a small open economy. Public Choice 51:221–239

Automatic Smoothing Parameter Selection: A Survey

By J. S. Marron[1]

Abstract: This is a survey of recent developments in smoothing parameter selection for curve estimation. The first goal of this paper is to provide an introduction to the methods available, with discussion at both a practical and also a nontechnical level, including comparison of methods. The second goal is to provide access to the literature, especially on smoothing parameter selection, but also on curve estimation in general. The two main settings considered here are nonparametric regression and probability density estimation, although the points made apply to other settings as well. These points also apply to many different estimators, although the focus is on kernel estimators, because they are the most easily understood and motivated, and have been at the heart of the development in the field.

1 Introduction

Choice of smoothing parameter is the central issue in the application of all types of nonparametric curve estimators. This is demonstrated in Fig. 1 which shows a simulated regression setup. In Fig. 1a, the curve is the underlying regression function, and simulated observations, taken at equally spaced design points, are represented by crosses. Figures 1b, 1c and 1d show the same curve and observations together with some moving weighted averages of the crosses, shown as dashed curves, corresponding to different window widths, as shown by the dashed curves representing the weights, which appear at the bottom of each plot. Note that in Fig. 1b, the window width is quite narrow, with the result that there are not enough observations appearing in each window for stability of the average, and the resulting estimate is overly subject to sample variability, i.e. is too "wiggly". Note that this is improved in Fig. 1c, where a larger window width has been used. In Fig. 1d, the window width is so large that observa-

---

[1] Dr. J. S. Marron, Department of Statistics, University of North Carolina, USA.

Research partially supported by NSF Grant DMS-8701201.

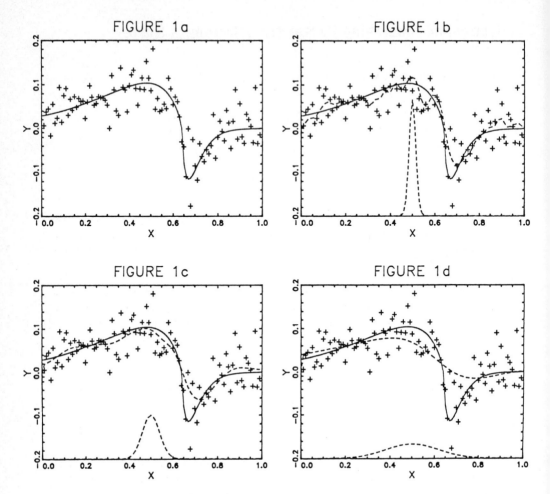

Fig. 1. Simulated regression setting. Solid curve is underlying regression. Residuals are Gaussian. Dashed curves are moving weighted averages, with Gaussian weights, represented at the bottom. Standard deviations in the weight functions are: Fig. 1b, 0.015; Fig. 1c, 0.04; Fig. 1d, 0.12

tions from too far away appear in the averages, with the effect of introducing some bias, or in other words features of the underlying curve that are actually present have been smoothed away.

The very large amount of flexibility in nonparametric curve estimators, demonstrated by changing the window width in the example of Fig. 1, allows great payoffs, because these estimators do not arbitrarily impose structure on the data, which is always done by parametric estimators. To see how this is the case, think of doing a simple linear regression least squares fit of the data in Fig. 1. Of course, if the structure imparted by a parametric model is appropriate, then that model should certainly be used for inference, as the decreased flexibility allows for much firmer results, in terms of more powerful hypothesis test, and smaller confidence intervals. However it is in cases where no model readily suggests itself, or there may be some doubt as to the model, that nonparametric curve estimation really comes to the fore. See Silverman (1986) and Härdle (1988) for interesting collections of effective data analyses carried out by these methods.

However there is a price to be paid for the great flexibility of nonparametric methods, which is that the smoothing parameter must be chosen. It is easy to see in Fig. 1 which window width is appropriate, because that is a simulation example, where the underlying curve is available, but for real data sets, when one has little idea of what the underlying curve is like, this issue clearly becomes more difficult.

Most effective data analysis using nonparametric curve estimators has been done by choosing the smoothing parameter by a trial and error approach consisting of look-ing at several different plots representing different amounts of smoothness. While this approach certainly allows one to learn a great deal about the set of data, it can never be used to convince a skeptic in the sense that a hypothesis test can. Hence there has been a search for methods which use the data in some objective, or "automatic" way to choose the smoothing parameter.

This paper is a survey of currently available automatic smoothing parameter selec-tion techniques. There are many settings in which smoothing type estimators have been proposed and studied. Attention will be focussed here on the two most widely studied, which are density and regression estimation, because the lessons seem to be about the same for all settings. These problems are formulated mathematically in Section 2.

There are also many different types of estimators which have been proposed in each setting, see for example Prakasa Rao (1983), Silverman (1986), and Härdle (1988). However all of these have the property that, as with the moving average estimator in Fig. 1, their performance is crucially dependent on choice of a smoothing parameter. Here again the lessons seem to be about the same, so focus is put on just one type of estimator, that is kernel based methods. These estimators are chosen be-cause they are simple, intuitively appealing, and best understood. The form of these are given in Section 2. Other important estimators, to which the ideas presented here also apply include histograms, the various types of splines, and those based on orthogo-nal series.

To find out more about the intuitive and data analytic aspects of nonparametric curve estimation, see Silverman (1986) for density estimation, and see Eubank (1988) and Härdle (1988) for regression (the former regression book requires more mathe-matical knowledge of the reader, and centers around smoothing splines, the latter is more applied in character, with the focus on kernel estimators). For an access to the rather large theoretical literature, the monograph by Prakasa Rao (1983) is recom-mended. Other monographs on curve estimation, some of which focus on some rather specialized topics, include Tapia and Thompson (1978), Wertz (1978), Devroye and Gyorfi (1984), Nadaraya (1983) and Devroye (1987). Survey papers have been written on density estimation by Wegman (1972), Tarter and Kronmal (1976), Fryer (1977), Wertz and Schneider (1978) and Bean and Tsokos (1980). Collomb (1982, 1985) and Bierens (1987) provide surveys of nonparametric regression. See Ullah (1987) for discussion of both settings as well as others.

Section 2 of this paper introduces notation. Section 3 discusses various possibilities for "the right amount of smoothing", and states an important asymptotic quantification of the smoothing problem. Section 4 introduces and discusses various methods for automatic bandwidth selection in the density estimation context. This is done for regression in Section 5. Section 6 discusses some hybrid methods and related topics.

2 Mathematical Formulation and Notation

The density estimation problem is mathematically formulated as follows. Use independent identically distributed observations, $X_1, ..., X_n$, from a probability density $f(x)$, to estimate $f(x)$. The kernel estimator of f, as proposed by Rosenblatt (1956) and Parzen (1962), is given by

$$\hat{f}_h(x) = n^{-1} \sum_{i=1}^{n} K_h(x - X_i),$$

where K is often taken to be a symmetric probability density, and $K_h(\cdot) = K(\cdot/h)/h$. See Chapter 3 of Silverman (1986) for a good discussion of the intuition behind this estimator and its properties. The smoothing parameter in this estimator is h, often called the bandwidth or window width. Note that the estimator could have been defined without h appearing as a separate parameter, however because the amount of smoothing is so crucial it is usually represented in this form.

One way of formulating the nonparametric regression problem is to think of using

$$Y_i = m(x_i) + \epsilon_i, \quad i = 1, ..., n,$$

where the ϵ_i are mean zero errors, to estimate the regression curve, $m(x)$. This setup is usually called "fixed design" regression. A widely studied alternative is "stochastic design" regression, in which the x_i's are treated as random variables. While mathematical analysis of the two settings requires different techniques, the smoothing aspects tend to correspond very closely, so only the fixed design is explicitly formulated here. See Chapter 2 of Härdle (1988) for a formulation of the stochastic design regression problem. Kernel estimators in regression were introduced by Nadaraya (1964) and Watson (1964). One way to formulate them is as a weighted average of the form

$$\hat{m}_h(x) = \sum_{i=1}^{n} W_i(x, h)Y_i,$$

where the weights are defined by

$$W_i(x, h) = K_h(x - X_i)/ \sum_{i=1}^{n} K_h(x - X_i).$$

See Section 3.1 of Härdle (1988) for discussion of this estimator, and a number of other ways of formulating a kernel regression estimator.

In both density and regression estimation, the choice of the kernel function, K, is of essentially negligible concern, compared to choice of the bandwidth h. This can be seen at an intuitive level by again considering Fig. 1. Note that if the shape of the weight functions appearing at the bottom is changed, the effect on the estimator will be far less than is caused by a change in window width. See Section 3.3.2 of Silverman (1986) and Section 4.5 of Härdle (1988) for a mathematical quantification and further discussion of this.

3 "Right" Answers

The traditional method of assessing the performance of estimators which use an automatic smoothing parameter selector, is to consider some sort of error criterion. The usual criteria may be separated into two classes, global and pointwise. As most applications of curve estimation call for a picture of an entire curve, instead of its value at one particular point, only global measures will be discussed here.

The most commonly considered global error criteria in density estimation are the Integrated Squared Error (i.e. the L^2 norm),

$$\text{ISE}(h) = \int [\hat{f}_h - f]^2,$$

and its expected value, the Mean Integrated Squared Error

$$\text{MISE} = E(\text{ISE}(h)).$$

Related criteria are the Integrated Absolute Error (i.e. the L^1 norm),

$$\text{IAE} = \int |\hat{f}_h - f|,$$

and its expected value,

$$\text{MIAE} = E(\text{IAE}(h)),$$

There are other possibilities such as weighted versions of the above, as well as the supremum norm, Hellinger distance, and the Kullback-Leibler distance.

In regression, one can study the obvious regression analog of the above norms, and in addition there are other possibilities, such as the Average Squared Error,

$$\text{ASE}(h) = n^{-1} \sum_{j=1}^{n} [\hat{m}_h(x_j) - m(x_j)]^2,$$

and its expected value,

$$\text{MASE}(h) = E(\text{ASE}(h)).$$

For the rest of this paper, the minimizers of these criteria will be denoted by an h with the appropriate subscript, e.g. h_{MISE}.

An important question is how much difference is there between these various criteria. In Section 6 of their Chapter 5, Devroye and Gyorfi (1984) report that there can be a very substantial difference between h_{MISE} and h_{MIAE} in density estimation. However, this issue is far from clear, as Hall and Wand (1988) point out that, for several specific densities, the difference betweeen h_{AMISE} and h_{AMIAE} is very small.

Given that there is an important difference between the squared error and the absolute error type criteria, there is no consensus on which should be taken as "the right answer". Devroye and Gyorfi (1984) point out a number of reasons for studying density estimation with absolute error methods. This has not gained wide acceptance though, one reason being that squared error criteria are much easier to work with from a technical point of view. The result of this is that all of the real theoretical break-throughs in density estimation have come first from considering squared error criteria, then with much more work, the idea is extended to the absolute error case.

The issue of the difference between the random criteria, such as ISE and IAE, and their expected values, such as MISE and MIAE, seems more clear. In particular it has been shown by Hall and Marron (1987a) that h_{ISE} and h_{MISE} do converge to each other asymptotically, but at a very slow rate, and may typically be expected to be quite far apart. Here again there is no consensus about which should be taken as "the right answer". ISE has the compelling advantage that minimizing it gives the smoothing parameter which is best, for the set of data at hand, as opposed to being best only with respect to the average over all possible data sets, as with MISE. However, acceptance of ISE as the "right answer" is controversial because ISE is random, and two different experimenters, whose data have the same underlying distributions, will have two different "right answers". This type of reason is why statistical decision theory (see for example Ferguson 1967) is based on "risk" instead of on "loss". See Scott (1988) and Carter, Eagleson and Smith (1986) for further discussion of this issue.

One advantage of MISE is that it allows a very clean asymptotic summary of the smoothing problem. In particular, for kernel density estimation, if K is a probability density and f has two continuous derivatives, then as $n \to \infty$ and $h \to 0$, with $nh \to \infty$,

$$MISE(h) = AMISE(h) + o(AMISE(h)),$$

where

$$AMISE(h) = n^{-1}h^{-1}(\int K^2) + h^4(\int x^2 K)^2 (\int (f'')^2)/4,$$

see for example (3.20) of Silverman (1986). Recall from Fig. 1, that too small a window width results in too much sample variability. Note that this is reflected by the first term (usually called the variance term) in AMISE becoming too large. On the other side, the fact that a too large window width gives too much bias, is reflected in the second term which gets large in that case.

There is a tendency to think of h_{AMISE} as being the same as h_{MISE}, and this seems to be usually nearly true, but can be quite far off sometimes. Scott (1986) has shown that for the lognormal density AMISE and MISE will still be very far apart even for sample sizes as large as a million. See Dodge (1986) for related results concerning pointwise error criteria.

4 Density Estimation

In this section most of the automatic bandwidth selectors proposed for kernel density estimation are presented and discussed. It should be noted that most of these have obvious analogs for other types of estimators as well.

4.1 Plug-in methods

The essential idea here is to work with AMISE(h) and plug in an estimate of the only unknown part, which is $\int (f'')^2$. Variations on this idea have been proposed and studied by Woodroofe (1970), Scott, Tapia and Thompson (1977), Scott and Factor (1981), Krieger and Pickands (1981), and Sheather (1983, 1986). Most of the above authors consider the case of pointwise density estimation, but the essential ideas carry over to the global case.

A drawback to this approach, is that estimation of $\int (f'')^2$ requires specification of a smoothing parameter. The argument is usually given that the final estimator is less dependent on this secondary smoothing parameter, but this does not seem to have been very carefully investigated. An interesting approach to the problem is given in Sheather (1986).

A second weakness of the plug-in estimator is that it targets AMISE, which can be substantially different from MISE.

A major strength of the plug-in selector is that, if strong enough smoothness assumptions are made, then it seems to have much better sample variability properties than many of the selectors in the rest of Section 4, see remark 4.6 of Hall and Marron (1987a).

For plug-in estimators in the absolute error setting, see Hall and Wand (1989). Related results, which can be applied to pointwise absolute error bandwidths can be found in Hall and Wand (1988).

4.2 Psuedo Likelihood Cross-Validation

Also called Kullback-Leibler cross-validation, this was proposed independently by Habbema, Hermans and van den Broek (1974) and by Duin (1976). The essential idea is to choose that value of h which maximizes the psuedo-likelihood,

$$\prod_{j=1}^{n} \hat{f}_h(X_j).$$

However this has a trivial minimum at $h = 0$, so the cross-validation principle is invoked by replacing $\hat{f}_h$ in each factor by the leave one out version,

$$\hat{f}_{h,j}(x) = (n-1)^{-1} \sum_{i \neq j}^{n} K_h(x - X_i).$$

Another viewpoint on why the leave-one-out estimator is appropriate here is that the original criterion may be considered to be using the same observations to construct the estimator, as well as assess its performance. When the cross-validation principle (see Stone 1974) is used to attack this problem, we arrive at the modification based on using the leave-one-out estimator.

Schuster and Gregory (1981) have shown that this selector is severely affected by the tail behavior of f. Chow, Geman, and Wu (1983) demonstrated that if both the kernel and the density are compactly supported then the resulting density estimator will be consistent. The fact that this consistency can be very slow, and the selected bandwidth very poor, was demonstrated by Marron (1985), who proposed an efficient modification of the psuedo-likelihood based on some modifications studied by Hall (1982). Hall (1987a, b) has provided a nice characterization of the pseudo-likelihood type of cross-validation, by showing that it targets the bandwidth which minimizes the Kullback-Leibler distance between $\hat{f}_h$ and f. Hall goes on to explore the properties of this bandwidth, and concludes that it may sometimes be appropriate for using a kernel estimate in the discrimination problem, but is usually not appropriate for curve estimation. For this reason, psuedo-likelihood currently seems to be of less current interest than the other smoothing parameter selectors considered here.

4.3 Least Squares Cross-Validation

This was proposed independently by Rudemo (1982a) and by Bowman (1984). The essential idea is to target

$$\text{ISE}(h) = \int \hat{f}_h^2 - 2 \int \hat{f}_h f + \int f^2 .$$

The first term of this expansion is available to the experimenter, and the last term is independent of h. Using a method of moments estimate of the second term results in the criterion.

$$\int \hat{f}_h^2 - 2 \sum_{j=1}^{n} \hat{f}_{h,j}(X_j).$$

which is then minimized to give a cross-validated smoothing parameter.

The fact that the bandwidth chosen in this fashion is asymptotically correct for ISE, MISE, and AMISE has been demonstrated, under various assumptions, by Hall (1983, 1985), Stone (1984), Burman (1985) and Nolan and Pollard (1987) (see Stone

1985 for the histogram analog of this). Marron and Padgett (1987) have established the analogous result in the case of randomly censored data. A comparison to an improved version of the Kullback-Leibler cross-validation was done by Marron (1987a).

The main strength of this bandwidth is that it is asymptotically correct under very weak smoothness assumptions on the underlying density. Stone (1984) uses assumptions so weak that there is no guarantee that $\hat{f}_h$ will even be consistent, but the bandwidth is still doing as well as possible in the limit. This translates in a practical sense into a type of robustness. The plug-in selector is crucially dependent on AMISE being a good approximation of MISE, but least squares cross-validation still gives good asymptotic performance, even in situations where the MISE $\approx$ AMISE approximation is very bad.

A drawback to least squares cross-validation is that the score function has a tendency towards having several local minima, with some spurious ones often quite far over on the side of undersmoothing. This does not seem to be only a small sample aberation, as Scott and Terrell (1987) noticed it in their simulation study even for very large samples. For this reason it is recommended that minimization be done by a grid search through a range of h's, instead of by some sort of computationally more efficient step-wise minimization algorithm (which will converge quite rapidly, but only to a local minimum). An unexplored possibility for approaching the local minimum problem is to select the bandwidth which is the largest value of h for which a local minimum occurs.

Another major weakness of the least squares cross-validated smoothing parameter is that it is usually subject to a great deal of sample variability, in the sense that for different data sets from the same distributions, it will typically give much different answers. This has been quantified asymptotically by Hall and Marron (1987a), who show that the relative rate of convergence of the cross-validated bandwidth to either of h_{ISE} or h_{MISE} is excruciatingly slow. It is interesting though that the noise level is of about the same order as the relative difference between h_{ISE} and h_{MISE}. This is the result referred to in Section 3, concerning the practical difference between random error criteria and their expected values.

While the noise level of the cross-validated bandwidth is very large it is rather heartening that the same level exists for the difference between the two candidates for "optimal", in the sense that the exponents in the algebraic rate of convergence are the same. This leads one to suspect that the rate of convergence calculated by Hall and Marron (1987a) is in fact the best possible. This was shown, in a certain minimax sense, by Hall and Marron (1987b). To keep this in perspective though, note that the constant multiplier of the rate of convergence of the optimal bandwidths to each other is typically smaller than for cross-validation. Since the rates are so slow, it is these constants which are really important. See Marron (1987b) for further discussion.

Recall that an attractive feature of the plug-in bandwidth selectors was their sample stability. These selectors have a faster rate of convergence to h_{AMISE} than the rate at which h_{ISE} and h_{MISE} come together. This does not contradict the above minimax result because this faster rate requires much stronger smoothness assumptions. In settings of the type which drive the minimax result, the plug-in selectors will be subject to much more sample noise, and also h_{AMISE} will be a very poor approximation to h_{MISE}.

A somewhat surprising fact about the least squares cross-validated bandwidth is that, although its goal is h_{ISE}, these two random variables are in fact negatively correlated! This means that for those data sets where h_{ISE} is smaller than usual, the cross-validated bandwidth tends to be bigger than usual, and vice versa. This phenomenon was first reported in Rudemo (1982a), and has been quantified theoretically by Hall and Marron (1987a). An intuitive explanation for it has also been provided by Rudemo, in terms of "clusterings" of the data. If the data set is such that there is more clustering than usual, note that h_{ISE} will be larger than usual, because the spurious structure needs to be smoothed away, while cross-validation will pick a smaller bandwidth than usual because it sees the clustering as some fine structure that can only be resolved with a smaller window. On the other hand, if the data set has less clustering than usual, then h_{ISE} will be smaller than usual, so as to cut down on bias, while cross-validation sees no structure, and hence takes a bigger bandwidth. An interesting consequence of this negative correlation is that if one could find a stable "centerpoint", then (if ISE is accepted as the right answer) it would be tempting to use a bandwidth which is on the opposite side of this from h_{CV}.

A last drawback of least squares cross-validation is that it can be very expensive to compute, especially when the recommended grid search minimization algorithm is used. Two approaches to this problem are the Fast Fourier Transform approximation ideas described in Section 3.5 of Silverman (1986), and the Average Shifted Histogram approximation ideas described in Section 5.3 of Scott and Terrell (1987).

Härdle, Marron and Wand (1988) have extended the least squares cross-validation idea to estimation of derivatives of a probability density.

4.4 Biased Cross-Validation

This was proposed and studied by Scott and Terrell (1987). It is a hybrid combining aspects of both plug-in methods, and also least squares cross-validation. The essential idea is to minimize, by choice of h, the following estimate of AMISE(h),

$$n^{-1}h^{-1}(\textstyle\int K^2) + h^4(\int x^2 K)^2 (\int (\hat{f}_h'')^2)/4.$$

Note that if the bandwidth used in the estimate of $\int (f'')^2$ were different from h, the bandwidth being assessed, then the selected bandwidth would be the same as the plug-in bandwidth discussed in Section 4.1. The fact that the same h is used in the estimate of $\int (f'')^2$ is what makes biased cross-validation substantially different.

Scott and Terrell (1987) show that the biased cross-validated bandwidth has sample variability with the same rate of convergence as least squares cross-validation, but with a typically much smaller constant coefficient. This is crucial as the rates are so slow that it is essentially the constant coefficients that determine performance of the selectors. Scott and Terrell (1987) also demonstrate the superior performance of biased cross-validation in some settings by simulation results.

A drawback of biased cross-validation is that, like the plug-in, its effective performance requires much stronger smoothness assumptions than required for least squares cross-validation. It seems possible that in settings where biased cross-validation is better than least squares cross-validation, the plug-in will be better yet, and in settings where the plug-in is inferior to least squares cross-validation, biased cross-validation will be as well, although this has not been investigated yet.

Another weak point of biased cross-validation is that for very small samples, on the order of $n = 25$, Scott and Terrell (1987) report that the method may sometimes fail all together, in the sense that there is no minimum. This seems to be not as bad as the spurious local minima that occur for least squares cross-validation, because at least it is immediately clear that something funny is going on. Also unlike the spurious minima in least squares cross-validation, this problem seems to disappear rapidly with increasing sample size.

4.5 Oversmoothing

This idea has been proposed in Chapter 5, Section 6 of Devroye and Györfi (1984) and by Terrell and Scott (1985). The essential idea is to note that

$$h_{\text{AMISE}} = \left(\frac{\int K^2}{(\int x^2 K)^2 \int (f'')^2} \right)^{1/5} n^{-1/5}.$$

The only part of this expression that is unavailable to the experimenter is $\int (f'')^2$. If one could find a lower bound for this quantity, then by substituting the lower bound, one would obtain a bandwidth which is asymptotically larger (oversmoothed) than any of the squared error notions of "optimal" described above. For such a lower bound to exist, it turns out to be enough that the scale of the f distribution is controlled, say by rescaling so that its variance is equal to one. Thus this oversmoothing idea can be reasonably implemented by rescaling through some estimate of the sample variance.

The version of the oversmoothed bandwidth described here is that of Terrell and Scott, the Devroye and Györfi version is the L^1 analog of this idea.

Terrell and Scott (1985) show that for unimodal densities, such as the Gaussian, the difference between the oversmoothed bandwidth and h_{AMISE} is often surprisingly small. Another benefit of this is that it is very stable accross samples because the only place the data even enter are through the scale estimate, which has a fast parametric rate of convergence.

Of course the oversmoothed bandwidth has the obvious drawback that it can be very inappropriate for multimodal data sets, which unfortunately are the ones that are most interesting when data is being analyzed by density estimation techniques.

A possible application of the oversmoothed bandwidth, that has been suggested in some oral presentations given by David Scott, is that it can be used to provide an upper bound to the range of bandwidths considered by minimization based techniques such as the various types of cross-validation. The usefulness of this idea has not yet been investigated.

5 Regression Estimation

Note that two of the ideas proposed above for density estimation, the plug-in selectors and biased cross-validation, can be directly carried over to the regression setting. Neither of these ideas has been investigated yet (although see Müller and Stadtmüller 1987 for a local criterion based plug-in selector). In this section most of the automatic bandwidth selectors that have been considered for kernel regression estimation are presented and discussed. Again note that the ideas here have obvious analogs for other types of estimators as well.

5.1 Cross-Validation

This was first considered in the nonparametric curve estimation context by Clark (1975) and Wahba and Wold (1975) for spline estimators. The essential idea is to use the fact that the regression function, $m(x)$ is the best mean square predictor of a new observation taken at x. This suggests choosing the bandwidth which makes $\hat{m}_h(x)$ a good predictor, or in other words taking the minimizer of the estimated prediction error,

$$\text{EPE}(h) = n^{-1} \sum_{j=1}^{n} [Y_j - \hat{m}_h(x_j)]^2.$$

This criterion has the same problem that was observed in Section 4.2, namely that it has a trivial minimum at $h = 0$. As above this can be viewed as being caused by using the same data to both construct and assess the estimator, and a reasonable approach to this problem is provided by the cross-validation principle. Hence the cross-validated bandwidth is the one which minimizes the criterion obtained by replacing $\hat{m}_h(x_j)$ by the obvious leave-one-out version. See Härdle and Marron (1985a) for a motivation of this criterion that is very similar in spirit to that for density estimation least squares cross-validation, as described in Section 4.3.

The fact that the bandwidth chosen in this fashion is asymptotically correct was established by Rice (1984) in the fixed design context, and by Härdle and Marron (1985a) in the stochastic design setting.

Härdle, Hall and Marron (1988) have shown that this method of bandwidth selection suffers from a large amount of sample variability, in a sense very similar to that described for the least squares cross-validated density estimation bandwidth in Section 4.3. In particular, the excruciatingly slow rate of convergence, and the negative correlation between the cross-validated and ASE optimal bandwidths are here also. See Marron (1987b) for further discussion.

One thing that deserves further comment is that Rudemo has provided an intuitive explanation of the cause of the negative correlation in this setting, which is closely related to his intuition for density estimation, as described near the end of Section 4.3. This time focus on the lag-one serial correlation of the actual residuals (i.e. on $\rho(\epsilon_i, \epsilon_{i+1})$). Under the assumptions of independent errors, this will be zero on the average, but for any particular data set, the empirical value will typically be either positive or negative. Note that for data sets where the empirical serial correlation is positive, there will be a tendency for residuals to be positive in "clumps" (corresponding to the "clusters" described in Section 4.3). This clumping will require h_{ASE} to be larger than usual, so as to smooth them away. Another effect is that cross-validation will feel there is some fine structure present, which can only be recovered by a smaller bandwidth. For those data sets with a negative empirical correlation, the residuals will tend to alternate between positive and negative. The effect of this is that the sample variability will be smaller than usual, so ASE can achieve a smaller value by taking a small bandwidth which eliminates bias. On the other hand, cross-validation does not sense any real structure, and hence selects a relatively large bandwidth.

Methods of relating these ideas to bandwidth selection for derivatives of regression functions have been proposed by Rice (1986) and Müller, Stadtmüller and Schmitt (1987).

5.2 Model Selection Methods

There has been a great deal of attention to a problem very closely related to non-parametric smoothing parameter selection, which is often called "model selection". The basic problem can perhaps be best understood in the context of choosing the degree of a polynomial, for a least squares fit of a polynomial regression function, although the largest literature concerns choice of the order of an ARMA fit in time series analysis. To see that these problems are very similar to bandwidth selection, note that when too many terms are entered into a polynomial regression, the resulting curve will be too wiggly, much as for the small bandwidth curve in Fig. 1. On the other hand if too few terms are used, there will not be enough flexibility to recover all the features of the underlying curve, resulting in an estimate rather similar to the large bandwidth curve in Fig. 1.

Given the close relationship between these problems, it is not surprising that there has been substantial cross-over between these two areas. The main benefit for non-parametric curve estimation has been motivation for a number of different bandwidth selectors. Rice (1984) has shown that the bandwidth selectors motivated by a number of these (based on the work of Akaike, Shibata and others), as well as the Generalized Cross Validation idea of Craven and Wahba (1979), all have the following structure. Choose the minimizer of a criterion of the form

$$\mathrm{EPE}(h)\psi(h),$$

where $\mathrm{EPE}(h)$ was defined in Section 5.1 above. The function $\psi(h)$ can be thought of as a correction factor, which has an effect similar to replacing the estimator by its leave-one-out version, as done by cross-validation, as described in Section 5.1 above. Rice (1984) shows that all of these bandwidths asymptotically come together, and also converge to h_{MASE}, see Li (1987) for a related result. Härdle and Marron (1985b) show that extra care needs to be taken with these selectors when the design is not equally spaced, and the errors are not heteroscedastic. See Silverman (1985) for related discussion in the context of spline estimation.

Deeper properties, concerning the sample variability of these bandwidths, have been investigated by Härdle, Hall and Marron (1988). It is shown there that, in a much deeper sense than that of Rice (1984), all of these bandwidths are asymptotically equivalent to each other and also to the cross-validated bandwidth discussed in Section 5.1. Hence all properties described for the cross-validated bandwidth apply to these as well.

5.3 Unbiased Risk Estimation

This consists of yet another method of adjusting the estimated prediction error defined in Section 5.1. This essential idea was proposed by Mallows (1973) in the model selection context, and comes from considering the expected value of EPE(h). When this is done, it becomes apparent that the bias towards h too small can be corrected by minimizing a criterion of the form

$$EPE(h) + 2\hat{\sigma}^2 K(0)/nh,$$

where $\hat{\sigma}^2$ is some estimate of the residual variance, $\sigma^2 = E[\epsilon_i^2]$. There has been substantial work done on the nonparametric estimation of σ^2, see for example Kendall (1976). For more recent references, see Rudemo (1982b), Rice (1984), Gasser, Sroka and Jennen (1986) and Eagleson and Buckley (1987) for discussion of possible estimates of σ^2.

The results of Rice (1984) and Härdle, Hall and Marron (1988), described above, apply here to this type of selector as well. For an interesting connection to Stein shrinkage estimation see Li (1985).

The main drawback to this type of selector is that it depends on an estimate of σ^2, although this should not be too troubling, because there are estimates available with a fast parametric convergence rate, so the amount of noise in this estimation is at least asymptotically negligible. Härdle, Hall and Marron (1988) have demonstrated that, in a rather strong sense, the bandwidth selectors discussed in Section 5.2 are essentially equivalent to the unbiased risk estimator. The one important difference is that the latter uses an explicit estimate of σ^2, while the former all essentially make use of the fact that EPE(h) provides an implicit estimate.

An advantage of this selector over the selectors in Sections 5.1 and 5.2 is that it appears to handle settings in which reasonable values of the bandwidth are close to $h = 0$. This happens typically when there is very small error variance, so not much local averaging needs to be done. It is immediately clear that cross-validation suffers in this type of context, but it can also be seen that the other selectors have similar problems. These issues have not been well investigated yet.

6 Extensions, Hybrids and Hopes for the Future

There are many possibilities for modifying the above selectors, in the hopes of improving them. Also ideas from one setting may be used to generate ideas in the other. For example, the density estimation plug-in idea discussed in Section 4.1 has been adapted to regression by Müller (1985) and Tsybakov (1987). Also biased cross-validation as discussed in Section 4.4 has an obvious regression analogue (on which David Scott reports he is currently working).

Bhattacharya and Mack (1987) have studied a stochastic process that is closely related to the plug-in bandwidth selectors (they work explicitly with the nearest neighbor density estimator, but it appears that analogous ideas should hold for conventional kernel density and regression estimators as well). This gives a certain linear model, which is then used to give an improved bandwidth. It seems there may be room for improvement of this type of some of the other bandwidth selectors described above as well.

Kappenman (1987) proposed a density estimation bandwidth selection method based on considering two estimates of $\int (f'')^2$. Mielniczuk and Vieu (1988) and Marron (1988) have shown that this bandwidth is not very useful in its present form, but it does provide a new set of ideas for finding bandwidth selection methods. For example, in Marron (1988) it is shown that a reasonable modification of Kappenman's bandwidth provides a new characterization of the least squares cross-validated bandwidth discussed in Section 4.3.

Burman (1988) provides a detailed analysis and suggests improvement of v-fold cross-validation. The basic idea here is to replace the leave-one-out estimators by leave-several-out versions, and then assess the performance against each of the left out observations. This has the distinct advantage that it cuts down dramatically on the amount of computation required, at least if direct implementation is used (there seems to be less gain if an algorithm of one of the types described at the end of Section 4.3 is used). If too many observations are left out, then note that the selected smoothing parameter should be reasonably good, except that it will be appropriate for the wrong sample size (the size of the sample minus those left out). Burman provides a nice quantification of this, and goes on to use the quantification to provide an appropriate correction factor. Burman also provides similar results for another modification of cross-validation based on "repeated learning testing" methods.

Another means of modifying cross-validation, and also a number of the other automatic bandwidth selectors, is through partitioning, as proposed by Marron (1987c). The basic idea here is to first partition the data into subsets. In density estimation this could be done randomly, while it may be more appropriate to take every k-th point in regression. Next construct the cross-validation score for each sample separately, and find the minimizer of the average of these score functions. When this is rescaled to adjust for the fact that the subset cross-validation scores are for much smaller sample sizes, the resulting bandwidth will often have, up to a point, much better sample stability than ordinary cross-validation. A drawback to this approach is that one must decide on the number of subsets to use, and this problem seems to closely parallel that of smoothing parameter selection.

N. I. Fisher has pointed out (in personal correspondence) that partitioned cross-validation seems subject to a certain inefficiency, caused by the fact that observations are not allowed to "interact" with observations in the other subsets. He then proposed overcoming this problem by replacing the average over cross-validation scores for the partition subsets by an average of the scores over all possible subsets of a given size. Of course there are far too many subsets to actually calculate this score function, so an average over some randomly selected subsets should probably be implemented. This idea has yet to be analyzed, although again the subsample size will clearly be an important issue.

Wolfgang Härdle has proposed another possibility along these lines, for density estimation. The idea is to minimize a cross-validation score based on a subsample consisting of say every k-th order statistic, or perhaps of averages of blocks of k order statistics. The resulting sample would be much more stable with respect to the type of clusterings which drive Rudemo's intuition, regarding the noise in least-squares cross-validation described near the end of Section 4.3. This idea has also not been investigated, and here again choice of k seems crucial.

7 Conclusions

It should be clear from the above that the field of smoothing parameter selection is still in its infancy. While many methods have been proposed, none has emerged as clearly superior. There is still much comparison to be done, and many other possibilities to be investigated.

The implications, in terms of actual data analysis, of what is known currently about automatic methods of smoothing parameter selection, are that there is still no sure-fire replacement for the traditional trial and error method. This is where one plots several smooths, and then chooses one based on personal experience and opinion. Indeed none of these automatic methods should be used without some sort of verification of this type.

Scott and Terrell (1987) have suggested the reasonable idea of looking at several automatically selected bandwidths, with the idea that they are probably acceptable when they agree, and there is at least a good indication that special care needs to be taken when they disagree. There are many things yet to be investigated in connection to this idea, especially in terms of how correlated all these automatically selected bandwidths are to each other. Also there is the issue of how many different bandwidths the user is willing to consider. Hopefully the field can at least be narrowed somewhat.

Acknowledgement: The author is grateful to a number of people who have pointed out oversights and inaccuracies in an earlier version of this paper.

8 References

Bean SJ Tsokos CP (1980) Developments in nonparametric density estimation. International Statistical Review 48:267–287

Bhattacharya PK, Mack KP (1987) Weak convergence of k-NN density and regression estimators with varying k and applications. Annals of Statistics 15:976–994

Bierens HJ (1987) Kernel estimation of regression function. In: Bewley TF (ed) Advances in econometrics. Canbridge University Press, New York; pp 99–144

Bowman A (1984) An alternative method of cross-validation for the smoothing of density estimates. Biometrika 65:521–528

Burman P (1985) A data dependent approach to density estimation. Zeitschrift für Wahrscheinlichkeitstheorie und verwandte Gebiete 69:609–628

Burman P (1988) Estimation of the optimal transformations using v-fold cross-validation and repeated learning testing methods. Unpublished manuscript

Chow YS, Geman S, Wu LD (1983) Consistent cross-validated density estimation. Annals of Statistics 11:25–38

Clark RM (1975) A calibration curve for radio carbon dates. Antiquity 49:251–266

Collomb G (1981) Estimation non parametrique de la regression: revue. International Statistical Review 49:75–93

Collomb G (1985) Nonparametric regressio: an up-to-date bibliography. Statistics 16:309–324

Craven P, Wahba G (1979) Smoothing noisy data with spline functions. Numerische Mathematik 31:377–403

Devroye L, Györfi L (1984) Nonparametric density estimation: The L_1 view. Wiley, New York

Devroye L (1987) A course in density estimation. Birkhauser, Boston

Dodge Y (1986) Some difficulties involving nonparametric estimation of a density function. Journal of Official Statistics 2:193–202

Duin RPW (1976) On the choice of smoothing parameters of Parzen estimators of probability density functions. IEEE Transactions on Computers C-25:1175–1179

Eagleson GK, Buckley MJ (1987) Estimating the variance in nonparametric regression. Unpublished manuscript

Eubank R (1988) Spline smoothing and nonparametric regression. Wiley, New York

Ferguson TS (1967) Mathematical statistics, a decision theoretic approach. Academic Press, New York

Fryer MJ (1977) A review of some non-parametric methods of density estimation. Journal of the Instiute of Mathematics and its Applications 20:335–354

Gasser T, Sroka L, Jennen C (1986) Residuals variance and residual pattern in nonlinear regression. Biometrika 73:625–633

Habbema JDF, Hermans J, van den Broek K (1984) A stepwise discrimination analysis program using density estimation. Compstat 1974: Proceedings in Computational Statistics. Physica Verlag, Vienna, pp 101–110

Härdle W (1988) Applied nonparametric regression

Härdle W, Marron JS (1985a) Optimal bandwidth selection in nonparametric regression function estimation. Annals of Statistics 12:1465–1481

Härdle W, Marron JS (1985b) Asymptotic nonequivalence of some bandwidth selectors in nonparametric regression. Biometrika 72:481–484

Härdle W, Hall P, Marron JS (1988) How far are automatically chosen regression smoothers from their optimum? Journal of the American Statistical Association 83:86–101, with discussion

Härdle W, Marron JS, Wand MP (1988) Bandwidth choice for density derivatives. Unpublished manuscript

Hall P (1982) Cross-validation in density estimation. Biometrika 69:383–390

Hall P (1983) Large sample optimality of least square cross-validation in density estimation, Annals of Statistics 11:1156–1174

Hall P (1985) Asymptotic theory of minimum integrated square error for multivariate density estimation. Proceedings of the Sixth International Symposium on Multivariate Analysis at Pittsburgh, 25–29

Hall P (1987a) On the estimation of probability densities using compactly supported kernels. Journal of Multivariate Analysis 23:131–158

Hall P (1987b) On Kullback-Leibler loss and density estimation. Annals of Statistics 15:1491–1519

Hall P, Marron JS (1987a) Extent to which least-squares cross-validation minimises integrated square error in nonparametric density estimation. Probability Theory and Related Fields 74:567–581

Hall P, Marron JS (1987b) On the amount of noise inherent in bandwidth selection for a kernel density estimator. Annals of Statistics 15:163–181

Hall P Marron JS (1987c) Estimation of integrated squared density derivatives. Statistics and Probability Letters 6:109–115

Hall P, Wand M (1988) On the minimization of absolute distance in kernel density estimation. To appear in Statistics and Probability Letters

Hall P, Wand M (1989) Minimizing L_1 distance in nonparametric density estimation. To appear in Journal of Multivariate Analysis

Kappenman RF (1987) A nonparametric data based univariate function estimate. Computational Statistics and Data Analysis 5:1–7

Kendall MS (1976) Time Series. Griffin, London

Krieger AM, Pickands J (1981) Weak convergence and efficient density estimation at a point. Annals of Statistics 9:1066–1078

Li KC, Hwang J (1984) The data smoothing aspects of Stein estimates. Annals of Statistics 12:887–897

Li KC (1985) From Stein's unbiased risk estimates to the method of generalized cross-validation. Annals of Statistics 13:1352–1377

Li KC (1987) Asymptotic optimality for C_p, C_L, cross-validation and generalized cross-validation: discrete index set. Annals of Statistics 15:958–975

Mallows CL (1973) Some comments on C_p, Technometrics 15:661–675

Marron JS (1985) An asymptotically efficient solution to the bandwidth problem of kernel density estimation. Annals of Statistics 13:1011–1023

Marron JS (1986) Will the art of smoothing ever become a science? Marron JS (ed) Function estimates. American Mathematical Society Series: Contemporary Mathematics 9:169–178

Marron JS (1987a) A comparison of cross-validation techniques in density estimation. Annals of Statistics 15:152–162

Marron JS (1987b) What does optimal bandwidth selection mean for nonparametric regression estimation. Dodge Y (ed) Statistical data analysis based on the L^1 norm and related methods. North Holland, Amsterdam

Marron JS (1987c) Partitioned cross-validation. North Carolina Institute of Statistics, Mimeo Series #1721

Marron JS (1988) Improvement of a data based bandwidth selector. Unpublished manuscript

Marron JS, Padgett WJ (1987) Asymptotically optimal bandwidth selection for kernel density estimators from randomly right-censored samples. Annals of Statistics 15:1520–1535

Mielniczuk J, Vieu P (1988) Asymptotic suboptimality of one method of cross-validatory bandwidth choice in density estimation. Unpublished manuscript

Müller HG (1985) Empirical bandwidth choice for nonparametric kernel regression by means of pilot estimators. Statistics and Decisions, Supplement Issue No. 2:193–206

Müller HG, Stadtmüller U (1987) Variable bandwidth kernel estimators of regression curves. Annals of Statistics 15:182–201

Müller HG, Stadtmüller U, Schmitt T (1987) Bandwidth choice and confidence intervals for derivatives of noisy data. Biometrika 74:743–749

Nadaraya EA (1964) On estimating regression. Theory of Probability and its Application 9:141–142

Nolan D, Pollard D (1987) U-processes: rates of convergence. Annals of Statistics 15:780–799

Parzen E (1962) On estimation of a probability density function and mode. Annals of Mathematical Statistics 33:1065–1076

Prakasa Rao BLS (1983) Nonparametric functional estimation. Academic Press, New York

Rice J (1984) Bandwidth choice for nonparametric regression. Annals of Statistics 12:1215–1230

Rice J (1986) Bandwidth choice for differentiation. Journal of Multivariate Analysis 19:251–264

Rosenblatt M (1956) Remarks on some non-parametric estimates of a density function. Annals of Mathematical Statistics 27:832–837

Rosenblatt M (1971) Curve estimates. Annals of Mathematical Statistics 42:1815–1842

Rudemo M (1982a) Empirical choice of histograms and kernel density estimators. Scandanavian Journal of Statistics 9:65–78

Rudemo M (1982b) Consistent choice of linear smoothing methods. Report 82-1, Department of Mathematics, Royal Danish Agricultural and Veterinary University, Copenhagen

Schuster EA, Gregory CG (1981) On the nonconsistency of maximum likelihood nonparametric density estimators. Eddy WF (ed) Computer Science and Statistics: Proceedings of the 13th Symposium on the Interface. Springer, New York, pp 295–298

Scott DW (1985) Handouts for ASA short course in density estimation. Rice University Technical Report 776-331-86-2

Scott DW (1986) Choosing smoothing parameters for density estimators. In: Allen DM (ed) Computer Science and Statistics: The Interface, pp 225–229

Scott DW (1988) Discussion of Härdle W, Hall P, Marron JS, How far are automatically chosen regression smoothers from their optimum? To appear Journal of the American Statistical Association

Scott DW, Factor LE (1981) Monte Carlo study of three data-based nonparametric probability density estimators. Journal of the American Statistical Association 76:9–15

Scott DW, Tapia RA, Thompson JR (1977) Kernel density estimation revisited. Nonlinear Analysis, Theory, Methods and Applications 1:339–372

Scott DW, Terrell GR (1987) Biased and unbiased cross-validation in density estimation. Journal of the American Statistical Association 82:1131–1146

Sheather SJ (1983) A data-based algorithm for choosing the window width when estimating the density at a point. Computational Statistics and Data Analysis 1:229–238

Sheather SJ (1986) An improved data-based algorithm for choosing the window width when estimating the density at a point Computational Statistics and Data Analysis 4:61–65

Silverman BW (1985) Some aspects of the spline smoothing approach to nonparametric regression curve fitting (with discussion). Journal of the Royal Statistical Society, Series B 46:1–52

Silverman BW (1986) Density estimation for statistics and data analysis. Chapman and Hall, New York

Stone CJ (1984) An asymptotically optimal window selection rule for kernel density estimates. Annals of Statistics 12:1285–1297

Stone CJ (1985) An asymptotically optimal histogram selection rule. Proceedings of the Berkeley Symposium in Honor of Jerzy Neyman and Jack Keifer

Stone M (1974) Cross-validatory choice and assessment of statistical predictions. Journal of the Royal Statistical Society, Series B 36:111–147

Tapia RA, Thompson JR (1978) Nonparametric probability density estimation. The Johns Hopkins University Press, Baltimore

Tarter ME, Kronmal RA (1976) An introduction to the implementation and theory of nonparametric density estimation. The American Statistician 30:105–112

Terrell GR, Scott DW (1985) Oversmoothed density estimates. Journal of the American Statistical Association 80:209–214

Tsybakov AB (1987) On the choice of the bandwidth in kernel nonparametric regression. Theory of Probability and Its Applications 32:142–148

Ullah A (1987) Nonparametric estimation of econometric functionals. Research Report 18, University of Western Ontario, to appear in Canadian Journal of Economics

Wahba G, Wold S (1975) A completely automatic fench curve: fitting spline functions by cross-validation. Communications in Statistics 4:1–17

Watson GS (1964) Smooth regression analysis. Sankhyā, series A 26:359–372

Wegman EJ (1972) Nonparametric probability density estimation: I. a summary of the available methods. Technometrics 14:533–546

Wertz W (1978) Statistical density estimation: a survey. Angewandte Statistique und Okonometrie 13, Vandenhoeck und Ruprecht

Wertz W, Schneider B (1979) Statistical density estimation: a bibliography. International Statistical Review 49:75–93

Woodroofe M (1970) On choosing a delta sequence. Annals of Mathematical Statistics 41:1665–1671

Bayes Prediction Density and Regression Estimation – A Semiparametric Approach

By R. C. Tiwari[1], S. R. Jammalamadaka[2] and S. Chib[3]

Abstract: This paper is concerned with the Bayes estimation of an arbitrary multivariate density, $f(x)$, $x \in R^k$. Such an $f(x)$ may be represented as a mixture of a given parametric family of densities $\{h(x|\theta)\}$ with support in R^k, where θ (in R^d) is chosen according to a mixing distribution G. We consider the semiparametric Bayes approach in which G, in turn, is chosen according to a Dirichlet process prior with given parameter α. We then specialize these results when f is expressed as a mixture of multivariate normal densities $\phi(x|\mu, \Lambda)$ where μ is the mean vector and Λ is the precision matrix. The results are finally applied to estimating a regression parameter.

1 Introduction

In a recent paper, Ferguson (1983) presents a nonparametric Bayes procedure for estimating an arbitrary density $f(x)$ on the real line. This paper extends the results of Ferguson to the multivariate case and considers the estimation of the predictive density as well as the regression parameter. Consider a $k \times 1$ random vector $X = (Y, X_2, ..., X_k)'$ where, in the regression context, Y may be regarded as the dependent variable and $(X_2, ..., X_k)$ as the set of independent variables. We assume that X has an *unknown* density $f(x)$, $x \in R^k$. Such an $f(x)$ may be represented as a mixture of a multivariate normal densities $\{\phi(x|\mu, \Lambda)\}$, i.e.,

$$f(x) = \int \phi(x|\mu, \Lambda)dG(\mu, \Lambda), \tag{1}$$

where μ, the mean vector and Λ, the precision (or the inverse of the variance) matrix of the normal density, are chosen according to a mixing distribution G. Note that any

---

[1] R C. Tiwari, University of North Carolina, Charlotte, USA.
[2] S. R. Jammalamadaka, University of California, Santa Barbara, USA.
[3] S. Chib, University of Missouri, Columbia, USA.

distribution on R^k can be approximated by such a mixture to any preassigned accuracy in the Levy metric, and any density on R^k can be approximated similarly in the L_1 norm (cf. Ferguson 1983).

We consider the semiparametric Bayes approach, in which the unknown mixing distribution G, is chosen according to a Dirichlet prior with parameter α, say $D(\alpha)$. Our objective is to find the Bayes estimate $f_n(x)$, of the density of a future observation X_{n+1} given a random sample $x_1, ..., x_n$ from $f(x)$; that is, to find the semiparametric Bayes prediction density

$$f_n(x) = E[f(x)|x_1, ..., x_n],\tag{2}$$

where, in view of representation (1), the expectation in (2) is with respect to the posterior distribution of G given the sample $(x_1, ..., x_n)$ which is a mixture of Dirichlet processes (see, equation (11)).

We also consider the problem of finding the Bayes estimate of the parameter β that minimizes the mean-squared prediction error

$$E\left[Y_{n+1} - \sum_{i=2}^{k} \beta_i X_{i,n+1}\right]^2 \tag{3}$$

over all $\beta = (\beta_2, ..., \beta_k) \in R^{k-1}$. Note that (3) is minimized when β is

$$\beta^* = D^{-1}a, \tag{4}$$

where

$$D_{(k-1)\times(k-1)} = ((d_{ij})) = ((E(X_{i,n+1} \cdot X_{j,n+1})))$$

and

$$a_{(k-1)\times 1} = (a_2, ..., a_k), \quad \text{with } a_i = E(X_{i,n+1} Y_{n+1}).$$

As stated in Poli (1985) (see also Tiwari, Chib and Jammalamadaka 1988), "the achieved estimate β^* provides the best linear prediction of Y_{n+1} in terms of $(X_{2,n+1}, ..., X_{k,n+1})$".

This paper is organized as follows. Section 2 contains preliminaries and some general results which are then specialized to the case of normal mixtures in Section 3. Section 4 contains the Bayes estimate of β^*, while the last section includes some comments on the computational aspects.

2 Preliminaries and General Results

This section provides the basic definitions and results that will be used in the sequel. Let X be a $k \times 1$ random vector. Then X has a k-variate normal distribution with mean vector μ and precision (the inverse of variance) matrix Λ, denoted by $X \sim N_k(\mu, \Lambda)$, if its pdf is given by

$$\phi(x \,|\, \mu, \Lambda) = (2\pi)^{-k/2} |\Lambda|^{1/2} \exp \{-(1/2)(x - \mu)'\Lambda(x - \mu)\}, \tag{5}$$

where $\mu \in R^k$, and Λ is a symmetric positive definite (s.p.d.) matrix of order k.

A $k \times k$ random matrix Λ has a Wishart distribution if its pdf is given by

$$f(\Lambda \,|\, \Lambda^*, \nu) = c \cdot |\Lambda^*|^{-\nu/2} |\Lambda|^{(\nu-k-1)/2} \cdot \exp \{-(1/2) \operatorname{tr} (\Lambda\Lambda^{*-1})\}, \tag{6}$$

where Λ^* is a scale matrix of order k, $\nu \geqslant k$ is the degrees of freedom, and c is the normalizing constant given by

$$c^{-1} = 2^{k\nu/2} \pi^{k(k-1)/4} \sum_{j=1}^{k} \Gamma(\nu + 1 - j/2).$$

We shall use the notation $\Lambda \sim W_k(\Lambda^*, \nu)$ to denote that Λ has the pdf given by (6).

The $k \times 1$ vector X has a multivariate Student's t-distribution if its density function is given by

$$f(x \,|\, \mu, \Lambda, \nu) = (\nu\pi)^{-k/2} \cdot \frac{\Gamma((\nu + k)/2)}{\Gamma(\nu/2)} \cdot |\Lambda|^{1/2} [1 + \nu^{-1}(x - \mu)'\Lambda(x - \mu)]^{-(k+\nu)/2} \tag{7}$$

where $\mu \in R^k$, $\nu > 0$ is the degrees of freedom and Λ is a s.p.d. matrix of order k. We use the notation $X \sim MVt_k(\mu, \Lambda, \nu)$ to denote that X has the pdf given by (7).

Let $\alpha(\cdot)$ be a finite non-null finitely additive measure on (R^d, R^d). A random probability measure P on (R^d, R^d) is a Dirichlet process with parameter α, and write $P \in D(\alpha)$, if for every finite s and every measurable partition $A_1, \ldots, A_s$ of R^d, the random variables $(P(A_1), \ldots, P(A_s))$ have the Dirichlet distribution with parameters $(\alpha(A_1), \ldots, \alpha(A_s))$ (cf. Ferguson 1973).

Let δ_θ represent the degenerate probability measure at a single point θ. Let G be the distribution function associated with the random probability measure P. Then, under $D(\alpha)$, G can expressed as (cf. Sethuraman and Tiwari 1982):

$$G = \sum_{i=1}^{\infty} p_i \delta_{\theta_i}, \tag{8}$$

where

(i) $\theta_1, \theta_2, \ldots,$ are iid on (R^d, R^d) with the common distribution $G_0 = \alpha(\cdot)/M$,

(ii) $(p_1, p_2, \ldots)$ and $(\theta_1, \theta_2, \ldots)$ are independent,

(iii) $q_1 = p_1, q_2 = p_2/(1 - p_1), q_3 = p_3/(1 - p_1 - p_2), \ldots$ are iid Beta $(1, M), M = \alpha(R^d)$.

More generally than (1), one may assume that the unknown density $\psi(x)$ is expressed as a mixture of a family of k-variate densities $\{h(x|\theta)\}$, with the mixing distribution G (on θ) in R^d, i.e.,

$$\psi(x) = \int h(x|\theta) dG(\theta). \tag{9}$$

If this mixing distribution G, is assumed to have a Dirichlet prior, then from (8)

$$\psi(x) = \sum_{i=1}^{\infty} p_i h(x|\theta_i). \tag{10}$$

Let $x_1, \ldots, x_n$ be a random sample from $\psi(x)$ given by (9). This is equivalent to first choosing $\theta_1, \ldots, \theta_n$ i.i.d. from $G_0(\theta)$, and then x_i from $h(x|\theta_i)$, $i = 1, \ldots, n$ independently. Then the posterior distribution of G given $x_1, \ldots, x_n$ is a mixture of Dirichlet processes (cf. Antoniak 1974)

$$G|x_1, \ldots x_n \in \int D\left(\alpha + \sum_{i=1}^{n} \delta_{\theta_i}\right) dH(\theta_1, \ldots, \theta_n | x_1, \ldots, x_n), \tag{11}$$

where $dH(\theta_1, ..., \theta_n | x_1, ..., x_n)$, the posterior density of $\theta_1, ..., \theta_n$ given $x_1, ..., x_n$, is

$$dH(\theta_1, ..., \theta_n | x_1, ..., x_n) \propto \left(\prod_{i=1}^{n} h(x_i | \theta_i) \right) \prod_{i=1}^{n} d\left(\alpha + \sum_{j=1}^{i-1} \delta_{\theta_j} \right) (\theta_i) / M^{(n)}$$

with the notation $M^{(n)} = M(M + 1) ... (M + n - 1)$. From (11) we have

$$E(G(\theta) | x_1, ..., x_n) = \frac{M}{M+n} G_0(\theta) + \frac{n}{M+n} \int \hat{G}_n(\theta) dH(\theta_1, ..., \theta_n | x_1, ..., x_n)$$
(12)

where $\hat{G}_n(\cdot) = \frac{1}{n} \sum_{i=1}^{n} \delta_{\theta_i}$, is the empirical measure of the observed $\theta_1, ..., \theta_n$ and G_0 corresponds to the normalized α-measure. Consequently we have the following:

Theorem 1: The Bayes estimator of $\psi(x)$ under squared error loss function, $\psi_n(x) = E[\psi(x) | x_1, ..., x_n]$, is given by

$$\psi_n(x) = \frac{M}{M+n} \psi_0(x) + \frac{n}{M+n} \hat{\psi}_n(x)$$
(13)

where $\psi_0(x)$, the estimate of $\psi(x)$ for no sample size, is given by

$$\psi_0(x) = E\psi(x) = \int h(x | \theta) dG_0(\theta)$$
(14)

and

$$\hat{\psi}_n(x) = \frac{1}{n} \sum_{i=1}^{n} \int ... \int h(x | \theta_i) dH(\theta_1, ..., \theta_n | x_1, ..., x_n).$$
(15)

The nonparametric Bayes estimate of $\psi(x)$ is, therefore, seen to be a weighted average of the prior guess $\psi_0(x)$ given in (14), and $\hat{\psi}_n(x)$ given in (15). Two special cases of interest as M, the strength in the prior goes to zero and infinity, may be considered as in Ferguson (1983).

In particular, as $M \to \infty$, the θ_i's are all distinct and the prediction density is given by

$$\psi^*(x) = \frac{1}{n} \sum_{i=1}^{n} \psi(x|x_i),$$ (16)

where

$$\psi(x|x_i) = \frac{\int h(x|\theta)h(x_i|\theta)dG_0(\theta)}{\int h(x_i|\theta)dG_0(\theta)}$$

is the Bayes prediction density of x given the one observation x_i.

3 Results for Normal Mixtures

In this section we specialize the results of the previous section by letting $\theta = (\mu, \Lambda)$ and $h(x|\theta)$ be a multivariate normal density with mean μ and the precision matrix Λ. We also let G_0 be the joint prior distribution of (μ, Λ) given by

$$\mu|\Lambda \sim N_k(\mu^*, \Lambda b^*), \quad b^* > 0$$ (17)

and

$$\Lambda \sim W_k(\Lambda^*, \nu^*).$$ (18)

Now, let the unknown density $f(x)$, be a random mixture of a multivariate normal densities as in (1) i.e.,

$$f(x) = \int \phi(x|\mu, \Lambda)dG(\mu, \Lambda)$$ (19)

where $\phi(\cdot|\mu, \Lambda)$ is the pdf in (5).

In (19), consider the special choice of a Dirichlet process prior for G with parameter $\alpha = MG_0$, where G_0 is the natural conjugate prior of (μ, Λ) given by (17) and (18) namely the normal-Wishart. It is important to note that nothing prevents us from choosing an arbitrary measure G_0, as the prior of θ.

Lemma 1: Let (μ, Λ) have a joint normal-Wishart prior given by (17) and (18). Then the prior guess of the prediction density at x, $f_0(x)$, is given by (see equation (14))

$$f_0(x) \alpha \left(1 + \frac{b^*}{b^* + 1}(x - \mu^*)'\Lambda^*(x - \mu^*)\right)^{-(k+\nu^* - k^* + 1)/2} \tag{20}$$

a k-variate *MVt* density with mean vector μ^*, precision matrix $\phi_0 = (\nu^* - k + 1)\Lambda^* b^*/ (b^* + 1)$, and $\nu_0 = (\nu^* - k + 1)$ degrees of freedom.

The proof of Lemma 1 is given in the Appendix.

Using Theorem 1 and Lemma 1, we are now able to provide the Bayes prediction density of a future observation X_{n+1}, given $x_1, ..., x_n$.

Theorem 2: Given $f(x) = \int \phi(x|\mu, \Lambda)dG(\mu, \Lambda)$, with $G \in D(\alpha)$, and $\alpha = MG_0$, where G_0 is the normal-Wishart prior specified in (17) and (18), the Bayes prediction density of X_{n+1} given $x_1, ..., x_n$ is

$$f_n(x) = \frac{M}{M + n} f_0(x) + \frac{n}{M + n} \hat{f}_n(x), \tag{21}$$

where $f_0(x)$ is the *MVt* density given in (20) and

$$\hat{f}_n(x) = \frac{1}{n} \sum_{i=1}^{n} \int ... \int \phi(x|\mu_i, \Lambda_i)dH((\mu_1, \Lambda_1), ..., (\mu_n, \Lambda_n)|x_1, ..., x_n). \tag{22}$$

The Bayes prediction density is therefore a weighted mixture of a multivariate-t density $f_0(x)$ and $\hat{f}_n(x)$, with the weights $M/(M + n)$ and $n/(M + n)$, respectively. The density $\hat{f}_n(x)$ can be evaluated numerically using the results of Section 5.

Two special cases which do not require a numerical evaluation are given next. The following Theorem 3 for $M \to 0$ yields the usual parametric result in which (μ, Λ) has the normal-Wishart prior and $x_1, ..., x_n$ is a random sample from $\phi(x|\mu, \Lambda)$.

Theorem 3: Let $x_i|\mu, \Lambda \sim N_k(\mu, \Lambda) \, i = 1, \ldots, n, \mu|\Lambda \sim N_k(\mu^*, \Lambda^*)$, and $\Lambda \sim W_k(\Lambda^*, \nu^*)$. Then as $M \to 0$, then density in (21) becomes

$$f_n^0(x) \propto [1 + [1 + (x - \mu^{**})'\phi^{**}(x - \mu^{**})]^{-(k+n+\nu^*-k+1)/2}, \tag{23}$$

where $\bar{x} = \sum_{i=1}^{n} x_i/n$ and $S = \sum_{i=1}^{n} (x_i - \bar{x})(x_i - \bar{x})'$. $\qquad\qquad\square$

A proof of this theorem is included in the Appendix. Note that $f_n^0(x)$ in (23) is a k-variate *MVt* density with mean vector $\mu^{**} = (b^*\mu^* + n\bar{x})/(b^* + n)$, precision matrix $\phi^{**} = (b^* + n)[nb^*(b^* + n)^{-1}(\bar{x} - \mu^*)(\bar{x} - \mu^*)' + \Lambda^{*-1} + S]^{-1}/(b^* + n + 1)$ and $n + \nu^* - k + 1$ degrees of freedom. Setting $n = 1$ and $\bar{x} = x_i$ in Theorem 3 gives the Bayes prediction density of X_{n+1} given one observation $x_i (i = 1, \ldots, n)$:

Corollary 1: Let $x_i|\mu, \Lambda \sim N_k(\mu, \Lambda)$, $\mu|\Lambda \sim N_k(\mu^*, b^*\Lambda)$ and $\Lambda \sim W_k(\Lambda^*, \nu^*)$. Then as $M \to 0$, the Bayes prediction density of X_{n+1} given x_i is

$$f_{1,i}(x) \propto [1 + (x - \mu_i^{\uparrow})'\psi_i^{\uparrow}(x - \mu_i^{\uparrow})]^{-(k+\nu-k+2)/2}$$

a k-variate multivariate-t pdf with mean vector $\mu_i^{\uparrow} = (b^*\mu^* + x_i)/(b^* + 1)$ precision matrix $\psi_i^{\uparrow} = (b^* + 1)[b^*(b^* + 1)^{-1}(x_i - \mu^*)(x_i - \mu^*)' + \Lambda^{*-1}]^{-1}/(b^* + 2)$ and $\nu - k + 2$ degrees of freedom.

The second special case, as $M \to \infty$, is covered by the following result which follows from Corollary 1 and (16).

Corollary 2: Let $x_i|\mu, \Lambda \sim N_k(\mu, \Lambda) \, i = 1, \ldots, n$, $\mu|\Lambda \sim N_k(\mu^*, b^*\Lambda)$, and $\Lambda \sim W_k(\Lambda^*, \nu^*)$ then as $M \to \infty$ the Bayes prediction density of X_{n+1} given $x_1, \ldots, x_n, f_n^{\infty}(x)$, is given by a finite mixture of multivariate-t densities i.e.,

$$f_n^{\infty}(x) \propto \frac{1}{n} \sum_{i=1}^{n} [1 + (x_i - \mu_i^{\uparrow})'\psi_i^{\uparrow}(x_i - \mu_i)]^{-(k+\nu-k+2)/2}.$$

4 Bayes Estimation of a Regression Parameter

The results obtained in the previous section allow us to find the estimate of β^* given in (4), where β^* minimizes the prediction mean-squared error that is specified in (3). Although the estimate of β^* using the Bayes prediction density in Theorem 2 cannot be computed in a closed form, the general principle can be illustrated with the following cases.

From (3) we have

$$\beta^* = D^{-1}a,$$

where for $1 \leqslant i, j \leqslant k - 1$, the typical elements of D and a are

$$d_{ij} = E(X_{i,n+1} \cdot X_{j,n+1})$$

and

$$a_i = E(X_{i,n+1} \cdot Y_{n+1}).$$

For an f which is a normal mixture, for the no-sample case, the estimate of β^* can be computed using the following. Let $\mu^* = (\mu_1^*, \dots, \mu_k^*)'$ and let $\Lambda^{*-1} = ((\Sigma_{ll'}^*))$, $1 \leqslant l$, $l' \leqslant k$, then the i, j-th element of D is

$$d_{ij} = (b^*(v^* - k - 1)/(b^* + 1))^{-1}\Sigma_{i+1,j+1}^* + \mu_{i+1}^*\mu_{j+1}^*, \quad 1 \leqslant i, j \leqslant k - 1$$

and the j-th element of a is

$$a_j = (b^*(v^* - k - 1)/(b^* + 1)^{-1}\Sigma_{1,j+1}^* + \mu_1^*\mu_{j+1}^*, \quad 1 \leqslant j \leqslant k - 1.$$

A similar procedure can be used to compute the estimate of β^* when $M \to 0$. Letting $\Lambda^{**-1} = ((\Sigma_{ll'}^{**}))$, $1 \leqslant l, l' \leqslant k$, and μ_l^{**} denote the l-th element of μ^{**} we have

$$d_{ij} = (n + v^* - k - 1)^{-1}\Sigma_{i+1,j+1}^{**} + \mu_{i+1}^{**}\mu_{j+1}^{**}$$

and

$$a_j = (n + v^* - k - 1)^{-1} \Sigma_{1,j+1}^{**} + \mu_1^{**} \mu_{j+1}^{**}, \quad 1 \leqslant j \leqslant k - 1.$$

Finally, for the $M \to \infty$ case, d_{ij}'s and a_j's can again be given explicitly. The details are ommitted.

5 Remarks and Computational Aspects

The usual issues in density estimation regarding the kernel and the window-length could be related to the choice of the prior α in our Bayes set-up, although the specifies need further investigation. In particular, the special form (16) corresponds to a variable kernel estimate, as Ferguson notes. Computation of (13), the Bayes estimator of the density can be done along the lines of Ferguson (1983), which contains an illustration for density on R^1. If we define

$$H(x_1, \ldots, x_n) = \int \ldots \int \left[\prod_{i=1}^{n} h(x_i | \theta_i) \right] \prod_{i=1}^{n} d\left(MG_0 + \prod_{j=1}^{i-1} \delta_{\theta_j} \right) (\theta_i) / M^{(n)}$$

then Lo (1978) provides the following representation of the function H

$$dH(\theta_1, \ldots, \theta_n | x_1, \ldots, x_n) = \frac{\left[\prod_{i=1}^{n} h(x_i | \theta_i) \right] \prod_{i=1}^{n} d\left(MG_0 + \prod_{j=1}^{i-1} \delta_{\theta_j} \right) (\theta_i)}{M^{(n)} \cdot h(x_1, \ldots, x_n)}$$

Using this, one can rewrite the expression for $\psi_{n,\alpha}(x)$ in (13) in terms of the function $h(\cdot)$ as

$$\psi_{n,\alpha}(x) = \frac{h(x, x_1, \ldots, x_n)}{h(x_1, \ldots, x_n)} \tag{24}$$

The computation of $\psi_{n,\alpha}(x)$ clearly depends on the evaluation of the ratio in equation (24).

If we expand the product measure which appears in equation (24), there are $n!$ terms and each term of the expansion determines a partition $Q = \{K_1, \ldots, K_n\}$ of the data set $\{x_1, \ldots, x_n\}$ with the property that $\theta_i = \theta_j$ if and only if $x_i \in K$, $x_j \in K$, for some set K in Q. Hence, we can write $h(x_1, \ldots, x_n)$ as

$$h(x_1, \ldots, x_n) = \sum_Q P_M(Q)Z(Q), \tag{25}$$

where

$$Z(Q) = \prod_{K \in Q} \int \prod_{x_i \in K} h(x_i|\theta)dG_0(\theta) \tag{26}$$

and $P_M(Q)$ is the probability of selecting a particular partition, Q. Define

$$Y(Q) = \frac{Z(Q)}{n} \sum_{K \in Q} |K| \frac{\int h(x|\theta) \prod_{x_i \in K} h(x_i|\theta)dG_0(\theta)}{\int \prod_{x_i \in K} h(x_i|\theta)dG_0(\theta)} \tag{27}$$

where $|K|$ is the cardinality of the set K. For the specific choice of G_0 that we use in (17) and (18), we can simplify the expression for $Z(Q)$ and $Y(Q)$ given in (26) and (27), respectively.

Given $x_1, \ldots, x_n$ the Monte Carlo procedure entails the following steps:

(i) *Select a partition:* This is done by using Kuo (1986)'s method. Start the first set of partitions with x_1, say. Then, for $i = 1, 2, \ldots, n - 1$, x_{i+1} starts a new set with probability $\dfrac{M}{M+i}$; otherwise it is placed in an existing set with probability $\left(\dfrac{r}{M+i}\right)$, where r is the number of elements already in that set. In the computations, we need only to record the number of the sets in a partition, and the indices in each class, and for this partitioning process, one may use the indices 1 through n and not the data themselves.

(ii) *Estimating* $\psi_{n,\alpha}$: Once a particular partition Q_i is randomly chosen, compute $Z(Q_i)$ and $Y(Q_i)$ using the equations (26) and (27). This process is replicated N times to give $Z(Q_i)$ and $Y(Q_i)$, $1 \leqslant i \leqslant N$, and the Monte Carlo estimate of $\hat{\psi}_n(x)$ in (13) is given by

$$\tilde{\psi}_n(x) = \sum_{i=1}^{N} Y(Q_i) \Big/ \sum_{i=1}^{N} Z(Q_i).$$

The estimate of $\psi_{n,\alpha}(x)$ is then computed using (13). The variance of this estimator can be computed using the asymptotic formula for the variance of the ratio of means (see, Cochran 1977, p. 155):

$$\text{Var}\left(\frac{\Sigma Y_i}{\Sigma Z_i}\right) = \text{Var}\left(\frac{\bar{Y}}{\bar{Z}}\right) = \frac{1}{N\mu_z^2}\left[\sigma_y^2 - 2\sigma_{yz}\frac{\mu_y}{\mu_z} + \sigma_z^2\frac{\mu_y^2}{\mu_z^2}\right]$$

where the estimates

$$\bar{Z}(Q) = \hat{\mu}_z = \sum_{i=1}^{N} Z(Q_i)/N, \quad \bar{Y}(Q) = \hat{\mu}_y = \sum_{i=1}^{N} Y(Q_i)/N,$$

$$\hat{\sigma}_z^2 = [N(N-1)]^{-1}\sum_{i=1}^{N}(Z(Q_i) - \bar{Z}(Q))^2,$$

$$\hat{\sigma}_y^2 = [N(N-1)]^{-1}\sum_{i=1}^{N}(Y(Q_i) - \bar{Y}(Q))^2,$$

and

$$\hat{\sigma}_{yz} = [N(N-1)]^{-1}[\Sigma Z(Q_i)Y(Q_i) - N\bar{Z}(Q)\cdot\bar{Y}(Q)]$$

are used in place of the corresponding parameters.

Appendix

Proof of Lemma 1: By using the definition in (14), we have that

$$f_0(x) = \int \phi(x|\mu, \Lambda)dG_0(\mu, \Lambda)$$

$$\alpha \int |\Lambda|^{(\nu^*-k)/2}e^{-1/2}\,\text{tr}\,\Lambda\left[(x-\mu^*)(x-\mu^*)'\frac{b^*}{b^*+1} + \Lambda^{*-1}\right]d\Lambda$$

$$\alpha\,|(x-\mu^*)(x-\mu^*)'\frac{b^*}{b^*+1} + \Lambda^{*-1}|^{(\nu^*+1)/2}$$

On using the normalizing constant of the Wishart distribution. Now using the result that if V is a nonsingular $(p \times p)$ matrix, a and $b \in R^p$ (cf. Press 1982, p. 20), then

$$|V + ab'| = |V|[1 + b'V^{-1}a],$$

we get that

$$f_0(x) \, \alpha \left[1 + \frac{b^*}{b^* + 1} (x - \mu^*)' \Lambda^* (x - \mu^*) \right]^{-(\nu^* + 1)/2},$$

This completes the proof.   □

Proof of Theorem 3: Notice that $f_n^0(x)$ is the expectation of $\phi(x|\mu, \Lambda)$ w.r.t. the posterior density of (μ, Λ) given $x_1, \ldots, x_n$. This posterior density is well known (e.g., see Press 1982, p. 187) and is given by

$$dG_0((\mu, \Lambda)|x_1, \ldots, x_n) \, \alpha \, dG_0(\mu, \Lambda) \cdot f(x_1, \ldots, x_n|\mu, \Lambda)$$

$$\alpha \, |\Lambda|^{1/2} \exp \left\{ -\frac{1}{2} (\mu - \mu^*)' \Lambda b^* (\mu - \mu^*) \right\} \times$$

$$\exp \left\{ -\frac{1}{2} (\mu - \bar{x})' n \Lambda (\mu - \bar{x}) \right\} \cdot |\Lambda|^{(n + \nu^* - k - 1)/2} \exp \left\{ -\frac{1}{2} \operatorname{tr} \Lambda [S + \Lambda^{*-1}] \right\}$$

from which we get that

$$\mu | x_1, \ldots, x_n, \Lambda \sim N_k(\mu^{**}, (\Lambda b^* + n\Lambda)), \tag{A.1}$$

and

$$\Lambda | x_1, \ldots, x_n, \Lambda^* \sim W_k((S + \Lambda^{*-1} + nb^*(b^* + n)^{-1}(\bar{x} - \mu^*)(\bar{x} - \mu^*)')^{-1}, n + \nu^*). \tag{A.2}$$

Using (A.1) and (A.2) it follows that

$$X_{n+1} | x_1, \ldots, x_n, \Lambda \sim N_k(\mu^{**}, \Lambda(b^* + n)/(b^* + n + 1)). \tag{A.3}$$

Let the pdf of in (A.3) be denoted by $f_n^0(\cdot|x_1, \ldots, x_n, \Lambda)$. Then, from (A.2) and (A.3) the Bayes prediction density of x_{n+1} is

$$f_n^0(x) = \int f_n^0(x|x_1, \ldots, x_n, \Lambda) \cdot W_k(d\Lambda|x_1, x_2, \ldots, x_n)$$

$$\alpha \int_\Lambda |\Lambda|^{1/2} \exp\left(-\frac{1}{2} \operatorname{tr} \Lambda[(b^* + n)(b^* + n + 1)^{-1}(x - \mu^{**})(x - \mu^{**})'\right)$$

$$\cdot |\Lambda|^{(n+\nu^*-k-1)/2} \exp\left(-\frac{1}{2} \operatorname{tr} \Lambda[S + \Lambda^{*-1} + nb^*(b^* + n)^{-1}(\bar{x} - \mu^*)(x - \mu^*)']\right) d\Lambda$$

from which the result follows. $\square$

References

Antoniak CE (1974) Mixtures of Dirichlet processes with applications to Bayesian nonparametric problems. Ann Statist 2:1152–1174

Cochran WG (1977) Sampling techniques. John Wiley & Sons, New York

Ferguson TS (1973) A Bayesian analysis of some nonparametric problems. Ann Statist 1:209–230

Ferguson TS (1983) Bayesian density estimation by mixtures of normal distributions. In: Rizvi MH, Rustagi JS, Siegmund (eds) Recent advances in statistics. Academic Press

Kuo L (1986) Computations of mixture of Dirichlet processes. SIAM J Scientific and Statistical Computing 7:60–71

Lo AY (1978) On a class of Bayesian nonparametric estimates: density estimates. Rutgers University, New Brunswick, NJ

Poli I (1985) A Bayesian nonparametric estimator for multivariate regression. Journal of Econometrics 28:171–182

Prakasa Rao BLS (1983) Nonparametric funvtional estimation. Academic Press

Press SJ (1982) Applied multivariate analysis: using Bayesian and frequentist methods of inference. Robert E. Krieger Publishing Co

Sethuraman J, Tiwari RC (1982) Convergence of Dirichlet measures and the interpretations of their parameter. In: Gupta SS, Berger JO (eds) Statistical decision theory and related topics, III, vol 2. Academic Press

Tiwari RC, Chib S, Jammalamadaka S Rao (1988) Nonparametric Bayes estimate for multivariate regression with a Dirichlet invariant prior. In: Ali Festschrift: Forthcoming

Wilks SS (1962) Mathematical statistics, 2nd ed. John Wiley, New York

Nonparametric Estimation and Hypothesis Testing in Econometric Models

By A. Ullah[1]

Abstract: In this paper we systematically review and develop nonparametric estimation and testing techniques in the context of econometric models. The results are discussed under the settings of regression model and kernel estimation, although as indicated in the paper these results can go through for other econometric models and for the nearest neighbor estimation. A nontechnical survey of the asymptotic properties of kernel regression estimation is also presented. The technique described in the paper are useful for the empirical analysis of the economic relations whose true functional forms are usually unknown.

1 Introduction

Consider an economic model

$$y = R(x) + u$$

where y is a dependent variable, x is a vector of regressors, u is the disturbance and $R(x) = E(y|x)$. Often, in practice, the estimation of the derivatives of $R(x)$ are of interest. For example, the first derivative indicates the response coefficient (regression coefficient) of y with respect to x, and the second derivative indicates the curvature of $R(x)$. In the parametric econometrics the estimation of these derivatives and testing

[1] Aman Ullah, Department of Economics, University of Western Ontario, London, Ontario, N6A 5C2, Canada.

I thank I. Ahmad, A. Bera, A. Pagan, C. Robinson, A. Zellner, and the participants of the workshops at the Universities of Chicago, Northern Illinois, Stanford, Riverside and Santa Barbara, for their comments on the subject matter of this paper. The work on this paper was done when the author was a vising scholar at the Stanford University. The SSHRC research grant and research facilities at the Stanford University are gratefully acknowledged.

of hypotheses related to them are carried out by assuming some functional form of $R(x)$, see e.g., Diewert (1971), Barnett and Lee (1985) and Gallant (1981). However, it is well known that any misspecification in the functional form of $R(x)$ leads to inconsistent estimates of the true derivatives, and affects the size and power of the test. In view of this, it is desirable to consider estimation and testing without assuming any functional form of $R(x)$. Essentially, the approach considered here is to first estimate $R(x)$ consistently by the nonparametric method, and then estimate the partial derivatives and test the relevant economic hypotheses.

When y and x are stochastic, the nonparametric kernel estimation of $R(x)$ was first proposed by Nadaraya (1964) and Watson (1964). Using this, Ullah and Vinod (1988), Vinod and Ullah (1988), and Rilstone and Ullah (1987) studied the estimator of the first derivative of $R(x)$; McMillan et al. (1987) and Rilstone (1987) considered the estimation of second derivative; and Ahmad and Ullah (1987) analyzed the higher order derivatives. In a related work Powell et al. (1986) proposed the kernel estimation of weighted averaged derivatives. Further, in a recent paper Rilstone (1988) considered the testing of a general set of economic restrictions on the first and second order derivatives.

When x's are fixed design regressors such as time or age, the kernel estimation of $R(x)$ was considered by Priestley and Chao (1972) and Beneditti (1977) for the univariate x, and by Ahmad and Lin (1984) for the multivariate x. Using Priestley and Chao type estimator, Schuster and Yakowitz (1979), Georgiev (1984) and Gasser and Muller (1984) proposed the estimation of derivatives of $R(x)$. The details can be found in the book by Hardle (1988). The other method of estimation in the fixed design case is the smoothing splines techniques, see e.g., Reinsch (1967) for the estimation of $R(x)$ and Cullum (1971) for the derivatives. For detail, see the book by Eubank (1988). Silverman (1984) has indicated the relationship between the kernel and smoothing spline techniques. Another method of estimating $R(x)$ is the local least squares regression, see Muller (1987) for recent work. Other developments are adaptive estimation (see the survey by Manski 1984), semiparametric estimation (see the survey by Robinson 1987), and signal extraction method (see e.g., Rao 1986 where $R(x)$ is simply treated as signals).

In this paper we consider the case of stochastic y and x, and systematically review and develop a purely nonparametric estimation and testing of hypothesis. Some new results are also presented. In Section 2 we present the model. Then in Section 3 we present the estimation of $R(x)$ and its derivatives. The least squares as well as the method of moment interpretation of Nadaraya-Watson estimator of $R(x)$ are given. Inequality and equality restricted estimation as well as testing of linear restrictions are considered. In Section 4 we briefly review the literature on asymptotic theory of $R(x)$ and its derivatives. Then in Section 5 we consider the nonparametric estimation of the structural equations where x and u are correlated.

2 The Model and Partial Derivatives

Suppose we have n-independent and identically distributed observations $(y_i, x_{i1}, ..., x_{ip})$ $i = 1, ..., n$ from an absolutely continuous $p + 1$ variate distribution with density $f(y, x_1, ..., x_p) = f(y, x)$. Here we consider y to be a dependent variable and x to be the vector of p regressors. If $E|y| < \infty$ then the conditional mean of y given x exists and it takes the form

$$E(y|x) = R(x) = \int y \frac{f(y, x)}{f_1(x)} \, dy \tag{2.1}$$

where $f_1(x)$ is the density of x marginal to $f(y, x)$ and $R(x)$ is a real valued function of x. $R(x)$ is called the regression function and it provides a formulation for the regression model as

$$y = R(x) + u = R(x_1, ..., x_p) + u \tag{2.2}$$

where, by construction, the disturbance term u is such that $E(u|x) = 0$.

The response or regression coefficient of y with respect to changes in a regressor, say $x_j (j = 1, ..., p)$, is defined as the first order partial derivative of $R(x)$ with respect to x_j. It is denoted by $\beta_j(x) = \beta(x)$ where

$$\beta(x) = \frac{\partial R(x)}{\partial x_j} = \lim_{h \to 0} \frac{R(x + h) - R(x - h)}{2h}, \tag{2.3}$$

$R(x - h) = R(x_1, ..., x_j - h, ..., x_p)$. Note that (2.3) is a varying response coefficient since it is a function of x. The fixed response coefficient can be defined as $\beta(\bar{x})$, i.e., $\beta(x)$ evaluated at $x = \bar{x} = (\bar{x}_1, ..., \bar{x}_p)$. Note that when $R(x)$ is linear, as often specified in the parametric econometrics, estimation of the first partials of $R(x)$ is equivalent to estimating regression coefficients.

Economic theory often imposes theoretical curvature conditions (concavity or convexity) on $R(x)$. For example, Slutsky matrix is symmetric and negative semi definite and demand elasticity is an increasing function of price. Thus the behavior of the second order partial of $R(x)$ is also of interest. This is

$$\beta^{(2)}(x) = \frac{\partial^2}{\partial x_j^2} R(x) = \lim_{h \to 0} \frac{R(x + 2h) - 2R(x) - R(x - 2h)}{(2h)^2} \tag{2.4}$$

In general the s-th order ($s = 1, 2, ...$) partial derivatives of $R(x)$ can be written as

$$\beta^{(s)}(x) = \frac{\partial^s}{\partial x_j^s} R(x) = \lim_{h \to 0} \left[\left(\frac{1}{2h} \right)^s \sum_{l=0}^{s} (-1)^l \binom{s}{l} R(x + (s - 2l)h) \right] \qquad (2.5)$$

Further, the cross derivatives can be written as

$$\frac{\partial^{s_1 + ... + s_r}}{\partial x_{j_1}^{s_1} ... \partial x_{j_r}^{s_r}} R(x) = \lim_{h \to 0} \left[\left(\frac{1}{2h} \right)^{s_1 + ... + s_r} \sum_{l_1=0}^{s_1} ... \sum_{l_r=0}^{s_r} (-1)^{l_1 + ... + l_r} \binom{s_1}{l_1} \right. \qquad (2.6)$$

$$\left. ... \binom{s_r}{l_r} R(x + (s_1 - 2l_1)h, ... x + (s_r - 2l_r)h) \right]$$

where each of $j_1, ..., j_r$ takes values 1 to p ($j_1 \neq j_2, ..., \neq j_r$), and $x + (s_1 - 2l_1)h = (x_1, ..., x_{j_1} + (s_1 - 2l_1)h ..., x_p)$ whereas $x + (s_r - 2l_r)h = (x_1, ..., x_{j_r} + (s_r - 2l_r)h ..., x_p)$. For $r = 1$ we get (2.5). Further for $r = 2$ we get various cross derivatives.

In what follows we consider the nonparametric estimation of the partial derivatives of $R(x)$ without specifying its form. This is done by first considering a nonparametric estimator of $R(x)$ and then taking its partial derivatives. Before presenting these we note that the partial derivatives discussed above are not confined to the regression model (2.2). In fact, although not considered here explicitly, the extension to dynamic models with stationary variables and system models are straightforward. For example, for the first order autoregressive model the regression functionin (2.1) becomes $E(y|y_{-1})$ where y_{-1} is the lagged value of the stationary variable y. Similarly for the system model y will be a vector of say q endogenous variables and $E(y|x)$ will be a vector regression function. We restrict ourselves to the model (2.2) for the sake of simplicity in exposition. The extension of the results to the simultaneous equations models is discussed in Section 5.

3 Estimation and Testing of Hypothesis

3.1 Estimation of Regression Function

First we consider the nonparametric kernel estimation of the regression function $R(x)$ in (2.2) or (2.1). This can be obtained by the following methods.

a) Nadaraya (1964) and Watson (1964) Method

We observe that $R(x)$ depends on the unknown densities. Thus, using the data on $p + 1$ variables $z = (y, x)$ we first note from Rosenblatt (1956) for $p = 1$ and Cacoullos (1966) for $p > 1$ that

$$f_n(y, x) = f_n(z) = \frac{1}{nh^q} \sum_1^n K\left(\frac{z_i - z}{h}\right), \quad q = p + 1 \tag{3.1}$$

and

$$f_{1n}(x) = \int f_n(z)dy = \frac{1}{nh^p} \sum_1^n K_1\left(\frac{x_i - x}{h}\right), \tag{3.2}$$

where h, the window-width (also called the smoothing parameter or band-width), is a positive function of the sample size n which goes to zero as $n \to \infty$, K is a kernel or weight function such that $\int K(z)dz = 1$, and $K_1(x) = \int K(z)dy$. The kernel K determines the shape of the curves and the window width h determines their width. For details on the kernel density estimation, see Prakasa-Rao (1983), Silverman (1986) and Ullah (1988).

Substituting (3.1) and (3.2) into (2.1) it can easily be verified that

$$R_n(x) = R_n = \int y \frac{f_n(y, x)}{f_{1n}(x)} dy = \sum_1^n y_i w_i(x) \tag{3.3}$$

where

$$w_i(x) = \frac{K_1\left(\dfrac{x_i - x}{h}\right)}{\displaystyle\sum_1^n K_1\left(\dfrac{x_i - x}{h}\right)} \tag{3.4}$$

R_n is known as the Nadaraya (1964) and Watson (1964) type regression function estimator. Thus kernel nonparametric regression estimates the unknown $R(x)$ be a weighted average of the observed values of y_i, where the weight of the i-th observation depends on the distance x_i to x through the kernel K. Note that in (3.3) the difference between

x_i and x is scaled by window width h surrounding the point x over which the data are averaged. Substituting R_n into (2.2) gives the nonparametric model:

$$y = R_n(x) + e \tag{3.5}$$

where e is the nonparametric residual. We observe that this nonparametric model (3.5) has been obtained without making assumptions about the functional form of the $R(x)$.

b) The Least Squares Method

The Nadaraya-Watson estimator R_n defined in (3.3) can be viewed as a weighted least squares (LS) estimator of $R(x)$. This is because R_n is the value of $R(x)$ for which the weighted squared error

$$S = \sum_1^n K\left(\frac{x_i - x}{h}\right)(y_i - R(x))^2 = \sum_1^n K\left(\frac{x_i - x}{h}\right)u_i^2 \tag{3.6}$$

is minimum. This is obtained by solving

$$\frac{\partial S}{\partial R(x)} = 2 \sum_1^n K\left(\frac{x_i - x}{h}\right)(y_i - R(x)) = 0 \tag{3.7}$$

or

$$\sum_1^n K\left(\frac{x_i - x}{h}\right)y_i = R(x) \sum_1^n K\left(\frac{x_i - x}{h}\right) \tag{3.8}$$

for $R(x)$. The solution is identical with (3.3).

c) Method of Moments

In (2.2), note that $E(u|x) = 0$ by construction. Thus for any kernel function of x we get the following moment condition.

$$EK\left(\frac{x - x_0}{h}\right)u = 0 \tag{3.9}$$

where x_0 is a fixed point. A sample estimate of this is

$$\frac{1}{n}\sum_1^n K\left(\frac{x_i - x_0}{h}\right)u_i = \frac{1}{n}\sum_1^n K\left(\frac{x_i - x_0}{h}\right)(y_i - R(x)) = 0, \tag{3.10}$$

and we would choose $R(x)$ for which this holds. The solution will be the same as (3.3).

We note that since R_n in (3.3) is a weighted average of the y_i it may be sensitive to fluctuations in the data. In such situations a robust family of estimators can be developed as a solution of R in

$$\sum_1^n K\left(\frac{x_i - x}{h}\right)\psi_x(y_i - R) = 0 \tag{3.11}$$

where ψ_n is a bounded function for all x satisfying some regularity conditions; see Collomb and Hardle (1986) and Hardle (1984). The choice of a family of bounded functions ψ_x in (3.11) guarantees bounded influence and suggests more stable prediction properties. The unbounded influence function $\psi_x(u) = u$ gives the classical Nadaraya-Watson estimator $R_n(x)$.

In the Nadaraya-Watson regression estimator, R_n, the window width h is the same under all the data points. An alternative is to consider

$$\hat{R}_n(x) = \frac{\sum\limits_1^n y_i h_i^{-p} K\left(\frac{x_i - x}{h_i}\right)}{\sum\limits_1^n h_i^{-p} K\left(\frac{x_i - x}{h_i}\right)}, \tag{3.12}$$

where h_i denotes a sequence of positive numbers. The estimator (3.12) is known as the recursive regression estimator. The h_i is assumed to satisfy $\sum h_i^p \to \infty$ as $n \to \infty$. This estimator was first examined by Ahmad and Lin (1976) and later by Greblicki and Krzyzak (1980), Devroye and Wagner (1980a), Györfi (1981), Krzyzak and Pawlak (1984) and Singh and Ullah (1986). For $h_i = h$ in (3.12) we get (3.3).

An alternative estimator, which suppresses h_i^{-p} from (3.12), is given as

$$\tilde{R}_n(x) = \frac{\sum\limits_1^n y_i K\left(\dfrac{x_i - x}{h_i}\right)}{\sum\limits_1^n K\left(\dfrac{x_i - x}{h_i}\right)} \tag{3.13}$$

This estimator has been studied by Devroye and Wagner (1980a), Krzyzak and Pawlak (1984) and Greblicki and Pawlak (1987). Note that this estimator is obtained by simply replacing h by h_i in (3.3).

We note that the estimators $\hat{R}_n(x)$ and $\tilde{R}_n(x)$ are recursive in the sense that when an additional data point becomes available it can be updated according to

$$\hat{R}_n(x) = \hat{R}_{n-1}(x) + \frac{y_n - \hat{R}_{n-1}(x)}{1 + (n-1)\hat{f}_{n-1}(x)/h_n^{-p} K\left(\dfrac{x_n - x}{h_n}\right)} \tag{3.14}$$

$$\tilde{R}_n(x) = \tilde{R}_{n-1}(x) + \gamma_n^{-1}(y_n - \tilde{R}_{n-1}(x)) K((x_n - x)/h_n) \tag{3.15}$$

where $\gamma_n = \gamma_{n-1} + K\left(\dfrac{x_n - x}{h_n}\right)$, $\gamma_0 = 0$. When γ_n in (3.15) is replaced by nh^p then the estimator $\tilde{R}_n$ is very similar to the recursive estimator obtained by the method of stochastic approximation (see Revesz 1977).

Note that $\hat{u}_n = y_n - \hat{R}_{n-1}(x)$ on the right hand of $\hat{R}_n(x)$ can be considered as one-step-ahead prediction error and it has been used to update the recursive estimator of $R(x)$ as each new data becomes available. The new information at time n comes in the form of $\hat{u}_n$ and R is estimated by updating $\hat{R}_{n-1}$. The residuals $\hat{u}$ so generated can be called as *nonparametric recursive residuals*.

Stone (1977) has considered a class of regression estimator (3.3) in which the weight function $w_i(x)$ is the weight with the property that values of i where x_i is close to x get higher weight than those that are far from x. The weight function w_i is said to be a probability weight function if $\sum w_i(x) = 1$ and nonnegative if $w_i \geq 0$. The k-nearest neighbor weight estimator is a special case and it is

$$R_n^*(x) = \sum_1^n y_i^* w_i \qquad (3.16)$$

where $w_i = 1/k$, $1 \leqslant i \leqslant k$ and $w_i = 0$ elsewhere, and y_i^* is the reordered data of y according to increasing values of the norm $\|x_i - x\|$.

Note that x's in (2.2) are stochastic. However, if they are fixed "design" variables such as time and age then $R(x)$ can be estimated by various nonparametric curve fitting procedures. Among the prominent methods are smoothing splines (Reinsch 1967); kernel estimator (Priestley and Chao 1972; Ahmad and Lin 1984); and local regression (Stone 1977; Muller 1987). Silverman (1984) has shown that smoothing splines are essentially equivalent to kernel estimates with certain kernels if the x_i are equidistantly spaced, where some sort of adaptation to local nonequidistance takes place if the x_i are not equidistancely spaced. In addition to above estimators, Johnston (1982) has considered the estimator of $R(x)$ when $f_1(x)$ is known. The properties of his estimator are discussed in Hardle and Kelly (1987).

Finally, we note here that the regression estimators discussed above are under the assumption that u_i in (2.2) have the same variances and they are independent. However if $V(u) = \Sigma$ is an $n \times n$ positive definite matrix either due to heteroskedasticity or serial correlation one could obtain the generalized least squares (GLS) estimator of $R(x)$. For this, it is convenient to note that the least squares estimator in vector notation, corresponding to (3.6), is to minimize

$$(y - LR(x))'K(y - LR(x)) = u'K^{1/2}K^{1/2}u \qquad (3.17)$$

with respect to $R(x)$, where $L = [1 \ldots 1]'$ and $K = D(K_1, \ldots, K_n)$ is an $n \times n$ diagonal matrix with $K_i = K((x_i - x)/h)$. This gives

$$R_n = (L'KL)^{-1}L'Ky \qquad (3.18)$$

which is equal to (3.3). In fact (3.18) can be calculated by the least squares regression of $K^{1/2}y$ on $K^{1/2}L$. Thus if $V(u) = \Sigma$ then the GLS estimator of $R(x)$ can be obtained by minimizing $u'K^{1/2}\Sigma^{-1}K^{1/2}u$. This gives

$$R_n^{GLS} = (L'K^{1/2}\Sigma^{-1}K^{1/2}L)^{-1}L'K^{1/2}\Sigma^{-1}K^{1/2}y \qquad (3.19)$$

For $\Sigma = I$, (3.19) reduces to (3.18).

Before turning to the estimation of partial derivatives we note that R_n is useful for nonparametric forecasting. Also, since R_n is the estimator of conditional expectation it provides a way out of specifying expectation variables appearing in various econometric variables, e.g., rational expectation models. For forecasting, see Ullah and Singh (1985) and Moschini et al. (1988).

3.2 Estimation of Partial Derivatives

A consistent estimator of the response coefficient $\beta(x)$ (first derivative of $R(x)$) in (2.3) is simply

$$\tilde{\beta}(x) = \frac{R(x + h) - R(x - h)}{2h}.$$ (3.20)

But this is not operational since $R(x \pm h)$ is not known. An operational version is

$$b_n(x) = \frac{R_n(x + h) - R_n(x - h)}{2h}$$ (3.21)

where $R_n(x)$ is the regression estimator given in (3.3)

Similarly the estimators of the s-th order derivative of $R(x)$ in (2.5) and the cross derivatives in (2.6) can be written by replacing $R(\ )$ with $Rn(\ )$. Thus, the estimator of $\beta^{(s)}(x)$ in (2.5) is

$$b_n^{(s)}(x) = \left(\frac{1}{2h}\right)^p \sum_{l=0}^{s} (-1)^l \binom{s}{l} R_n(x + (s - 2l)h),$$ (3.22)

and that of cross derivatives, following (2.5), is

$$b_n^{(s_1 + \ldots + s_r)} = \left(\frac{1}{2h}\right)^{s_1 + \ldots + s_r} \sum_{l_1=0}^{s_1} \ldots \sum_{l_r=0}^{s_r} (-1)^{l_1 + \ldots + l_r} \binom{s_1}{l_1} \ldots \binom{s_r}{l_r}$$

$$\times R(x + (s_1 - 2l_1)h, \ldots x + (s_r - 2l_r)h).$$

The estimator (3.22) and its properties have been considered in Ahmad and Ullah (1987). For $s = 1$, (3.21) reduces to (3.20) and this has been considered in Rilstone (1987) and Rilstone and Ullah (1987).

Ullah and Vinod (1988) proposed the estimator of $\beta(x) = \partial R(x)/\partial x$ as an analytical derivative of $R_n(x)$ in (3.3). Their estimator is

$$\hat{\beta}_n(x) = \frac{\partial}{\partial x} R_n(x) = \sum_1^n y_i(w_{1i} - w_{2i})$$

(3.23)

where $w_{1i} = K'((x_i - x)/h)/\Sigma\, K(x_i - x)/h)$ and $w_{2i} = w_i(x)\, \Sigma\, w_{1i}$; $w_i(x)$ is as in (3.4) and $K'((x_i - x)/h) = \partial K((x_i - x)/h)/\partial x_j$. Numerically $\hat{\beta}_n(x) = b_n(x)$. However in contrast to $b_n(x)$, the derivation of asymptotic properties as well as calculations of $\hat{\beta}_n(x)$ (especially of higher order derivatives) would be difficult.

An alternative derivation of $\hat{\beta}_n(x)$ and its generalization for higher order derivatives can be obtained as below. Let us write from (2.1), using $f_1(x) = f(x)$,

$$R(x) = \frac{\int yf(y, x)dy}{f_1(x)} = \frac{g(x)}{f(x)}$$

(3.24)

or $R(x)f(x) = g(x)$. Differentiating it with respect to x_j we get s-th order derivative of $R(x)$, $\beta^{(s)}(x)$, as a solution of

$$\sum_{l=0}^{s} \binom{s}{l} \beta^{(l)}(x) f^{(s-l)}(x) = g^{(s)}(x).$$

(3.25)

The estimator of $\beta^{(s)}(x)$ is then a solution of

$$\sum_{l=0}^{s} \binom{s}{l} \beta_n^{(l)}(x) f_n^{(s-l)}(x) = g_n^{(s)}(x).$$

(3.26)

For example, if $s = 1$, we get Vinod and Ullah (1988) estimator

$$\beta_n(x) = (f_n(x))^{-1}[g_n^{(1)}(x) - f_n^{(1)}(x)R_n(x)]$$

(3.27)

where $g_n^{(1)}(x) = (nh^p)^{-1}\, \Sigma\, y_i K'((x_i - x)/h)$ and $f_n^{(1)}(x) = (nh^p)^{-1}\, \Sigma\, K'((x_i - x)/h)$; $K'(\ )$ is as defined by (3.23). It is easy to verify that (3.27) is the same as $\hat{\beta}_n(x)$ in

(3.23). However, an alternative estimator, which is different from $\beta_n(x)$, may be obtained by using the estimators of $f^{(s-1)}(x)$ and $g^{(s)}(x)$ as given in Singh (1981).

The recursive estimators of $\beta^{(s)}(x)$ can be developed by replacing $R_n(\;)$ in (3.22) with the recursive estimators $\hat{R}_n(\;)$ and $\tilde{R}_n(\;)$ given in (3.12) and (3.13), respectively. For example, using $\hat{R}_n(\;)$, we can write

$$b_n^{(s)}(x) = \frac{n-1}{n} b_{n-1}^{(s)}(x) + \left(\frac{1}{2}\right)^s \sum_{l=0}^{s} (-1)^l \binom{s}{l} \frac{1}{n(h_n^p)^s} R_n(x + (s-2l)h_n). \tag{3.28}$$

Gasser and Muller (1984) and Georgiev (1984) were perhaps the first to consider the partial derivatives of Priestley and Chao (1972) type kernel regression estimator. However, their estimator is restricted to fixed "design" variable case whose domain can be transformed into the $(0, 1)$ interval. The estimator, for $p = 1$, is

$$\beta_n^*(x) = \frac{1}{h} \sum_1^n y_i \int_{s_{i-1}}^{s_i} K'\left(\frac{x-u}{h}\right) du. \tag{3.29}$$

where $0 = s_0 \leqslant \ldots \leqslant s_n = 1$ and $s_{i-1} \leqslant x_i \leqslant s_i$. For $p > 1$, the estimator corresponding to $\beta_n^*(x)$ can be written by using the Ahmad and Lin (1984) estimator of $R(x)$ for the fixed regressors case.

An alternative idea developed in Powell et al. (1986) is the kernel estimation of the "average" derivative over the sample space. That is,

$$\bar{\beta} = E(f_1(x)\beta(x)) = \int \left(\frac{\partial}{\partial x} R(x)\right) f_1^2(x) dx \tag{3.30}$$

$$= -2E\left(y \frac{\partial f_1(x)}{\partial x_j}\right)$$

where the last equality is obtained using integration by parts. A moment estimator of (3.30) is then

$$\bar{\beta}_n = -\frac{2}{n} \sum_1^n y_i \frac{\partial f_{1,n}(x_i)}{\partial x_j}. \tag{3.31}$$

Powell et al. (1986) have shown that $\bar{\beta}_n$ is $\sqrt{n}$ convergent, and it is proportional to an estimator of β in "single index" models of the form $R = R(x\beta)$. Finally, we note that the estimator of derivatives in (3.22) can easily be written for the nearest neighbor estimator by substituting R_n in (3.22) with R_n^* given in (3.16).

3.3 Restricted Estimation

Economic theory often imposes certain a priori restrictions on the partial derivative $\beta(x)$. Let there be m such exact linear restrictions $A\,\beta(x) = r$ at a point x; A is an $m \times p$ matrix of constants and r is an $m \times 1$ known vector. If these restrictions are ignored then the estimators of $\beta(x)$ in 3.2 will be biased. An asymptotically unbiased estimator of $\beta(x)$ subject to $A\beta(x) = r$ can, however, be obtained. This is the restricted least squares estimator of $\beta(x)$ and it is obtained by minimizing (3.6) subject to $A\beta(x) = r$. The estimator is given as

$$\hat{b}_n(x) = b_n(x) - A'(AA')^{-1}(Ab_n(x) - r), \tag{3.32}$$

where $b_n(x)$ is given in (3.21).

Now consider the case of inequality restrictions on, say, the j-th response coefficient $\beta_j(x)$ as $\beta_j(x) \geqslant r$ where r is a known scalar. The decision rule or the inequality restricted estimator which combines both the sample and linear inequality restriction in estimating $\beta_j(x)$ may be expressed as

$$\beta_{j,n}(x) = rI_{(-\infty,\,r)}(b_{j,n}(x)) + b_{j,n}(x)I_{[r,\infty)}(b_{j,n}(x)) \tag{3.33}$$

where $I_{(a,\,b)}(x)$ represents an indicator function which takes the value 1 if the random variable x falls within $(a,\,b)$ and is zero otherwise.

In the general case of m linear inequality restrictions $A\beta(x) \geqslant r$, the inequality restricted estimator is

$$\beta_n(x) = \hat{b}_n(x)I_{(-\infty,\,r)}(b_n(x)) + b_n(x)I_{[r,\infty)}(b_n(x)), \tag{3.34}$$

where $\hat{b}_n(x)$ is as given in (3.32). The estimators (3.33) and (3.34) are similar to those given in the parametric econometrics, see Judge and Yancey (1986) for details.

3.4 Hypothesis Testing

Suppose we want to test m linear restrictions

$$H_0: \quad A\beta(x) = r \quad \text{against} \quad H_1: \quad A\beta(x) \neq r \qquad (3.35)$$

at a point x, where A and r are as defined in 3.3. The test for (3.35) can be carried out by using the Wald Statistic

$$W = (Ab_n(x) - r)'[AV(b_n(x))A']^{-1}(Ab_n(x) - r) \qquad (3.36)$$

where $V(b_n(x))$ is the variance covariance matrix of $b_n(x)$ given in Section 4. It follows from the asymptotic normality result of $b_n(x)$ in Section 4 that $Ab_n(x) - r$ is asymptotically normal, and hence W in (3.36) is asymptotically a central χ^2_m under H_0. Rilstone (1988) has considered the testing of m linear restrictions in (3.35) for all x, and has shown how the rate of convergence of W to central χ^2 can be improved in this case. In addition the test of $H_0: g(\beta(x), H(x)) = 0$ against $H_1: g(\beta(x), H(x)) \neq 0$ is considered, where $g(\ )$ represents the function of $\beta(x)$ and the Hessian matrix $H(x)$.

Another hypothesis of interest is that $R(x)$ is linear, that is, $H_0: R(x) = x\beta$ against $H_1: R(x) \neq x\beta$. Ullah (1985) proposed a test statistic which compares the parametric residual sum of squares with the nonparametric one. Recently, Lee (1987) has studied asymptotic distribution of this test statistic. Finally, for the test of independence of x and u and some other testing problems, see Ullah and Singh (1985).

4 Asymptotic Properties

4.1 Regression Estimators

There is an enormous literature on the proofs of the asymptotic properties of regression estimators, the details of which can be found in review articles of Collomb (1981), Gyorfi (1981) and Bierens (1987), and in the books by Prakasa Rao (1983) and Hardle (1988). Our aim here is merely to describe the basic assumptions and asymptotic results which may provide some understanding of the large sample behavior of the kernel regression estimator. In addition, we present the asymptotic standard errors and normality results for the partial derivatives considered in Section 3. These will be useful for the applied work. Below, we first consider the i.i.d. case and then time dependent but identically distributed case.

The asymptotic properties of the regression estimators can be established under some regularity assumptions about the kernel K and the density f. We also require that the window width $h = h_n$ depend on the sample size n in some way. The assumptions we make are:

A.1 Let K be the class of all Borel-measurable bounded real functions $K(x), x = (x_1, ..., x_p)'$ such that (i) $\int K(x)dx = 1$, (ii) $\int |K(x)|dx < \infty$, (iii) $\|x\|^p|K(x)| \to 0$ as $\|x\| \to \infty$, and (iv) $\sup |K(x)| < \infty$, where $\|x\|$ is the usual Euclidean norm of x.

A.2 $h_n \to 0$ as $n \to \infty$

A.3 $nh_n^p \to \infty$ as $n \to \infty$

The assumption A.1 implies that K is a bounded density with $\|x\|^p|K(x)| \to 0$. This assumption is satisfied by a large class of functions; for example, the p variate standard normal density, and the function $K(x_1, ..., x_p) = 2^{-p} \prod_1^p I(x_j)$, where $I(x_j) = 1$ if $|x_j| < 1$ and 0 otherwise. Furthermore, the assumptions A.2 and A.3 imply that as n increases h should decrease but in a way such that nh^p is still large.

The weak consistency of R_n ($R_n \to R$ in probability at any point, as $n \to \infty$), under the assumptions A.1 to A.3 and $Ey^2 < \infty$, follow at every continuity point x of the functions $f_1(x)$, $R(x)$, $\sigma^2(x) = V(y|x)$. This has been treated in Watson (1964), Rosenblatt (1969) and Noda (1976) for $p = 1$ and by Gredblécki and Krzyzak (1980) for $p > 1$. In econometrics this result is discussed in Bierens (1987) and Singh et al. (1987). Nadaraya (1964) and Noda (1976) give strong consistency result; i.e., $R_n \to R$ with probability one (almost surely) for $p = 1$. A rigorous proof of pointwise consistency (weak as well as strong) was first given by Devroye (1981). His results imply that weak consistency follows if $E|y| < \infty$, A.2 and A.3 hold, and there exists r, c_1, c_2 such that

A.4 $c_1 I(x) \leqslant K(x) \leqslant c_2 I(x)$

where I is an indicator function which takes the value 1 when $\|x\| \leqslant r$ and 0 otherwise. Moreover, if $|y| < \infty$ a.s. (almost surely) and

A.5 $nh^p(\log n)^{-1} \to \infty$ as $n \to \infty$

then $R_n \to R$ a.s. for almost all x. Devroye's (1981) weak consistency condition A.4 on K is weaker than A.1. Also his results hold for continuous as well as discrete distributions $F(x)$ of x. However, note that Devroye's kernels are practically confined to the window kernels, i.e., kernels which equal 1 for $\|x\| \leqslant 1$ and 0 otherwise. This problem is overcome by Greblicki et al. (1984) and Krzyzak and Pawlak (1984) who give the consistency results by replacing $I(x)$ in A.4 with a nonnegative nonincreasing function $H(\|x\|)$ having bounded support with a positive radius, and $0 < H(0) < \infty$. The kernels satisfying this are

$$K(x) = (1 - \|x\|^\delta)I(x), \quad 0 \leqslant \delta < \infty \tag{4.1}$$

where $I(x)$ is as in A.4 with $r = 1$. For other kernels, see Greblicki and Krzyzak (1980). Greblicki et al. (1984, p. 1574) results also allow the kernels with unbounded support, e.g., for $p = 1$, $K(x) = e^{-1}$ for $|x| \leqslant e$ and $(|x| \log |x|)^{-1}$ otherwise. For the proof of strong consistency, also see Zhao and Fang (1985).

Uniform weak consistency of R_n, i.e., $\sup_{x} |R_n - R|$ tends to zero as $n \to \infty$ in probability describes the behavior of R_n for the entire x space. This is treated in Bierens (1987). The uniform weak consistency follows under the assumptions A.1, A.2, the characteristic function of K is absolutely integrable, R is uniformly continuous in R^p and

A.6 $nh^{2p} \to \infty$ as $n \to \infty$

The uniform strong consistency results, i.e.

$$\sup_{a \leqslant x \leqslant b} |R_n - R| \to 0 \text{ a.s.}$$

follows under A.1, A.2, K is of bounded variation on $a \leqslant x \leqslant b$, f_1 is continuous with $\min_{a \leqslant x \leqslant b} f_1(x) > 0$, R is continuous on R^p, $|y| \leqslant c \leqslant \infty$ a.s. and

A.7 $\displaystyle\sum_{n=1}^{\infty} \exp(-\alpha nh^{2p}) < \infty$ for all $\alpha > 0$.

This result was given by Nadaraya (1965, 1970) for $p = 1$. Devroye (1978) extended the results to the multidimensional case under weaker conditions. The main result of his paper is that for the uniform strong consistency bounded variation of K is not needed and that the rest of the conditions of Nadaraya can be relaxed considerably. In particular, his proof does not assume that x or y have densities, K is just needed to be radial type and instead of A.7, A.5 holds. Mack and Silverman (1982) provide the rate of weak and strong (uniform) consistency as $0((nh_n^p)^{-1} \log h_n^{-p})^{1/2}$. They assumed a moment condition on y and considered K to be uniformly continuous and of bounded variation. Their rate is better than uniform weak convergence rate of $0(n^{-1/2}h_n^{-1})$ given by Schuster and Yakowitz (1979) for $p = 1$.

The conditions for consistency under the global L_1 criterion, i.e., conditions under which $L_1 = \int |R_n - R| F(dx) \to 0$ in probability or almost surely ($F(dx)$ represents probability measure of x) are discussed in the work of Devroye and Wagner (1980a). They have shown that under the conditions A.2, F is absolutely continuous probability measure of x on R^p, $|y| \leqslant C \leqslant \infty$ a.s. and K is a nonnegative bounded integrable function on R^p whose radial majorant ψ is integrable, i.e.,

$$\psi(x) \equiv \sup_{\|y\| \geqslant \|x\|} K(y), \quad \int \psi(x)dx < \infty, \tag{4.2}$$

the L_1 consistency (weak) follows if (A.3) holds. Moreover the strong consistency follows if

A.8 $\quad \sum_{n=1}^{\infty} \exp(-\alpha nh^p) < \infty \quad$ for all $\alpha > 0$

Note that A.5 implies A.8. Further the condition (4.2) is equivalent to $\|x\|^p \psi(x) \to 0$ as $\|x\| \to \infty$ and thus related to A.1(iii). For example, (4.2) holds if K is a bounded function and either has compact support, or satisfies $\|x\|^{p+\epsilon}K(x) \to 0$ as $\|x\| \to \infty$, $\epsilon > 0$. We also note that the above L_1 consistency result is distribution free in the sense that there is no condition on (y, x) other than boundedness of y and the absolute continuity of F. No continuity restrictions are put on R as well as on the density corresponding to F.

Distribution free consistency results were first established by Stone (1977) when he showed that a large class of weighted regression estimates (for example, (3.16)) satisfy $EL_1 \to 0$ for all possible distribution of (y, x) with $E|y| < \infty$. Similar results were later established for kernel estimator R_n by Devroye and Wagner (1980b) and Spiegelman and Sacks (1980). In particular, Devroye and Wagner (1980b) showed that $EL_1 \to 0$ under A.2, A.3 and K is a bounded nonnegative function with compact support such that for a small sphere S about the origin $\inf_{x \in S} K(x) > 0$. Note that this result imposes stronger condition on K compared to (4.2) but weaker conditions on the distribution of (y, x). The results for $E \int |R_n - R|^p F(dx) \to 0$ as $n \to \infty$ are also discussed in Stone (1977) and Deveroye and Wagner (1980b) under the same conditions as for $p = 1$, with $E|y|^p < \infty$.

In the recent paper Zhao (1985) has provided the exponential bounds for the EL_1 based on the kernel and nearest neighborhood estimators of regressions. For example, for the kernel estimator, he has shown that

$$P[EL_1 \geqslant \epsilon] \leqslant \exp(-Cn) \tag{4.3}$$

where $C > 0$ is a constant independent of n.

The joint asymptotic normality of $R_n(x_1), \ldots, R_n(x_m)$ at the m fixed points $x_1, \ldots, x_m$ was first shown by Schuster (1972) for $p = 1$ and later by Bierens (1987), Singh et al. (1987) and Rilstone (1987) for $p > 1$. At a single point x where $f_1(x) > 0$ the results of Schuster (1972) and Rilstone (1987) show that if (A.1) holds $Ey^3 < \infty$, first and second order derivatives of $f_1(x)$ and $l_1(x) = \int yf(y, x)dy$ and first order derivative of $l_2(x) = \int y^2 f(y, x)dy$ exist and are bounded, and

A.9 $nh^{2+p} \to \infty$ and $nh^{4+p} \to 0$ as $n \to \infty$

A.10 $\int xK(x)dx = 0$, $\int xx'K(x)dx = \Omega$ is finite,

then

$$(nh^p)^{1/2}(R_n - R) \sim N(0, \Lambda(x)) \tag{4.4}$$

where

$$\Lambda(x) = \frac{\sigma^2(x)}{f_1(x)} \int K^2(u)du; \quad \sigma^2(x) = V(y \mid x). \tag{4.5}$$

Note that the condition $nh^{4+p} \to 0$ is needed for the $(nh^p)^{1/2}$ Bias $(R_n) \to 0$ as $n \to \infty$. Bierens (1987) suggests using jackknife estimator of R to eliminate this bias.

In practice $\sigma^2(x)$ in (4.5) can be replaced by its consistent nonparametric estimator

$$\hat{\sigma}^2(x) = \frac{\sum y_i^2 K\left(\dfrac{x_i - x}{h}\right)}{\sum K\left(\dfrac{x_i - x}{h}\right)} - \hat{R}_n^2. \tag{4.6}$$

For details see Ullah (1988). Using $\hat{\sigma}^2(x)$ one can calculate standard errors of R_n, and also the confidence intervals.

Now we turn to the recursive estimators $\hat{R}_n$ and $\tilde{R}_n$ given in (3.14) and (3.15) Ahmad and Lin (1976) were the first to treat consistency results for $\hat{R}_n$ and later Greblicki and Krzyzak (1980) considered weak consistency of $\hat{R}_n$ and $\tilde{R}_n$. Essentially, for the weak consistency results of $\hat{R}_n$ and $\tilde{R}_n$ compared to R_n one needs to replace A.3 by $\Sigma\, h_i^p \rightarrow \infty$ (Greblicki and Krzyzak 1980), or by the weaker condition $n^{-2} \Sigma\, h_i^{-p} \rightarrow 0$ (Devroye and Wagner 1980a) under L_1 criterion. For the strong consistency (A.5)

gets replaced by $\sum\limits_{n=1}^{\infty} n^{-2} h_n^{-p} < \infty$ or $n h_n^p/\log\log n \rightarrow \infty$ as $n \rightarrow \infty$ (Devroye and Wagner

1980a) under the L_1 criterion. Krzyzak and Pawlak (1984) have considered consistency results (weak and strong) under the weaker condition on the kernel described before in (4.1). Note that all the conditions for the consistency, discussed above so far, are the sufficient conditions. In the recent papers Greblicki (1987) and Greblicki and Pawlak (1987) have provided the necessary and sufficient conditions for the consistency.

As far as the author is aware the asymptotic normality of $\tilde{R}_n$ and $\hat{R}_n$ has not been established in the literature. This is also true for the estimators based on the stochastic approximations as well as the general weighted estimators of Stone (1977) described in 3.1.

4.2 Partial Derivatives

First we note that the partial derivative estimator $\tilde{\beta}(x)$ in (3.20) converges to $\beta(x) = \partial R(x)/\partial x$ as $n \rightarrow \infty$ ($h = h_n \rightarrow 0$). Thus the asymptotic behavior of the operational partial derivative estimator $b_n(x)$ in (3.10) depends on the asymptotic behavior of the differences

$$\frac{R_n(x - mh) - R(x - mh)}{2h} \tag{4.7}$$

for $m = -1, 0, 1$. The consistency and asymptotic normality of the differences $R_n(x - mh) - R(x - mh)$ have been described in 4.1. Using these results it is straightforward to prove various consistencies of $b_n(x)$ and show that, under the conditions similar to the case of $R_n(x)$,

$$(nh^{2+p})^{1/2}(b_n(x) - \beta(x)) \sim N(0, \Lambda_1(x)), \quad \Lambda_1(x) = \frac{\sigma^2(x)}{f_1(x)} \int (K'(u))^2 du \tag{4.8}$$

where $K'(u) = \partial K(u)/\partial u_j$ and $\sigma^2(x)$ is as given in (4.5). Note that the expression of the variance $\Lambda_1(x)$ is the same as $\Lambda(x)$ appearing in (4.5) with the K replaced by K'. The result (4.8) has been proven in Rilstone (1987) and Rilstone and Ullah (1987) by alternative methods.

Following the same arguments, consistencies and asymptotic normality results of the s-th derivatives can easily be established. The following result is from Ahmad and Ullah (1987):

$$(nh^{2s+p})^{1/2}(b^{(s)}(x) - \beta(x)) \sim N(0, \Lambda_s(x)) \tag{4.9}$$

where $\Lambda_s(x)$ is $\Lambda_1(x)$ with $K'(u)$ replaced by the s-th derivative $K^{(s)}(u)$. For the cross partial derivatives, following (3.22), the result is the same as (4.9) except that we get the square of cross partial derivatives of K in $\Lambda_s(x)$.

For the partial derivatives estimators in the fixed design variable case given in (3.29), the result in (4.9) holds except that $f_1(x)$ drops out; see Gasser and Muller (1984).

4.3 Dependent Observations

Most of the asymptotic results for the i.i.d. case discussed above go through for the case of dependent observations. However, as expected, in the case of dependent observations one requires certain conditions on the nature of dependence (mixing conditions) of the stationary processes. We define these mixing conditions below.

The process $\{z_i\}$ is said to be *strongly mixing* if α_t, the mixing coefficient, defined by

$$\alpha_t = \sup_{A,B} |P(A \cdot B) - P(A)P(B)|$$

converges to zero as $t \to \infty$, where $A \in B^i_{-\infty}$ and $B \in B^{\infty}_{i+t}$; $B^{l'}_l$ is the σ-field of events generated by $z_l, z_{l+1}, \ldots, z_{l'}$. The process $\{z_i\}$ is said to be ϕ-mixing if the mixing coefficient $\phi_t \to 0$ as $t \to \infty$, where $\phi_t = \sup_{A,B} |P(B|A) - P(B)|$ and A and B are as defined above. Notice that every ϕ-mixing process is a α-mixing. Further details about these can be found in White (1984).

The weak pointwise consistency of R_n has been shown under α and ϕ-mixings in Robinson (1986); and by Bierens (1987) under ν-stability in L^2 with respect to a ϕ-mixing base. In addition to the conditions A.1 to A.3 and the regularity conditions on $R(x)$ and $f_1(x)$, the weak consistency under α-mixing follows if $(nh^{2p})^{-1} \sum_1^n \alpha_t \downarrow 0$ and under ϕ-mixing if $(nh^p)^{-1} \sum_1^n \phi_t \downarrow 0$ as $n \rightarrow \infty$.

The uniform weak consistency of R_n has been shown by Bierens (1983) under the condition $nh^{2p} \sum_0^n \phi_t^{1/2} \rightarrow \infty$ as $n \rightarrow \infty$. Under α-mixing we require $nh^{2p} \rightarrow \infty$ and $\sum_0^\infty \alpha_t^{(1-2/\theta)} < \infty$ where $\theta > 2$ moment of y_t is assumed to be bounded. Note that the rate of uniform convergence is the same as in the i.i.d. case. The uniform strong consistency of R_n has been studied by Collomb and Hardle (1986) under ϕ-mixing. Their results are the extension of Mack and Silverman (1982) results in the i.i.d. case. Recently Roussas (1988) has established pointwise as well as uniform strong consistencies under various types of mixing.

The asymptotic normality of R_n has been studied by Robinson (1983) and Bierens (1987). From Robinson (1983) the asymptotic normality of R_n in (4.4) holds, under α-mixing, when $|y| \leqslant c < \infty$ a.s. if $N \sum_N^\infty \alpha_t = o(1)$. If we relax boundedness of y but assume $E|y|^\theta < \infty, \theta > 2$ then the normality holds if $N \sum_N^\infty \alpha_t^{1-2/\theta} = 0(1)$.

Using theresults for R_n, the asymptotic properties of the partial derivative could be developed as in the i.i.d. case. The details will appear in a future paper.

The asymptotic properties of the R_n and partial derivatives discussed above depend on the mixing conditions which, in practice, may be difficult to verify. In view of this Castellana and Leadbetter (1986) have developed the asymptotic theory of the density estimators under an alternative measure of dependence. It would be a useful subject of future study to develop the similar asymptotic results for the R_n and the partial derivatives.

4.4 Selection of h and K

It follows from Collomb (1981) and Singh et al. (1987) that if we choose kernel K whose first $r - 1$ order moments are zero then, under certain conditions and for large sample,

$$\text{Bias } R_n(x) = ER_n(x) - R(x) = \lambda(x)h^r = 0(h^r) \tag{4.10}$$

where $\lambda(x)$ depends upon unknown functions $R(x)$ and $F_1(x)$. Further from (4.4) $V(R_n(x)) = 0(nh^p)^{-1}$. Thus the asymptotic mean squared error (MSE) of $R_n(x) =$

$0(h^{2r}) + 0(nh^p)^{-1}$. The optimal value of h, therefore, is $h = \lambda_0(x)n^{-1/(p+2r)}$, where $\lambda_0(x)$ is unknown but it can be determined by cross validation technique. For this value of h, the MSE is of $0(n^{-2r/(2r+p)})$. For details on various selection techniques of h, see the book by Hardle (1988) and the survey paper by Marron (1988).

Using (4.10) it can be shown that, under certain conditions and for large sample

$$\text{Bias } (b_n^s(x)) = 0(h^{r-s}) \tag{4.11}$$

Further from (4.9), $V(b_n^{(s)}(x)) = 0(nh^{p+2s})^{-1}$ which makes the asymptotic MSE = $0(h^{2(r-s)}) + 0(nh^{p+2s})^{-1}$. This gives the optimal $h \alpha n^{-1/(2r+p)}$, and for this h the MSE is of $0(n^{-2(r-s)/(2r+p)})$. For $s = 0$, we get the result for $R_n(x)$ as given above.

Note that the speed of convergence of the MSE is less than the usual n^{-1}. This implies that the nonparametric estimates could be imprecise for small samples. Further, the speed of convergence gets slower when p, the number of regressors, is large. Also, note that for higher order derivatives we require $r - s > 0$. Thus, if we are considering $s = 2$ then we require kernel whose at leat first two moments are zero, otherwise the second derivative will not be asymptotically unbiased. The selections of kernels whose $(r - 1)$ moments are zero has been discussed in Singh (1981), Ullah and Singh (1985), Bierens (1987), and Muller (1984) among others.

5 Structural Models

Suppose $y = R(x) + u$ in (2.2) is a single equation out of the system of M simultaneous equation model, where x is now referred as a vector of right hand endogenous variables. Let w be the vector of stochastic exogenous variables (instruments) which appear in the remaining $M - 1$ equations. The w's are such that $Ewu = 0$ but as is the case in such models $E x u \neq 0$. Thus $R(x) = E(y|x)$ is not the proper conditioning and the estimator $b_n(x)$ of $dy/dx = dR(x)/dx = \beta(x)$ in (3.2)) is not consistent. A way out is to rewrite the above model as

$$y = g(w) + v, \quad v = u + R(x) - g(w) \tag{5.1}$$

where $g(w) = E(R(x)|w$ such that $E(v|w) = 0$. The parameter of interest remains $dy/dx = \beta(x)$, and we discuss its estimation below.

Note that the reduced forms for y and x are

$$y = E(y|w) + \epsilon_1$$

$$x = E(x|w) + \epsilon_2 \tag{5.2}$$

where ϵ_1 and ϵ_2 are disturbances. Thus, the identification condition is

$$g(w) = E(y|w) \tag{5.3}$$

Further the parameter of interest can be written as

$$\frac{dy}{dx} = \beta(x) = \frac{dE(y|w)}{dE(x|w)} = \frac{dy^*(w)}{dx^*(w)} \tag{5.4}$$

where $y^*(w) = E(y/w)$ and $x^*(w) = E(x/w)$. This implies that in the structural equation case we may consider the regression of $y^* = y^*(w)$ on $x^* = x^*(w)$ instead of x on x, as

$$y^* = R(x^*) + u^* = E(y^*|x^*) + u^* \tag{5.5}$$

and estimate the parameter

$$\beta(x^*) = \frac{dR(x^*)}{dx_j^*}. \tag{5.6}$$

The estimator corresponding to (3.21) is

$$b_n(x^*) = \frac{dRn(x^*)}{dx_j^*} = \frac{Rn(x^* + h) - Rn(x^* - h)}{2h} \tag{5.7}$$

where $Rn(x^* + h)$ is the same as R_n in (3.3) with x replaced by x^*. In practice, using (3.3), we can replace $y^* = E(y|w) = R_y(w)$ and $x^* = E(x|w) = R_x(w)$ by their estimators $R_{n,y}(w)$ and $R_{n,x}(w)$, respectively. The operational estimator $b_n(x^*)$ so obtained is the nonparametric two stage estimator. In the case where both y^* and x^* are the linear functions of w, and (5.5) is linear we get Theil's two stage least squares estimator of $\beta(x^*) = \beta$. Further details on the estimator in (5.7) are given in Robinson and Ullah (1987).

References

Ahmad I, Lin P (1976) Nonparametric sequential estimation of a multiple regression function. Bull Math Statist 17:63–75

Ahmad I, Lin P (1984) Fitting a multiple regression. Journal of Statistical Planning and Inference 2:163–176

Ahmad I, Ullah A (1987) Nonparametric estimation of the p-th order derivative of regression function. Mimeo, Univ. of Western Ontario

Barnett WA, Lee YW (1985) The global properties of minflex laurent, generalized leontief, and translog flexible functional forms. Econometrica 52:1421–1437

Beneditti JK (1977) On the nonparametric estimates of regression functions. Journal of the Royal Statistcal Society 00:248–253

Bierens HJ (1983) Uniform consistency of Kernel estimators of a regression function under generalized conditions. Journal of the American Statistical Association 77:699–707

Bierens HJ (1987) Kernel estimation of regression function. In: Bewley TF (ed) Advances in econometrics. Cambridge University Press, New York, pp 99–144

Cacoullos T (1966) Estimation of a multivariate density. Annals Institute of Statistical Mathematics 18:179–189

Castellana JV, Leadbetter MR (1986) On smooth probability density estimation for stationary processes. Stochastic Theory and Their Applications 21:179–193

Collomb A (1981) Estimation nonparametrique de la regression, revue bibliographique. International Statistical Review 49:73–93

Collomb A, Hardle W (1986) Strong uniform convergence rates in robust nonparametric time series analysis and prediction: Kernel regression estimation from dependent observations. Stochastic Processes and Their Applications 23:77–89

Cullum J (1981) Numerical differentiation and regularization, Siam J Numet Annal 8:254–265

Devroye LP (1978) The uniform convergence of the Nadaraya-Watson regression function estimats. Canadian Journal of Statistics 00:179–191

Devroye LP (1981) On the amost everywhere convergence of nonparametric regression function estimates. The Annals of Statistics 19:1310–1319

Devroye LP, Wagner TJ (1980a) On the L_1-convergence of Kernel estimators of regression functions with applications in discrimination. Wahrsch Verw Gabiete 51:15–25

Devroye LP, Wagner TJ (1980b) Distribution free consistency results in nonparametric discrimination and regression function estimates. Annals of Statistics 00:231–239

Diewert WE (1971) An application of the Sheperd duality theorem: a generalized leontif production function. Journal of Political Economy 49:481–507

Eubank R (1988) Spline smoothing and nonparametric regression. Wiley, New York

Gallant AR (1981) On the bias in flexible functional forms and an essentially unbiased form: the fourier flexible form. Journal of Econometrics 15:211–245

Gasser T, Muller HG (1984) Estimating regression functions and their derivatives by the Kernel method. Scandinavian Journal of Statistics 11:171–185

Georgiev AA (1984) Speed of convergence in nonparametric Kernel estimation of a regression function and its derivatives. Annals of the Institute of Statistical Mathematics 00:455–462

Greblicki W, Krzyzak A (1980) Asymptotic properties of Kernel estimates of a regression function. Journal of Statistics, Planning Inference 00:81–89

Greblicki W (1987) Decomposition of the recursive Kernel regression estimate. Mimeo, University of Manitoba

Greblicki W, Pawlak M (1987) Necessary and sufficient consistency conditions for a recursive Kernel regression estimate. Journal of Multivariate Analysis (forthcoming)

Greblicki W, Krzyzak A, Pawlak M (1984) Distribution-free pointwise consistency of Kernel regression estimate. The annals of Statistics 12:1570–1575

Gyorfi L (1981) On recent results on nonparametric regression estimates and multiple classification. Problems Control Information Theory 10:43–52

Hardle W (1984) Robust regression function estimation. Journal of Multivariate Analysis 14:169–180

Hardle W (1988) Applied nonparametric regression. Mimeo

Hardle W, Kelly G (1987) Nonparametric Kernel regression estimation – optimal choice of bandwidth. Statistics 18:21–35

Hardle W, Marron JS (1985) Optimal bandwidth selection in nonparametric regression function estimation. The Annals of Statistics 13:1465–1481

Johnston GJ (1982) Probabilities of maximal deviations for nonparametric regression function estimates. Journal of Multivariate Analysis 12:402–414

Judge G, Yancey TA (1986) Improved methods of interence in econometrics. North Holland, Amsterdam

Krzyzak A, Pawlak M (1984) Distribution-free consistency of a nonparametric Kernel regression estimate and classification. IEEE Trans Inform Theory 30:78–81

Lee BJ (1987) A nonparametric model specification test using the Kernel estimation method. Mimeo, University of Wisconsin-Madison

Mack YP, Silverman BW (1982) Weak and strong unitarian consisteny of Kernel regression estimates. Z Wahrsche Verw Gebiete 61:405–415

Manski CF (1984) Adaptive estimation of nonlinear regression models. Econometric Reviews 3(2):145–194

Marron JS (1988) Automatic smoothing parameter selection: a survey. Mimeo, University of North Carolina

McMillan J, Ullah A, Vinod HD (1986) The shape of the demand curve. University of Western Ontario, manuscript

Moschini G, Stengos T, Prescott D (1988) Nonparametric Kernel estimation applied to forecasting: an evaluation based on the bookstrap. Research Report, University of Guelph

Muller HG (1984) Smooth optimum kernel estimators of densities, regression curves and modes. Annals of Statistics 3:1329–1348

Muller HG (1987) Weighted local regression and Kernel methods for nonparametric curve fitting. Journal of the American Statistical Association, March, p 221

Nadaraya E (1964) On regression estimators. Theory of Probability and Applications 9:157–159

Nadaraya E (1965) On nonparametric estimation of density functions and regression. Theory of Probability and Applications 10:186–190

Nadaraya E (1970) Remarks on nonparametric estimates of density functions and regression curves. Theory of Probability and Applications 15:139–142

Noda K (1976) Estimation of a regression function by the Parzen Kernel type density estimators. American Institute of Statistics and Mathematics 28:221–234

Priestley MB, Chao MT (1972) Nonparametric function fitting, Journal of Royal Statistical Society B 34:385–392

Powell J, Stock JM, Stoker TM (1986) Semiparametric estimation of weighted average derivatives. Working paper 1793-86, M.I.T.

Prakasa Rao BLS (1983) Nonparametric functional estimation. Academic Press, Orlando

Rao CR (1986) Some recent results in signal detection. Research Report 23, University of Pittsburgh

Reinsch H (1967) Smoothing by spline functions. Numerische Mathematik 10:177–183

Revesz P (1977) How to apply the method of stochastic approximation in the nonparametric estimation of a regression function. Math Operations for Sch Statist Serv Statistics 8:119–126

Rice J (1984) Bandwidth choice for nonparametric regression. Annals of Statistics 12:1215–1231

Rilstone P (1987) Nonparametric partial derivative estimation. Unpublished PhD DIssertation, University of Western Ontario

Rilstone P (1988) A nonparametric approach to general econometric hypotheses tests. Mimeo, Université Laval

Rilstone P, Ullah A (1987) Nonparametric estimation of response coefficients. University of Western Ontario manuscript

Robinson C, Ullah A (1987) Nonparametric estimation of the simultaneous equations model. Mimeo, University of Western Ontario

Robinson PM (1983) Nonparametric estimators for time series. Journal of Time Series Analysis 4:85–208

Robinson PM (1986) On the consistency and finite sample properties of nonparametric Kernel time series regression, autoregression and density estimations. Annals of the Institute of Statistical Mathematics 38:539–549

Robinson PM (1987) Semiparametric econometrics: a survey. Journal of Applied Econometrics

Rosenblatt M (1956) Remarks on some nonparametric estimates of density function. Annals of Mathematical Statistics 27:832–837

Rosenblatt M (1969) Conditional probability density and regression estimators. J of Multivariate Analysis 2:25–31

Roussas GG (1988) Nonparametric regression estimation under mixing conditions. Research Report 101, University of California, Davis

Schuster EF, Yakowitz S (1979) Contributions to the theory of nonparametric regression with applications to system identification. Annals of Statistics 7:139–149

Silverman BW (1984) Spline smoothing: the equivalent variable Kernel method. The Annals of Statistics 12:898–916

Silverman BW (1986) Density estimation for statistics and data analysis. Chapman and Hall, New York

Singh RS (1981) Speed of convergence in nonparametric estimation of a multivariate mu-density and its mixed partial derivatives. Journal of Statistical Planning and Inference 5:287–298

Singh RS, Ullah A (1986) Nonparametric recursive estimation of a multivariate, marginal and conditional DGP with an application to specification of econometric models. Communications in Statistics, Theory and Methods 15:3489–3513

Singh RS, Ullah A, Carter RAL (1987) Nonparametric inference in econometrics: new applications. In: MacNeill I, Umphrey G (eds) Time series and econometric modelling. D. Reidell, Holland

Speigelman C, Sacks J (1980) Consistent window estimation in nonparametric regression. The Annals of Statistics 8:240–246

Stone CJ (1977) Consistent nonparametric regression. The Annals of Statistics 5:595–645

Ullah A (1988) Nonparametric estimation of econometric functions. Canadian Journal of Economics

Ullah A (1985) Specification analysis of econometric models. Journal of Quantitative Economics 1:187–210

Ullah A, Singh RS (1985) The estimation of probability density functions and its applications in econometrics. Technical Report 6, University of Western Ontario

Ullah A, Vinod HD (1988) Nonparametric estimation of econometric parameters. Journal of Quantitative Economics

Vinod HD, Ullah A (1988) Flexible production estimation by nonparametric Kernel estimators. In: Fomby TB, Rhodes CF (eds) Advances in econometrics: robust and nonparametric statistical inference. JAI Press

Watson GS (1964) Smooth regression analysis. Sanikhya, Series A 26:15, 175–184

White H (1984) Asymptotic theory for econometricians. Academic Press

Zhao LC (1985) Exponential bounds of mean error for the Kernel estimates of regression functions. University of Pittsburgh

Zhao LC, Fang Z (1985) Strong convergence of Kernel estimates of nonparametric regression functions. Chinese Annals of Mathematics, Ser B 6:147–155

Some Simulation Studies of Nonparametric Estimators[1]

By Y. Hong and A. Pagan[2]

Abstract: This paper constructs a number of Monte Carlo studies to assess the quality of various nonparametric estimators that have been proposed recently for the estimation of nonlinear econometric models. We consider both kernel and Fourier series based methods of estimation, and also examine techniques that have been suggested to improve the bias properties of the kernel estimator. The two models examined are a production function and a model emphasising the effects of risk. The Fourier estimator does very well in estimating the first of these, but not the second, while the kernel estimator shows substantial bias for the first, which is only partially alleviated by the procedures advocated for bias correction, and good results for the second.

1 Introduction

Many problems in econometrics are characterized by an unknown functional form, and a wide variety of specificaitions has emerged to give empirical researchers the needed flexibility when estimating relations between observed data. For capturing production relations there are the Cobb-Douglas, CES, transcendental log, quadratic etc., functions. For demand studies using household data a variety of transformations such as Box-Cox, semi-log etc., have all emerged to estimate Engel curves. Finally, in macroeconomic models a key variable is frequently the expectation of a random variable with respect to an information set, in which case it is common to assume that the expectation is a linear function of observed variables. More recently conditional variances have assumed importance and for this quadratic formulations such as Engle's (1982) ARCH have found favor.

This parametric emphasis to modeling has been challenged in recent years with the advent of nonparametric procedures. Gallant (1982) advocated and applied a Fourier

[1] This material is based upon work supported by the National Science Foundation under Grant No. SES-8719520.
[2] Y. Hong and A. Pagan, Dept. of Economics, University of Rochester, Rochester, N.Y. 14627, USA.

approximation approach to the determination of production technologies while Rilstone and Ullah (1987) estimated marginal products of factors with the kernel estimator of Nadaraya (1964) and Watson (1964). Deaton (1988) applied the kernel technique to the estimation of Engel curves while Pagan and Hong (1988) employed both kernel and Fourier based methods when modeling the conditional variance of equity yields and the excess holding yield on Treasury bills. In all cases the studies seemed to show that considerable gains could be had over existing parametric formulations.

The asymptotic theory justifying these estimators is now well developed. For kernel estimators, conditions under which the estimators are consistent and asymptotically normal are summarized in Bierens (1987), while a recent paper by Andrews (1988) has provided a detailed treatment of consistency and asymptotic normality of Fourier-based estimators if data is independently and identically distributed (i.i.d), although he indicates that his results would extend to dependent observations. Frequently, it emerges from this analysis that the rate of convergence of the estimators is quite slow, and this raises an issue of whether sample sizes are sufficiently large in practice that one could take the asymptotic theory as being an accurate predictor of the sampling distributions of the estimators. Some simulation studies have appeared to examine this question e.g., Chalfont and Gallant (1985) for testing production restrictions and Rilstone and Ullah (1987) for estimating CES production functions, with generally good findings. Nevertheless, much remain to be done before these estimators could be recommended for widespread use.

This paper looks at a slightly different question, namely the relative performance of kernel and Fourier based methods in estimating a number of models that could arise in practice. Section 2 formally defines the variety of estimators employed in the later simulation work and lists what is to be expected of the estimators. Section 3 considers the comparative performance of both estimators in estimating a CES production function, with the design of the study being derivative from White (1980). As a special case one of the variables (the capital stock) is fixed, leaving only an univariate relation between output and labor to be determined, and this produces a situation reminiscent of Engel curve studies. In Section 4 we consider the estimation of the risk premium by nonparametric methods as advocated in Pagan and Ullah (1988). This experiment is of interest in its own right, but is also meant to be representative of a range of situations which are "semi-parametric", and in which the rate of convergence of the estimators of the set of parameters of interest is the same as for parametric models.

The range of models employed here is small and the purpose of the paper is to try to get some insight into how well the estimators work, whether one is superior to another in different circumstances, and what theoretical issues arise from the results. Thus our purpose is a very modest one, but we think that the results are of some interest and fill a gap in the existing literature.

2 The Estimators

Consider an unknown relation between a variable y_i and another variable x_i:

$$y_i = g(x_i) + u_i \tag{1}$$

where u_i, $(i = 1, ..., N)$, is assumed i.i.d. $(0, \sigma^2)$ and is a martingale difference with respect to $F_i = \{y_{i-1}, y_{i-2}, ..., x_i, x_{i-1}, ...\}$. For simplicity results are stated in terms of a scalar x_i, with comments being made, where necessary, about what modifications are needed when x_i is a vector of variables.

The objective is to estimate $m^* = g(x^*)$ i.e., the conditional expectation $E(y|x = x^*)$. If x_i took only discrete values $x_1^*, ..., x_p^*$, a simple estimator of $E(y|x = x_j^*)$ is the sample average

$$\hat{m}^* = (N_j^*)^{-1} \sum_{i \in S_j^*} y_i \quad j = 1, ..., p \tag{2}$$

where S_j^* is the set of i corresponding to x_j^* and N_j^* is the number in this set. Provided $N_j^* \to \infty$, this would be a consistent and asymptotically normal estimator of $g(x_j^*)$ since $y_i(i \in S_j^*)$ has $y_i \sim$ i.i.d. $(g(x_j^*), \sigma^2)$. Let us define the indicator function $I(z_i)$ as being unity if $-1/2 \leqslant z_i \leqslant 1/2$ and zero otherwise, and set $z_i = ((x_i - x_j^*)/h)$, where h is chosen to be smaller than one half of the minimum distance between any of the $x_j^*(j = 1, ..., p)$ so that $I(z_i) = 1$ only when $x_i = x_j^*$. With these definitions (2) could be re-written as

$$\hat{m}^* = \left[\sum_{i=1}^{N} I_i \right]^{-1} \sum_{i=1}^{N} I_i y_i, \tag{3}$$

since the restriction on h ensures that only those observations corresponding to $x_i = x_j^*$ actually appear in the sample average (all others have $I_i = 0$).

When x_i is a continuous random variable the indicator function approach above cannot apply since x_i assumes particular values with probability zero. Nadaraya (1964) and Watson (1964) therefore suggested that $I(z)$ be replaced by a continuous function of z, $K(z)$, but with the same properties that $K(z) \geqslant 0$, $\int K(z)dz = 1$ (in fact it is also necessary that $K(z)$ be symmetric but the heuristic argument given here to justify the kernel estimator cannot easily capture that requirement). (3) then becomes

$$\hat{m}^* = \left(\sum_{i=1}^{N} K_i \right)^{-1} \sum_{i=1}^{N} K_i y_i. \tag{4}$$

Since these properties characterize density functions, there is a wide range of possible choices for K. Popular ones are the Gaussian kernel $K(z) = (2\pi)^{-1/2} \exp(-(1/2)z^2)$ and the Epanechnikov kernel $K(z) = (3/4h)(1 - z^2)I(|z| \leqslant 1)$ where $I(z_i)$ is an indicator function and $z_i = ((x_i - x^*)/h)$. The former has been used in Rilstone and Ullah (1987) and Pagan and Hong (1988) while the latter was adopted by Deaton (1988). As observed by many authors the choice of a kernel is not as crucial as the choice of h, the bandwidth. Of course in the discrete case it was obvious what h should be, but in the continuous case $g(x^*)$ will need to be estimated by "borrowing" observations on y_i corresponding to x close to x^*, where "closeness" is measured by the size of h. Clearly, if h is made too large one is getting a blurred image of $g(x^*)$ (technically the bias will be large), whereas if h is made too small few observations on "x_j^*" will be available and so the variability of the estimator will be high. For this reason the selection of h can be quite important to the properties of an estimator.

The multivariate case where x_i is a $q \times 1$ vector is easily dealt with the replacing univariate densities with multivariate ones. Hence the multivariate Gaussian kernel is

$$(2\pi)^{-q/2}|H|^{-1/2} \exp\left(-\frac{1}{2}(x_i - x^*)'H^{-1}(x_i - x^*)\right),$$ while the multivariate Epanechni-

kov is proportional to $(1 - z'z)I(z'z \leqslant 1)$, where $z = (x_i - x^*)/h$. Notice from (4) that factors such as $|H|^{-1/2}$ appear on both the numerator and denominator (4) and so disappear. In later work H is set to diag $(N^{-1(4+q)}\hat{\sigma}_j)$, where $\hat{\sigma}_j (j = 1, ..., q)$ is the sample standard deviation of the j-th element in x_i. The optimal choice of bandwidth has been extensively discussed in Bierens (1987), and found to be $cN^{-1/(4+q)}$, so that we are just choosing c to be the sample standard deviation. There are many ways of selecting h, either automatically (as in cross-validation) or by intervention ("eyeballing"), but the computational burdens of simulation mean that a fixed bandwidth is necessary. Further discussion is available in Singh and Ullah (1985).

The kernel is an easy way to estimate $g(x^*)$ and can be done by data transformations allied with some way of computing sums. Most standard econometric programs are therefore well designed to calculate it, and in programs such as GAUSS it is very easily implementable.

Perhaps the major problem with the kernel estimator is that asymptotically it is no centered at $g(x^*)$ unless special care is taken i.e., the limiting theory implies that $(Nh^q)^{1/2}(\hat{m}^* - E(\hat{m}^*))$ is asymptotically normal with a zero mean, but $(Nh^q)^{1/2}(E(\hat{m}^*) - g(x^*))$ need not tend to zero. In theory it is possible to force this latter term to converge to zero by choosing h such that $\lim_{N \to \infty} h^2(Nh^q)^{1/2} \to 0$ (see Bierens 1987) but,

in practice, for observations in the 200 or so range this makes no difference to the results i.e., the bias remains.

As will be seen in the next section this bias can be a problem for the kernel estimator, and the formulation of methods to ameliorate it need to have high priority. A number of suggestions have been made. Schucany and Sommers (1977) used a jacknifing method that entails the averaging of two estimators with different bandwidths.

Thus if h_1 is set to $cN^{-1/(q+4)}$ and h_2 to $cN^{-\delta/(q+4)}(\delta \in (0, 1))$, with corresponding estimates $\hat{m}_1^*$ and $\hat{m}_2^*$, the estimator

$$\hat{m}^* = \{m_1^* - N^{-2(1-\delta)/(q+4)}\hat{m}_2^*\}/(1 - N^{-2(1-\delta)/(q+4)}) \tag{5}$$

is asymptotically centered on $g(x^*)$.

An alternative proposal involves the construction of "higher order bias reducing" kernels that are linear combinations of a basic kernel and which can eliminate bias under certain conditions. Generally when $K(z)$ is chosen in this way it is not possible to ensure that it is non-negative and hence a density function. Bartlett (1963) initiated this idea and Robinson (1987) has recently used it in our context. To construct such a kernel let $K'(z)$ be a base kernel e.g., the Gaussian, and define ($l = 2, 4, 6, ...$)

$$K(z) = \sum_{j=0}^{1/2(l-2)} c_j z^{2j} K'(z), \tag{6}$$

where c_j are solutions to the system of $1/2(l-2) + 1$ linear equations $\sum_{j=0}^{1/2(l-2)} c_j \mu_{2(i+j)}$
$= \delta_{i0}$ $0 \leqslant i \leqslant 1/2(l-2)$ (δ_{i0} is the Kronecker delta) and $\mu_{2j} = \int z^{2j} K'(z)dz$. Table 1 below gives values of c_j for the Gaussian kernel and a range of values for l. The idea behind this suggestion is that the Taylor series expansion of $E(\hat{m}^*) - m^*$ involves a power seris in h, and the coefficients of h_j will be zero if all moments of the kernel up to and including the j-th are zero. When l is the order of the first non-zero moment of the kernel, $(Nh^q)^{1/2}(E(\hat{m}^*) - m^*)$ will converge to zero provided $(Nh^q)^{1/2}h^l \to 0$ as $N \to \infty$. Putting $h = N^{-(1/(q+4))}$ will satisfy this restriction for any $l > 2$.

Another variant of nonparametric estimation is the Fourier method advocated by Gallant (1982). In this (1) is approximated by a quadratic polynomial in x_i and a linear combination of cosine and sine terms in x_i

$$y_i = \beta_0 + \beta_1 x_i + \beta_2 x_i^2 + \sum_{j=1}^{M} (\gamma_j \cos jx_i + \delta_j \sin jx_i) + v_i. \tag{7}$$

Table 1. Values of c to Construct Kernel in (6)

	$l = 2$	$l = 4$	$l = 6$	$l = 8$
c_0	1	1.5	1.875	2.1875
c_1		−0.5	−1.25	−2.1875
c_2			0.125	0.4375
c_3				−0.02083

The formulation has its origins in approximation theory where it is known that a Fourier series can approximate $g(x_i)$ arbitrarily well over the range $(0, 2\pi)$ (in fact to use this method data *must* be scaled to be in this range). For economic analysis the Fourier technique has the extra advantage that it also approximates derivatives of $g(x_i)$ with respect to x_i arbitrarily well, and this is important as these derivatives correspond to economic quantities of interest such as the marginal product. Provided M is chosen such that $M \to \infty$ as $N \to \infty$ and $g(\cdot)$ is sufficiently smooth, the estimator of $g(x^*)$ formed as the OLS predictions from (7) is consistent. Andrews (1988) shows that, if M is set to cN^r, where c is a constant and $0 < r < 1$, $(N^{1-r})^{1/2}(\hat{g}(x^*) - g(x^*))$ is asymptotically normal. The choice of r is therefore akin to that of the bandwidth in kernel regression. If the problem of bias is ignored or eliminated by bias reducing methods $N^{2/(q+4)}(\hat{m}^* - m^*)$ is asymptotically normal, and writing the normalizing factor as $(N \cdot N^{(-q/(q+4))})$ suggests that $r = (q/q + 4)$ would be appropriate when comparing kernel and Fourier estimators. It is interesting to observe that the Fourier approach does not suffer the bias problems of the kernel (in theory) and this makes it attractive. Eastwood and Gallant (1987) however found that the rate of convergence to asymptotic normality could be very slow unless M was chosen as a function of the data. In our later experiments we have pre-assigned M, but the question of a "best choice" clearly deserves further investigation.

When x_i is multivariate of order q the first three terms in (7) are a quadratic form in the vector x_i i.e., they would be $\beta_0 + x_i'\beta + x_i'Bx_i$ where β is a $(q \times 1)$ vector and B is a $(q \times q)$ matrix. The Fourier terms are made functions of scalars $k_j'x_i$ where k_j are $(q \times 1)$ vectors termed "multi-indexes". The first q of these are the q elementary vectors, and an algorithm for constructing them is described in Gallant (1982) with a computer code available in Monahan (1981). An important feature of the Fourier procedure is that it is asymptotically unbiased and therefore has a potential advantage over the kernel estimator. Against this is the fact that the number of parameters to be estimated in (7) multiply rapidly as the dimension of x_i rises, and this may limit its use to small dimensional problems. In fact, past users, such as Gallant, overcome this problem of a profligate number of parameters by estimating systems of equations and imposing cross-equation constraints from economic theory.

The above discussion has concentrated upon estimating a conditional mean, but there are models estimated in econometrics which demand that a conditional variance be estimated. These are models which incorporate a risk premium and which have the generic form

$$y_i = z_i\beta + \sigma_i^2\delta + e_i \tag{8}$$

where z_i is weakly exogenous for β and δ and σ_i^2 represents the variance of some random variable ψ_i conditional upon an information set F_i. Pagan and Ullah (1988) survey the ways in which it has been suggested that the unobserved variable σ_i^2 be replaced by a function of data. One popular solution has been to assume that the conditional expectation of ψ_i is a linear function of some weakly exogenous variables w_i, that is $E(\psi_i | F_i) = w_i \gamma$, and to then assume σ_i^2 is a function of ϕ_{i-j}^2, where $\phi_i = \psi_i - E(\psi_i | F_i)$.

Engle's (1982) ARCH model for example sets $\sigma_i^2 = \alpha_0 + \sum_{j=1}^{r} \alpha_j \phi_{i-j}^2$.

Pagan and Ullah (1988) advance an estimation strategy that seeks to avoid the parameterization of σ_i^2. The basic idea advanced in that paper was to replace σ_i^2 by $\phi_i^2 = (\psi_i - E(\psi_i | F_i))^2$, and to then consistently estimate β and δ by applying IV with instruments constructed from F_i (including x_i as its own instrument). Of course instrument construction needs to be done carefully, since they must be as highly correlated with ϕ_i^2 as possible. In fact, because $E(\phi_i^2 | F_i) = \sigma_i^2$, σ_i^2 appeals as a good instrument, making it desirable to estimate σ_i^2 for this purpose. An important facet of the IV strategy is that it only requires $m_i = E(\psi_i | F_i)$ to be estimated accurately; truncation of the instrument set to (say) $\bar{\sigma}_i^2 = E(\phi_i^2 | F_i')$, where $F_i' \in F_i$, does not affect the consistency of the estimators of β and δ, although efficiency might be affected if $\bar{\sigma}_i^2$ has only a weak correlation with ϕ_i^2. Overall, there is a trade-off between maximizing instrument correlation and restricting F_i' to be small enough to get estimates $\bar{\sigma}_i^2$ that are not "too noisy".

Basically the IV approach requires the computation of $m_i = E(\psi_i / F_i)$ and some estimate of σ_i^2 (although as noted above it is not crucial that the latter be accurate). As described earlier, m_i might be linear in the members of F_i i.e., $w_i \gamma$, and this is a frequent assumption in VAR modeling. If so $\hat{m}_i$ can be estimated as the predictions from the regression of ψ_i against w_i. However, in some instances it may be desirable to allow m_i to be a non-linear function of F_i, and then it could be estimated in the same way as $g(x^*)$ was estimated earlier. Whichever way an estimate for m_i, $\hat{m}_i$, is generated, $\hat{\phi}_i^2 = (\psi_i - \hat{m}_i)^2$ replaces σ_i^2 and an instrument $\hat{\sigma}_i^2$ is used for $\hat{\phi}_i^2$. In Section 4 we use as instruments the nonparametric estimate of the conditional variance of ψ_i given F_i.

Now although neither $\hat{m}_i$ nor $\hat{\sigma}_i^2$ is likely to be estimated very precisely unless dim (F_i) is small or the number of observations is large, these quantities are only being used as "regressors" in (8), and so the IV estimator of β and δ should be root-N consistent and asymptotically normal. To get this result, following Pagan and Ullah (1988) it is necessary to show that $N^{-1/2} \sum z_i (\hat{\phi}_i^2 - \phi_i^2) \xrightarrow{p} 0$, where z_i are the chosen instruments. When the conditional mean is parameterized as $w_i \gamma$ this is true, as discussed in Pagan (1984) and exploited in tests for heteroskedasticity, but no general proof currently exists when ϕ_i is estimated nonparametrically, particular when ψ_i is a time series. An alternative estimator, if $F_i' = F_i$, might be to regress y_i against x_i and $\hat{\sigma}_i^2$, as this would give a consistent estimator of δ, β, but the standard errors would need to be adjusted because of a "generated regressor" bias arising from the use of $\hat{\sigma}_i^2$ rather than σ_i^2. Just as in the case when $\hat{\sigma}_i^2$ is constructed parametrically from F_i, Pagan (1984), the appropriate adjustment may be difficult to do directly, but is easily done with the IV procedure. Hence, estimation and inference is naturally performed within the IV framework.

The final issue to be addressed concerns which nonparametric method should be used to construct $\hat{m}_i$ and $\hat{\sigma}_i^2$. In Section 4 we employ both the kernel based approach and the Fourier method. Both are easy to apply and have advantages. It should be noted that for the Fourier technique, $\hat{\sigma}_i^2$ is estimated as the predictions obtained by fitting a Fourier approximation to $(\psi_i - \hat{m}_i)^2$, since $E(\psi_i - m_i)^2 = \sigma_i^2$ is the basis of such a regression.

3 Kernel and Fourier Estimation of a CES Production Function

White (1980) set up a simulation experiment to evaluate the ability of flexible functional forms to adequately approximate unknown regression functions. He simulated data from a CES production function

$$y_i = (L_i^\rho + 2K^\rho)^{1/\rho} + u_i. \tag{9}$$

In our first experiment K was fixed at the value 1.71, $\log L_i$ was distributed uniformly over $[0, 1]$, u_i was i.i.d. $(0, 0.01)$ and ρ was set to be -5. This gives an unknown functional relation between y_i and $x_i = L_i$. The variance of u_i was chosen so as to get an R^2 of around 0.9 when (9) is fitted with both L_i and K_i.

Our aim is to estimate the functional relation $g_i = (L_i^{-5} + 2(1.71)^{-5})^{-(1/5)}$ at selected points $L^* = 1.284, 1.568, 1.852, 2.136, 2.420$. A variety of estimators was applied. Because of the bias problem the kernel estimator was computed with jack-knifing ($\delta = 0.25, 0.5$ and 0.75) as in (5) and higher order kernels ($l = 4, 6, 8$) as in (6). The number of terms in the Fourier approximation (7) (M) was set to 2, making it independent of sample size. Three sample sizes $N = 60, 100$ and 200 were used and 500 replications performed.

Fig. 1, 2 and 3 graph g_i evaluated at the five points L^* detailed above along with the average estimates provided by the standard kernel ($l = 2$), jack-knifing ($\delta = 0.75$), a higher-order kernel ($l = 8$) and Fourier series estimators; the values of δ and l represented the choices with smallest average bias. The bias problem with standard kernel estimators is immediately apparent, but neither of the bias reducing procedures is particularly successful in samples of size 60, with noticable bias at the lower end of the grid. As the sample grows the higher order kernel approach improves but the jack-knifed estimator does not. Of course for this set of parameters the relative magnitude of the bias is small: what is important is its resilience to an increase in sample size. With other parameter combinations the magnitude of the bias could probably be made much greater.

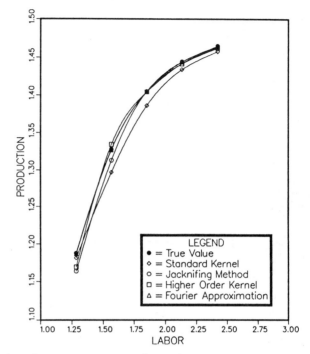

Fig. 1. Nonparametric Estimates of a CES Production Function $\{N = 60\}$

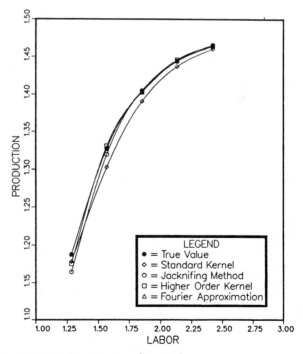

Fig. 2. Nonparametric Estimates of a CES Production Function $\{N = 100\}$

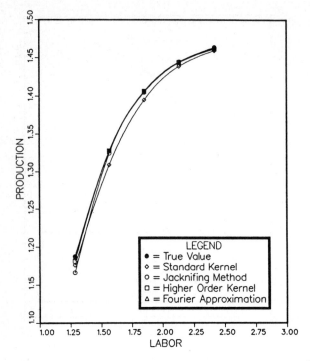

Fig. 3. Nonparametric Estimates of a CES Production Function $\{N = 200\}$

In contrast to the poor performance of the kernel estimators the Fourier method exhibits very small bias at all points in the L-space. In fact, simulations with N as low as 30 did not change this conclusion. Hence, for problems characterized by a single regressor in x_i, the Fourier estimator would seem to produce estimates of m^* that are

Table 2. Average Estimates of $g(\cdot)$ for (9), Various Estimators, $N = 60$

	$L^* = K^* = 1.284$	$L^* = K^* = 1.852$	$L^* = K^* = 2.420$
$g(\cdot)$	1.0307	1.4867	1.9426
Fourier	1.0207	1.4758	1.9479
$\delta = 0.25$	1.0000	1.4634	1.9303
$\delta = 0.5$	0.9979	1.4713	1.9339
$\delta = 0.75$	0.9964	1.4776	1.9364
$l = 2$	1.0264	1.4231	1.8520
$l = 4$	0.9871	1.6257	2.0040
$l = 6$	0.9814	1.4980	1.9603
$l = 8$	3.4396	1.3363	1.5865

Table 3. Average Estimates of $g(\cdot)$ for (9), Various Estimators, $N = 100$

	$L^* = K^* = 1.284$	$L^* = K^* = 1.852$	$L^* = K^* = 2.420$
$g(\cdot)$	1.0307	1.4867	1.9426
Fourier	1.0197	1.4777	1.9336
$\delta = 0.25$	1.005	1.4680	1.9413
$\delta = 0.5$	0.9989	1.4753	1.9446
$\delta = 0.75$	0.9980	1.4805	1.9470
$l = 2$	1.0225	1.4317	1.8735
$l = 4$	0.9917	1.6828	1.9871
$l = 6$	0.9950	1.4701	1.9456
$l = 8$	1.0056	1.5267	1.8561

Table 4. Average Estimates of $g(\cdot)$ for (9), Various Estimators, $N = 200$

	$L^* = K^* = 1.284$	$L^* = K^* = 1.852$	$L^* = K^* = 2.420$
$g(\cdot)$	1.0307	1.4867	1.9426
Fourier	1.0196	1.4747	1.9376
$\delta = 0.25$	1.000	1.4728	1.9498
$\delta = 0.5$	0.9989	1.4789	1.9532
$\delta = 0.75$	0.9991	1.4822	1.9556
$l = 2$	1.0176	1.4421	1.8939
$l = 4$	0.9957	1.5635	1.9935
$l = 6$	1.0053	1.5706	1.9862
$l = 8$	1.0287	1.5497	1.9336

much closer to the true values than any of the kernel based procedures. Of course one might improve upon the kernel estimates by using variable bandwidths or selecting these by cross-validation: what the experiment emphasis is that bias is a potentially serious problem for kernel methods.

When the complete production function is estimated, results are rather similar. In this instance log K_i is distributed uniformly over [0, 1] and a grid of 25 points was taken corresponding to all bivariate combinations of the points (1.284, 1.568, 1.852, 2.136, 2.420) for L^* and K^*. Tables 2, 3 and 4 show the average estimates of m^* obtained for three of the combinations $(L^*, K^*) = (1.284, 1.284)$, $(1.852, 1.852)$ and $(2.420, 2.420)$. A complete tabulation is available on request. Generally, the Fourier approximation does reasonably well, although it is noticeable that the bias does not reduce very much with the sample size and it may be that M should have been increased. The basic kernel estimator ($l = 2$) is not dominated by the Fourier estimator as much as it was when x_i was a scalar, while the bias reduction methods perform well for large values of K and L but remain very poor at the left end of the grid. Indeed the best strategy might well be to stay with the raw kernel, as some of the higher-order kernel estimators ($l > 2$) are incredibly variable, with extreme outliers in a number of replications.

These limited experiments emphasize the problem of asymptotic bias in the kernel estimator and, at least for a small number of conditioning variables, suggest that Fourier methods may well be the best way to approximate $g(\cdot)$. What is very disappointing in the results is the relatively poor performance of methods that have been proposed to reduce the bias of standard kernel estimators. Perhaps these methods would work better in larger sample sizes, but it is obvious by comparing the first columns of Tables 2 and 4 that the improvement seems very slight, even when the sample size tripled. A much more detailed comparison between the estimators as well as investigation of other ways to reduce bias is therefore warranted.

4 Risk Estimation and ARCH Models

In these experiments the parameter δ in equation (8), with $\beta = 0$ and so z_i excluded, was estimated by nonparametric methods. The conditional variance of ψ_i, σ_i^2, followed variants of Engle's (1982) ARCH model, while $\psi_i = \mu + \phi_i$. The density of the error term ϕ_i, conditional upon past information, was taken to be $N(0, \sigma_i^2)$, with δ, the location parameter μ, and σ_e^2 all being set to unity. Two experiments were performed, with σ_i^2 being either an ARCH (1) or an ARCH (4) of the type used by Engle et al. (1987) when modeling the excess holding yield on U.S. Treasury Bills.

$$\sigma_i^2 = \alpha_0 + \alpha_1 \phi_{i-1}^2 \tag{10}$$

$$\sigma_i^2 = \alpha_0 + \alpha_1 \sum_{j=1}^{4} ((5-j)/10)\phi_{i-j}^2 \tag{11}$$

Four estimators of δ were considered.

A) Estimate σ_i^2 by a kernel estimator, with conditioning variables $\psi_{i-1}, ..., \psi_{i-r}$, r being the order of the ARCH process, and regress y_i against $\hat{\sigma}_i^2$.

B) Replace σ_i^2 in (8) by $\hat{\phi}_i^2 = (\psi_i - \hat{\mu})^2$, $\hat{\mu}$ being the sample mean of ψ_i, and then do instrumental variables with $\hat{\sigma}_i^2$ as instrument for $\hat{\phi}_i^2$.

C) Fit the Fourier approximation to (7) with y_i replaced by $\hat{\phi}_i^2$, take the predictions, $\tilde{\sigma}_i^2$, as an estimator of σ_i^2, and regress y_i against $\tilde{\sigma}_i^2$.

D) Fit the parameters α_0, α_1 in (10) and (11) and μ using M.L.E., compute $\tilde{\sigma}_i^2$ and regress y_i against $\tilde{\sigma}_i^2$.

Estimator D is meant to be a benchmark since it would be as efficient as any two-stage estimator could be, in that it exploits the fact that the conditional variance is generated by an ARCH process and the conditional density is normal. The Fourier approximation might be expected to be a good one when $r = 1$ since $\sigma_i^2 = \alpha_0 + \alpha_1(\psi_{i-1} - \mu)^2$ $= \alpha_0 + \alpha_1 \psi_{i-1}^2 - 2\alpha_1 \mu\psi_{i-1} + \alpha_1\mu^2$, and therefore the quadratic terms that lead the Fourier approximation are all that is needed to estimate σ_i^2. However, it will lose something owing to the addition of unnecessary trigonometric terms. Because of this feature M was varied with the sample size, being 1 for $N = 30$, 2 for $N = 60$, 100, and 3 for $N = 200$. In the case of equation (11) only the diagonal terms in the quadratic form derived from $(\psi_{i-1}, \psi_{i-2}, \psi_{i-3}, \psi_{i-4})$ were retained.

Table 5 gives the mean and standard deviations (in parentheses) of the estimated δ from the four estimators for $\alpha_1 = 0.2$ and 0.5, σ_i^2 as in (10), and for sample sizes $N = 60$, 100 and 200. Table 6 gives comparable results when σ_i^2 is from (11). The kernel based estimators do quite well in estimating δ, although it is noticeable that

Table 5. Mean and Standard Deviation of Estimators of δ in (8) $\sigma_i^2 = \alpha_0 + \alpha_1\phi_{i-1}^2$

	Estimator			
	A	B	C	D
$\alpha_1 = 0.2$				
$N = 60$	1.0728	1.1223	0.8749	1.0235
	(0.2392)	(0.2578)	(0.2459)	(0.1827)
$N = 100$	1.0458	1.0718	0.8902	1.0124
	(0.1782)	(0.1940)	(0.2117)	(0.1393)
$N = 200$	1.0269	1.0388	0.9012	1.0126
	(0.1246)	(0.1351)	(0.1626)	(0.0986)
$\alpha_1 = 0.5$				
$N = 60$	1.2076	1.1960	0.8963	1.0570
	(0.2435)	(0.2923)	(0.2734)	(0.2047)
$N = 100$	1.1589	1.1433	0.8939	1.0364
	(0.1984)	(0.2630)	(0.2599)	(0.1748)
$N = 200$	1.1223	1.0901	0.8606	1.0305
	(0.1600)	(0.1882)	(0.2341)	(0.1304)

Table 6. Mean and Standard Deviation of Estimators of δ in (8) $\sigma_i^2 = \alpha_0 + \alpha_1 \sum\limits_{j=1}^{4} ((5-j)/10)\phi_{i-j}^2$

	Estimator			
	A	B	C	D
$\alpha_1 = 0.2$				
$N = 60$	1.0497	1.1176	0.6978	0.9954
	(0.2818)	(0.2943)	(0.2027)	(0.1914)
$N = 100$	1.0181	1.0603	0.7758	1.0015
	(0.2036)	(0.2169)	(0.1780)	(0.1404)
$N = 200$	0.9980)	1.0274	0.8521	1.0048
	(0.1378)	(0.1418)	(0.1302)	(0.0930)
$\alpha_1 = 0.5$				
$N = 60$	1.1686	1.1442	0.7016	0.9991
	(0.2793)	(0.2927)	(0.2023)	(0.1847)
$N = 100$	1.1344	1.0786	0.7648	1.0074
	(0.2009)	(0.2135)	(0.1892)	(0.1420)
$N = 200$	1.1008	1.0346	0.8234	1.0157
	(0.1460)	(0.1553)	(0.1649)	(0.0975)

there is a small sample bias which is declining only slowly and that this worsens as α_1 rises. However, the move from a single (ψ_{i-1}) to four conditioning variables ($\psi_{i-1}, ..., \psi_{i-4}$) did not affect the performance of the estimator at all. This is to be expected from the theory, arising from the fact that the nonparametric estimators are effectively being averaged, and therefore root-N consistency should hold. It is hard to be certain if this prediction is correct or not, but the ratio of the standard error of $\hat{\delta}$ at $N = 100$ to that at $N = 200$ is generally around 1.2–1.3, so that the variance would be in ratio 1.4–1.7, compared to the theoretical requirement of $\sqrt{2}$. It is also noticeable that the benchmark estimator D gives good results and it is certainly more efficient than any of the kernel methods, although the efficiency loss might be acceptable given the greater robustness of the kernel procedures to specification errors in σ_i^2.

Perhaps the most disappointing result from Tables 5 and 6 was the poor performance of the Fourier based estimator. When $r = 4$ this might be expected since a very large number of terms appear in the expansion. But the fact that δ is poorly estimated when $r = 1$, relative to that from the kernel and ARCH methods, when $r = 1$ is surprising, as it has already been noted that performance might have been expected to be good in this context, in that one is merely adding on superfluous trigonometric regressors in the first stage when estimating σ_i^4. In fact, if the trigonometric terms are dropped i.e. σ_i^2 is estimated by regressing $\hat{\phi}_i^2$ against a constant, ψ_{i-1} and ψ_{i-1}^2, the average values of $\hat{\delta}$ for the three sample sizes were $1.0102, 0.995$ and 0.996 ($\alpha_1 = 0.2$) and $1.1079, 1.0922$ and 1.0837 ($\alpha_1 = 0.5$). Hence the bias stems directly from the addition of the Fourier terms. No simple explanation of this outcome could be found and it clearly will repay further study.

5 Conclusion

This paper has tried to present some evidence upon the relative performance of kernel and Fourier based nonparametric estimators. When estimating a conditional mean theoretical considerations point to an asymptotic bias problem for kernel methods, and this was borne out in our experiments with a production function. More disturbing however was the fact that some of the methods suggested to overcome this problem were not very effective, and in some instances the bias in the estimated mean could be worse than if no adjustment was made at all. The bias problem afflicting the kernel estimator was not present for the Fourier method and this must make it a strong candidate when the context requires the estimation of a conditional mean, If kernel methods are to be used better procedures for bias correction will need to be developed.

In contrast to this outcome, when the nonparametric estimators of a conditional variance were "averaged" by their employment in a regression to estimate the effects of risk, the kernel estimators were much superior to the Fourier ones. It is significant that, in this semi-nonparametric setting, the OLS estimator of the risk coefficient exhibits no asymptotic bias, even when the kernel method is used to generate a conditional variance for use as a proxy for the missing true variance. Hence, kernel procedures look attractive in this situation, although a wider range of specifications will need to be examined before one could confidently recommend them.

Our experiments show that nonparametric estimation may be a useful tool in econometric analysis, even in relatively small sample sizes. We have also found that there are differences in performance between the different nonparametric estimators and it will be important to determine the most effective one in any particular case. Certainly a lot more needs to be done so as to attain a good understanding of the performance of various estimators before one is likely to see them in widespread application.

References

Andrews D (1988) Asymptotic normality of series estimators for various nonparametric and semi-parametric models. Mimeo, Yale University

Bartlett MS (1963) Statistical estimation of density functions. Sankhya A 25:145–154

Bierens H (1987) Kernel estimators of regression functions. Ch. 3 in Bewley T (ed) Advances in econometrics, fifth world congress, vol I, pp 99–144

Chalfont JA, Gallant AR (1985) Estimating substitution elasticities with the Fourier cost function. Journal of Econometrics 28:205–222

Deaton A (1988) Agricultural pricing policies and demand patterns in thailand. Mimeo, Princeton University

Eastwood BJ, Gallant AR (1987) Adaptive truncation rules for seminonparametric estimators that achieve asymptotic normality. Mimeo, North Carolina State University

Engle RF (1982) Autoregressive conditional heteroscedasticity with estimates of the variance of United Kingdom inflation. Econometrica 50:987–1008

Engle RF, Lillien DM, Robins RP: Estimating time varying risk premia in the term structure: the ARCH-M model. Econometrica 55:391–408

Gallant AR (1982) Unbiased determination of production technologies. Journal of Econometrics 20:285–323

Monahan JF (1981) Enumeration of elementary multi-indexes for multivariate Fourier series. Institute of Statistics Mimeograph Series No. 1338, North Carolina State University

Nadaraya EA (1964) On estimating regression. Theory of Probability and its Applications 9:141–142

Pagan AR (1984) Econometric issues in the analysis of regressions with generated regressors. International Economic Review 25:221–247

Pagan AR, Ullah A (1988) The econometric analysis of models with risk terms. Journal of Applied Econometrics 3:87–105

Pagan AR, Hong Y (1988) Non-parametric estimation and the risk premium. Rochester Center for Economic Research Working Paper no. 135, University of Rochester

Rilstone P, Ullah A (1987) Non-parametric estimation of response coefficients. Mimeo, University of Western Ontario

Robinson P (1987) Root-N-consistent semiparametric regression. Discussion Paper No. R.9, London School of Economics

Schucany WR, Sommers JP (1977) Improvement of Kernel type density estimators. Journal of the American Statistical Association 72:420–423

Singh RS, Ullah A (1985) Nonparametric time series estimation of joint DGP, conditional DGP and vector autoregression. Econometric Theory 1:27–52

Watson GS (1964) Smooth regression analysis. Sankhya, Series A 26:359–372

White H (1980) Using least squares to approximate unknown regression functions. International Economic Review 21:149–170

Estimating a Hedonic Earnings Function with a Nonparametric Method

By J. Hartog[1] and H. J. Bierens[2]

Abstract: In this paper we apply the nonparametric approach of Bierens and Hartog (1988) to estimating and testing an earnings function which emphasizes the simultaneous impact of supply characteristics (like education) and demand characteristics (like job level). The data support this emphasis and point to significant non-linearities. In particular, job level comes out as an important variable.

1 Introduction

In this paper, we use the nonparametric econometric theory for specifying, estimating and testing regression models with discrete explanatory variables, developed in Bierens and Hartog (1988) to estimating and testing an earnings function.

The empirical application in Bierens and Hartog (1988) merely served as an illustration of the econometric theory. In the present paper the focus is on the empirical application and its consequence for the theory on earnings differentials. We take the theory of hedonic prices as our point of departure. An important extension of the present paper is to add job level as an explanatory variable and to demonstrate the important interaction with the other explanatory variables. This extension is in tune with earlier work (Hartog 1981, 1985, 1986a, b), stressing that allocation of workers to jobs, and hence, the demand side of the labor market, cannot be neglected in explaining earnings differentials.

A typical feature of the explanatory variables in this earnings function is that they take on a finite number of values. In Bierens and Hartog (1988) it has been shown that such regression models take the form of a finite-order polynomial of a linear function

[1] Joop Hartog, University of Amsterdam, Jodenbreestraat 23, 1011 NH Amsterdam, The Netherlands.
[2] Herman J. Bierens, Free University, De Boelelaan 1105, 1081 HV Amsterdam, The Netherlands.
We gratefully acknowledge the comments of an anonymous referee.

of the regressors. Therefore we proposed a two-stage estimation procedure, where in the first stage the linear function involved is estimated by OLS and in the second-stage the polynomial involved is estimated by regression on orthogonal polynomials. Moreover, we proposed a number of tests for testing the order of the polynomial and the redundancy of explanatory variables. For convenience of the reader this econometric theory will be reviewed.

The plan of the paper is as follows. In Section 2 we discuss our earnings function and the ideas behind it, and the data are described in Section 3. In Section 4 we show that regression models with discrete explanatory variables take the form of a polynomial of a linear combination of the regressors. Section 5 is devoted to estimation procedures and Section 6 deals with testing the regression function. In Section 7 we apply the approach involved to our earnings function, and in Section 8 our empirical findings are interpreted.

2 Allocation and the Earnings Function

An earnings function specifies the relation between an individual's earnings in the labor market and relevant characteristics of the worker and the job. Generally, in a market interpretation, such an earnings function emerges from the interaction of supply and demand behavior. In this section, a particular specification of the market interpretation will be presented.

Consider, as a start, the following simplified situation. All workers are identical in potential productivity and in preferences. Jobs differ in only one characteristic, the level of difficulty and complexity of the task to be performed, or job level, for short. Job levels are ranked, with level 1 the simplest and level J the most complex. Suppose, workers have a reservation wage for participating at all in the labor market, and have reservation wages ω^j that make them indifferent for work at any job level j, $j = 1, 2, \ldots J$. The reservation wages ω^j are identical for all individuals, and fixed, independent of any other variable in the model. An example of such reservation wages, or iso-utility wages, is given in Fig. 1. Now it is clear that if workers have unrestricted, costless access to all jobs, the observed wage rate at any job level j will equal ω^j. Any deviations would be corrected by supply movements between jobs.

Which points in this set ω^j will be observed, depends on the conditions of the demand side. Suppose, all firms are identical, producing a homogeneous commodity, and all face the same choice of technology. The production process can be either organized with jobs of level 1, or of 2, or of any other level j. Higher job levels put higher demands on the workers, but generate higher productivity, like an intellectual analogue of the speed of an assembly line. Suppose, the firm's options can be represented with iso-profit wages $\lambda^j(\Pi)$, i.e. wages paid to a worker in an organization with

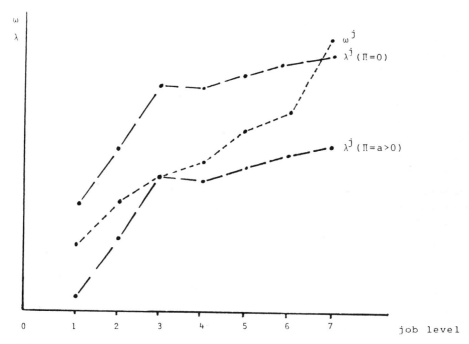

Fig. 1. Reservation wages and iso-profit points

jobs at level j that would all leave the same profit level Π to the firm. In Fig. 1, an illustration is given for equivalence at a profit level $\Pi = 0$. If iso-profit wage lines (or rather, iso-profit points) were always parallel to the one at $\Pi = 0$, all firms would select on organization with $j = 3$, as this would generate the highest profit. In fact, what the firm does is select the organization that realizes a point on the best iso-profit line compatible with the wage function, that was already derived to be equal to ω^j. The location of the iso-profit points will presumably be determined by other variables as well, like e.g. the number of workers hired, the volume of output and the number of firms in the market. For example, free entry of firms may adjust the location of iso-profit points to make $\Pi = 0$ the only feasible (long-run) equilibrium. This may affect the optimal job level, but as long as firms are identical, only one organization cum job level is selected (and only one wage-job level combination is observed), unless ω^j and λ^j have equal distances at different j, i.e. have "parallel curves" over a range containing an optimum.

The location of the iso-profit points may differ between firms, if firms differ in one or more characteristics: given supplies of other relevant inputs, input prices, product market characteristics in case of heterogeneous products, etc. It is conceivable that firms have, in the short run, a given organization, with given job levels. Then, if the maximum wage λ^j that the firm can pay for this job level is higher than the reservation wage ω^j, workers can be profitably hired at this job level; competition will drive the wage level down to ω^j. If $\lambda^j < \omega^j$, workers are not observed at the job level, for the firm under consideration. Differences between firms, due to their different characteristics, may create a set of feasible job levels, with observed wage rates equal to the wages ω^j. The distribution of firms by shift characteristics will determine the observed allocation. This result is not really different if firms do have a choice as to the job level at which they operate.

The situation becomes more complicated if the reservation wages ω^j are dependent on one or more endogenous variables. Suppose, for example, that firms' isoprofit wages λ^j depend on the size of the firm, through economies of scale, and that individuals' reservation wages ω^j also depend on firm size, as they prefer work in smaller units, say. Then, realized ω^j curves are segments of curves conditional on different firm sizes. Now, the distribution of firms by size also determines the selection of observed wages among the conditional ω^j curves. With a given distribution of firm sizes, this generalizes the earlier rule that the demand side determines the selection of observed wages from an exogenous reservation wage structure. But if firm size is subject to choice by firms, there is full interaction between the selection and matching of characteristics and the wage structure; the firms' choice of scale will also depend on the wage structure, that is, on the preferences of the individuals. The distribution of firms by size becomes endogenous.

An analogous argument can be developed by starting from the supply side. If individuals differ in levels of education, with a fixed level for any worker, and if the iso-profit line is completely fixed, independent of any endogenous variable, observed wages will always lie on this unique iso-profit line.

In earlier work (Hartog 1986a, b), a short-run framework was assumed, with individuals' education levels and firms' job levels fixed. This allowed the interpretation of the estimated earnings function as revealing the demand price for education and the supply price for job level. Generally speaking, the theory outlined above leads to an earnings function that contains supply characteristics and demand characteristics simultaneously, and is not restricted a priori to either the first (like in the pure human capital model) or to the second set (like in pure segmentation models). Explicit models, specifying a utility and a profit structure and deriving the implied equilibrium earnings function are technically very complicated and only a few examples exist (Epple 1987). Rosen (1974) has suggested a method, for the case of characteristics that assume continuous values, to derive supply and demand functions, in a two-step procedure. First, estimate an earnings function relating wages to characteristics and next, compute the partial derivatives of the function to obtain marginal characteristics prices. Then, take these marginal prices at the sample points as the dependent variables for supply prices and demand prices for each characteristic, and relate these to explanatory variables. Then, the usual identification conditions for supply and demand functions apply. Hartog (1986a) is in fact an application of this approach for discrete variables. Epple (1987) and Bartik (1987) have recently demonstrated that OLS may not be the appropriate technique for estimating demand and supply functions.

In this paper, we will not attempt to identify supply and demand functions. Rather, we will content ourselves with estimating the earnings function. From the outlined theory of job-worker matching and the associated theory of hedonic prices, we take the message that both supply and demand variables are relevant in explaining wages and that the resulting equilibrium earnings function may be quite complex. Essentially, the theory claims that we cannot expect marginal characteristics prices to be uniform throughout the labor market. This an important reason for preferring a semi-parametric method, in which the functional form is determined by the data rather than by the investigator. The method, developed by Bierens and first presented in Bierens and Hartog (1988) will be outlined in Sections 4, 5 and 6.

3 The Data

The data are taken from the Dutch Wage Structure Survey 1979 (CBS 1979) collected by the national statistical office, CBS. The Wage Structure Survey (WSS) is a representative wage survey, where data on individual workers are taken from the administration of firms and institutions. In comparison to individual surveys, this allows a careful observation of earnings, using well-defined concepts. For privacy reasons however, the wages of top-level officials are not available; the cut-off level is a monthly wage of Dfl. 11,500,- , more than 4 times the median wage in the Netherlands, surpassed by less than 1% of the workers (CBS 1980, p. 312). Hence, the sample is truncated at the top; we did not attempt any correction. We used hourly earnings, found from dividing reported earnings per payment interval (week, month, etc.) by reported hours of work.

The WSS contains some 700,000 observations, but CBS has agreed to compile a special data tape, created as a random sample from WSS. This sample contains 30,612 observations. Restricting the analysis to individuals who work full-time, have received their wage continuously (no interruptions due to illness, working short-time, etc.), worked at their present employer during the full year and for whom level of education is known, leaves 13,986 observations (the largest reductions in the number of observations are due to "working only part of the year", $n = 9,811$, and to missing observations on annual earnings, $n = 3,526$). From these 13,986 observations a random subsample of size 2,000 has been drawn, to meet the constraint on computer cost.

Most of the explanatory variables used are rather conventional and need no explanation. Job level however, is a new variable, requiring elaboration. The scale used consists of 9 job levels; instructions about the assignment of jobs to job levels were included in the original survey. To quote the instruction: "The assignment should be as precise as possible on the basis of the activities performed, taking into account the necessary education or knowledge, the difficulty and the degree of responsibility. It is not the actual education of the worker that determines the assignment to job level, but the education or knowledge that is required for the job. In practice, the distinction of workers by function, salary scale or rank that your firm may use, can provide guidance". A detailed description of the job levels can be found in Hartog (1986a).

The point to be stressed here is the emphasis placed by the instruction, on *required* levels of education. That is precisely the emphasis needed for the present approach. The models stressing allocation effects assume that the demand side of the labor market is heterogeneous, and that the productivity of a worker depends on the nature of the job. This implies the potential existence of comparative advantage, where relative differences between individuals change with the type of employment. Detecting such effects requires measurement of the demand side and this can be done by a scale for job difficulty. Somewhat disturbingly, the instruction also refers to the salary scale as an auxiliary indicator of the job level. That seems to make the explanatory variable dependent on the variable that is to be explained. The problem is less serious than it may seem. First, the detailed instruction will in many cases enable to determine the job level without recourse to the salary scale. And second, the firm may indeed have constructed its salary structure precisely to express the dependence of earnings on the required capabilities of the worker, in line with the theory promoted above. In other words, the causality may very well run from job requirements to earnings, even though the grading instruction allows to use the information in reversed order.

4 Specification of the Earnings Function

We shall estimate an earnings function relating the log of gross hourly wages (measured in 0.01 guilders) to the following six explanatory variables:

$x^{(1)}$ = job level, ranging from 1 to 9
(see Hartog 1986a for details):

1: lowest level, not even requiring limited specific training.

. . . .

9: highest level, personnel with authority and responsibility for the whole firm, for example members of the board of directors.

$x^{(2)}$ = level of education, ranging from 1 to 7:

    1: basic
    2: lower vocational
    3: intermediate general
    4: intermediate vocational
    5: higher general
    6: higher vocational
    7: university

$x^{(3)}$ = sex

    1: male
    2: female

$x^{(4)}$ = age class[3], ranging from 1 to 10:

    1: age $\leqslant 20$
    2: $20 < $ age $\leqslant 25$
    3: $25 < $ age $\leqslant 30$
    4: $30 < $ age $\leqslant 35$
    5: $35 < $ age $\leqslant 40$
    6: $40 < $ age $\leqslant 45$
    7: $45 < $ age $\leqslant 50$
    8: $50 < $ age $\leqslant 55$
    9: $55 < $ age $\leqslant 60$
   10: $60 < $ age $\leqslant 64$

$x^{(5)}$ = experience with the present employer, in year classes[3], ranging from 1 to 10:

    1: 1–5
    2: 6–10
    3: 11–15
    4: 16–20
    5: 21–25
    6: 26–30
    7: 31–35
    8: 36–40
    9: 41–45
   10: 46–50

---

[3] This variable is also available in years. The main reason for working with classes is to accommodate the analysis of cross-effects, in Section 8.

$x^{(6)} = $ collective agreement

    1: wages set in a collective agreement

    2: wages not set in a collective agreement

The actual data set we work with consists of 2,000 i.i.d. observations $(y_j, x_j), j = 1,$ $2, ..., n = 2,000$, where y_j is the natural logarithm of gross hourly wages of individual j, and $x'_j = (x_j^{(1)}, ..., x_j^{(7)}) \in X$ is the corresponding vector of explanatory variables specified above, including a constant term $x_j^{(7)} = 1$, with

$$X = \{(x^{(1)}, ..., x^{(7)})' : x^{(1)} \in \{1, 2, ..., 9\}, x^{(2)} \in \{1, 2, ..., 7\},$$

$$x^{(3)} \in \{1, 2\}, x^{(4)} \in \{1, 2, ..., 10\}, x^{(5)} \in \{1, 2, ..., 10\},$$

$$x^{(6)} \in \{1, 2\}, x^{(7)} = 1\} \tag{4}$$

the space of regressors.

Now the earnings function is the response function $g(x)$ of the (non)linear regression model

$$y_j = g(x_j) + u_j, \quad j = 1, 2, ..., n, ..., \tag{5}$$

where each u_j satisfies the standard regression condition that its conditional expectation relative to x_j equals zero with probability 1, that is:

$$E(u_j | x_j) = 0 \quad \text{a.s.}^4 \quad \text{for } j = 1, 2, ... \tag{6}$$

A typical feature of this earnings function, and in fact of all empirical earnings functions considered in the literature, is that the explanatory variables are discrete. In particular in the present case the space of explanatory variables, X, is finite. As has been shown in Bierens and Hartog (1988), this feature enables us to determine the *exact* functional form of the regression function $g(x)$, namely as a finite polynomial of a linear function of the regressors.

In order to illustrate this point, consider the following nonlinear regression model:

$$y_j = g(x_{1,j}, x_{2,j}) + u_j, \quad j = 1, 2, ..., \tag{7}$$

---

4   a.s. stands for "almost surely", which means that the event involved holds with probability 1.

where $E(u_j | x_{1,j}, x_{2,j}) = 0$ a.s., $x_j' = (x_{1,j}, x_{2,j})$ is a two-components vector contained with probability 1 in the set

$$X = \left\{ \begin{pmatrix} 0 \\ 0 \end{pmatrix}, \begin{pmatrix} 1 \\ 0 \end{pmatrix}, \begin{pmatrix} 0 \\ 1 \end{pmatrix}, \begin{pmatrix} 1 \\ 1 \end{pmatrix} \right\} = \left\{ x_1, x_2, x_3, x_4 \right\} \tag{8}$$

and g is *any* real function defined on X. Moreover, let

$$\theta' = (1, -2). \tag{9}$$

Then it is easy to verify that

$$g(x) = \alpha_0 + \alpha_1 (\theta'x) + \alpha_2 (\theta'x)^2 + \alpha_3 (\theta'x)^3 \quad \text{for } x \in X, \tag{10}$$

where

$$\begin{pmatrix} \alpha_0 \\ \alpha_1 \\ \alpha_2 \\ \alpha_3 \end{pmatrix} = \begin{pmatrix} 1 & 0 & 0 & 0 \\ 1 & 1 & 1 & 1 \\ 1 & -2 & 4 & -8 \\ 1 & -1 & 1 & -1 \end{pmatrix}^{-1} \begin{pmatrix} g(x_1) \\ g(x_2) \\ g(x_3) \\ g(x_4) \end{pmatrix} \tag{11}$$

This easy result is not specific for this particular θ, but it holds for all linear functions $\theta'x$ which are one-to-one mappings from X into R. Such vectors θ will be called *linear separators* of X. More generally:

Definition 1: A vector $\theta \in R^k$ is a linear separator of a countable subset X of R^k if for all pairs $(x_1, x_2) \in X \times X$, $\theta'x_1 = \theta'x_2$ implies $x_1 = x_2$.

The existence of a linear separator of a countable set is always guaranteed. In fact the set of all linear separators is uncountable. Cf. Bierens and Hartog (1988, Theorem 1).

From Definition 1 it follows that for any linear separator θ of X each point in the range of $\theta'x$ $(x \in X)$ can uniquely be associated to a point in the domain X, and vice versa. In other words, if the value of $\theta'x$ is known then $x \in X$ is known too. Consequently we have by the definition of conditional expectations (see, for example, Chung 1974, Ch. 9) that for any random vector $(y, x) \in R \times X$,

$$E(y | x) = E(y | \theta'x) \quad \text{a.s.,} \tag{12}$$

Consequently, model (5) now takes the form

$$y = \varphi_\theta(\theta'x) + u, \tag{13}$$

where the function φ_θ depends on θ. Since the space X of regressors is finite it is easy to verify, similarly to (10), that φ_θ is a polynomial of order the size of X minus 1, or less. Thus, for any linear separator θ of X the regression model (5) takes the form

$$y_j = \sum_{l=0}^{m-1} \alpha_l(\theta)(\theta'x_j)^l + u_j, \tag{14}$$

where m is less than or equal to the size of X.

In Bierens and Hartog (1988) we have proposed to choose as linear separator the vector $\hat\theta$ of OLS estimators of the parameters of the linear model with constant term, as then $\hat\theta'x$ will be "close" to the true regression function $g(x)$, hence model (14) might then be true for m less than the size of X. The choice of $\hat\theta$ as a linear separator is admissable if its probability limit θ_0 is a linear separator of X. Since the set of vectors in R^k that are not linear separators of X has Lebesgue measure zero, this is not too strong a condition. Table 1 gives the OLS estimation results involved, together with the usual statistics. In particular, the t-statistics have been calculated according to the approach of White (1980).

We recall that these OLS results only concern the best linear approximation of the earnings function, as the true model might be nonlinear. Consequently, the error ϵ_j in

Table 1. OLS results for $y = ln$ (hourly wage x 100)

No. Explanatory variables	OLS estim.	t-values
1: job level (1-9)	.08439	22.22
2: level of education (1-7)	.06222	12.69
3: sex (male=1, female=2)	-.13760	-11.13
4: age class (1-10)	.04491	15.05
5: experience class (1-10)	.00651	1.64
6: collective agreement (=1) or not (=2)	-.03647	-3.08
7: constant term (=1)	6.83100	240.60
residual variance =	.0445	
residual s.e. =	.2111	
R^2 =	.6933	
n =	2000	

the linear model $y_j = \theta_0' x_j + \epsilon_j$ does not necessarily satisfy the standard condition $E(\epsilon_j | x_j) = 0$ a.s., but merely the weaker condition $E\epsilon_j x_j = 0$. The latter condition defines θ_0 as:

$$\theta_0 = (E x_j x_j')^{-1} E x_j y_j$$

The results in Table 1 allow some tentative conclusions about the impact of the explanatory variables on the log of the wages. Firstly, it appears that with one exception the explanatory variables have significant OLS parameters. The exception involved is company experience. Secondly, the signs of the OLS parameters conform to our expectations: negative for females, positive for education, age, experience and non-collective bargaining. However, an extensive discussion of the results will be postponed until we have presented the complete estimation results, in Sections 7 and 8.

5 Estimation

Using the OLS statistic $\hat\theta$ as a linear separator the model becomes a linear model in the parameters $\alpha_0, \alpha_1, ..., \alpha_{m-1}$ and the variables $\hat\theta' x_j, (\hat\theta' x_j)^2, ..., (\hat\theta' x_j)^{m-1}$. However, applying OLS to estimate the α may be hampered by numerical instability if m is large, due to the fact that then the matrix with elements

$$\frac{1}{n} \sum_{j=1}^{n} (\hat\theta' x_j)^{l_1 + l_2}, \quad l_1, l_2 = 0, 1, ..., m - 1$$

will probably be nearly singular (see Seber 1977, Section 8.1). A neat cure for this problem is suggested by Forsythe (1957) and others, namely to use orthogonal polynomials. Moreover, numerical stability of polynomial regressions can be further improved by standardizing the variables into the interval $[-1, 1]$. In our case the variables involved are $\theta' x_j$ with θ a linear separator, which will be standardized into the interval $[-1, 1]$ by using the transformation

$$z(x, \theta) = \frac{2\theta' x - M_1(\theta) - M_2(\theta)}{M_1(\theta) - M_2(\theta)}, \tag{15}$$

where

$$M_1(\theta) = \sum_{i=1}^{k} \max_{x \in X} \theta_i x^{(i)} \tag{16}$$

and

$$M_2(\theta) = \sum_{i=1}^{k} \min_{x \in X} \theta_i x^{(i)}, \tag{17}$$

with

$$(\theta_1 \ldots, \theta_k)' = \theta \in R^k \quad \text{and} \quad (x^{(1)}, \ldots, x^{(k)})' = x \in X.$$

Thus we now propose to rewrite model (14) as

$$y_j = \sum_{l=0}^{m-1} \gamma_l(r)\psi_l(z(x_j, \theta)|\theta) + u_j, \quad \text{with}$$

$$E(u_j|x_j) = 0 \quad \text{a.s.} \quad (j = 1, 2, \ldots, n), \tag{18}$$

where the $\psi_l(z|\theta)$ are orthogonal polynomials of order l, respectively. Thus

$$\frac{1}{n} \sum_{j=1}^{n} \psi_{r_1}(z(x_j, \theta)|\theta)\psi_{r_2}(z(x_j, \theta)|\theta) = \begin{cases} 1 & \text{if } r_1 = r_2, \\ 0 & \text{if } r_1 \neq r_2. \end{cases} \tag{19}$$

By virtue of (19) the least squares estimators of the parameters $\psi_l(\theta)$ of model (18) can now simply be calculated by

$$\hat{\gamma}_l(\theta) = \frac{1}{n} \sum_{j=1}^{n} y_j \psi_l(z(x_j, \theta)|\theta), \quad l = 0, 1, 2, \ldots \tag{20}$$

In practice we will use $\hat{\theta}$ instead of a fixed θ as a linear separator. Assuming that

$$\theta_0 = \text{plim } \hat{\theta} \tag{21}$$

is a linear separator of X, we then have for $l = 0, 1, \ldots, m - 1$.

$$\text{plim } \hat{\gamma}_l(\hat{\theta}) = \text{plim } \hat{\gamma}_l(\theta_0) \tag{22}$$

Moreover, if m is large enough then

$$\text{plim} \sum_{l=0}^{m-1} \hat{\gamma}_l(\hat{\theta}) \psi_l(z(x, \hat{\theta})|\hat{\theta}) = g(x) = E(y_j|x_j = x) \tag{23}$$

for every $x \in X$ with positive probability.

6 Model Specification Testing

Next we consider the problem of how to test whether m is sufficiently large and θ_0 is a linear separator. The test we present here is a further elaboration of a model specification test proposed by Bierens (1982). For further details we refer to Bierens and Hartog (1988).

Let for $\theta^* \in R^k$ and $\tau \in R$,

$$\hat{z}(x_j, \theta^*) = \frac{2\theta^{*\prime}x_j - \max_{1 \leqslant j \leqslant n} (\theta^{*\prime}x_j) - \min_{1 \leqslant j \leqslant n} \theta^{*\prime}x_j}{\min_{1 \leqslant j \leqslant n} (\theta^{*\prime}x_j) - \min_{1 \leqslant j \leqslant n} (\theta^{*\prime}x_j)}, \tag{24}$$

$$\hat{\rho}_{m,j}(\tau|\theta^*) = e^{\tau\hat{z}(x_j,\theta^*)}$$

$$-\sum_{l=0}^{m-1} \{\psi_l(z(x_j, \hat{\theta})|\hat{\theta}) \frac{1}{n} \sum_{j_0=1}^{n} \psi_l(z(x_{j_0}, \hat{\theta})|\hat{\theta})e^{\tau\hat{z}(x_{j_0},\theta^*)}\}. \tag{25}$$

$$\hat{\xi}_m(\tau|\theta^*) = \frac{1}{n} \sum_{j=1}^{n} (\partial/\partial\theta')\hat{g}_m(x_j|\hat{\theta})e^{\tau\hat{z}(x_j,\theta^*)} {}^5 \tag{26}$$

---

[5] By $(\partial/\partial\theta)f(\theta^*)$ we denote the *row* vector of partial derivations of the function $f(\theta)$ evaluated at $\theta = \theta^*$, and the corresponding *column* vector is denoted by $(\partial/\partial\theta')f(\theta^*)$. The derivatives involved can be calculated by numerical differentiation.

$$\hat{s}_m^2(\tau|\theta^*) = \frac{1}{n} \sum_{j=1}^{n} (y_j - \hat{g}_m(x_j|\hat{\theta}))^2 \hat{\rho}_{m,j}(\tau|\theta^*)^2$$

$$-2\frac{1}{n}\sum_{j=1}^{n}(y_j - \hat{g}_m(x_j|\hat{\theta}))(y_j - \hat{\theta}'x_j)\hat{\rho}_{m,j}(\tau|\theta^*)x_j'\left(\frac{1}{n}\sum_{j=1}^{n}x_jx_j'\right)^{-1}\hat{\xi}_m(\tau|\theta^*)$$

$$+\hat{\xi}_m(\tau|\theta^*)'\hat{\Omega}\hat{\xi}_m(\tau|\theta^*), \tag{27}$$

and

$$\hat{\eta}_m(\tau|\theta^*) = \frac{(1/\sqrt{n})\sum_{j=1}^{n}(y_j - \hat{g}_m(x_j|\hat{\theta}))e^{\tau\hat{z}(x_j,\theta^*)}}{\sqrt{\hat{s}_m^2(\tau|\theta^*)}} \tag{28}$$

where $\hat{\Omega}$ is defined by

$$\hat{\Omega} = \left(\frac{1}{n}\sum_{j=1}^{n}x_jx_j'\right)^{-1}\left(\frac{1}{n}\sum_{j=1}^{n}(y_j - \hat{\theta}'z_j)^2x_jx_j'\right)\left(\frac{1}{n}\sum_{j=1}^{n}x_jx_j'\right)^{-1} \tag{29}$$

Moreover, let θ^* be an arbitrary linear separator of X. If

$$H_0 : m \text{ and } \theta = \theta_0 \text{ are such that model (14) is true} \tag{30}$$

then for $n \to \infty$ and $\tau \neq 0$

$$\hat{\eta}_m(\tau|\theta^*) \to N(0, 1) \text{ in distr.} \tag{31}$$

due to the central limit theorem and the asymptotic normality of $\hat{\theta}$. If the null hypothesis (30) is false then there exists a $\delta > 0$ such that for every $\tau \in (-\delta, 0) \cup (0, \delta)$.

$$|\hat{\eta}_m(\tau|\theta^*)| \to \infty \quad \text{a.s.} \tag{32}$$

Moreover, under the maintained hypothesis that θ_0 is a linear separator the above conclusions also hold for $\theta^* = \hat{\theta}$.

The result (32) follows from the fact that if m is too small then for every $\tau \in (-\delta, 0) \cup (0, \delta)$, plim $(1/\sqrt{n})\eta_m(\tau|\theta^*) \neq 0$, which in its turn follows from plim $\left(\frac{1}{n}\right) \sum_{j=1}^{n} (g(x_j) - g_m(x_j|\theta_0))e^{\tau \hat{z}(x_j, \theta^*)} \neq 0$. See Bierens and Hartog (1988).

Thus conducting the test at say the 5% significance level we accept the null hypothesis if for an a priori chosen linear separator θ^* and a small number τ_0, $|\eta_m(\tau_0|\theta^*)| < 1.96$, and we reject the null if not.

The power of the test depends on the appropriate choice of τ and θ^*. Although we may substitute $\theta^* = \hat{\theta}$, the test might then no longer be consistent, as we then only test whether the polynomoal $\sum_{l=0}^{m-1} \gamma_l(\theta_0)\psi_l(z(x_j, \theta_0)|\theta_0)$ equals $E(y_j|\theta_0'x_j)$ a.s. However, if θ_0 is not a linear separator this conditional expectation need no longer be equal to $E(y_j|x_j)$. Thus, in the first instance, we should not use $\theta^* = \hat{\theta}$. We recall that almost any $\theta \in R^k$ is a linear separator of a finite set X in R^k. This suggests that we may choose θ^* randomly from a continuous distribution. But how does this random choice of θ^* affect the asymptotic properties of the test statistic involved? The following theorem shows that it doesn't, and that we may even choose τ randomly from a continuous distribution.

Theorem 1: Let θ^* be a random drawing from a k-variate continuous distribution, and let τ be an independent random drawing from a continuous distribution on R. Then (31) holds if (30) is true and (32) holds if (30) is false.

Proof: The separate Appendix to Bierens and Hartog (1988), which is available from the second author on request.

Thus we may for example draw τ and the components of θ^* independently from a uniform distribution, and then conduct the test in the same way as before.

Having tested and accepted a particular m in the above way, we might reduce m to m_*, say, where $0 \leqslant m_* < m$, by testing whether

$$H_0 : \gamma_{m*}(\theta_0) = \ldots = \gamma_{m-1}(\theta_0) = 0 \tag{33}$$

This test can be conducted by using the well-known Wald test. See Bierens and Hartog (1988, Theorem 8).

The ultimate purpose of most empirical econometric analysis is to determine which explanatory variables are important in the model under review and which are not. However, since the models (14) and (18) are true for any linear separator, provided m is sufficiently large, it is clear that the OLS results in Table 1 are not conclusive with respect to this question. The test we proposed is similar to the test in Theorem 1, i.e. calculate the test statistic $\eta_m(\tau|\hat{\theta})$ with the p-th component of the x_j's fixed on its minimum or maximum level.

Denoting the resulting test statistic by $\eta_m(\tau|\hat{\theta},p)$, we have

Theorem 2: Let the hypothesis (30) be true and let τ be an independent random drawing from a continuous distribution on R. Then

$$\hat{\eta}_m(\tau|\hat{\theta},p) \to N(0,1) \quad \text{in distr.} \tag{34}$$

if the component p of x_j is redundant, and

$$|\hat{\eta}_m(\tau|\hat{\theta},p)| \to \infty \text{ a.s.} \tag{35}$$

if it is not redundant.

Proof: The separate Appendix to Bierens and Hartog (1988).

In our empirical application we shall sequentially apply the above approach with an increasing critical level in order to determine m. The reason for working with an increasing critical level is to prevent problems associated with pretesting, as then the type I and II errors of the test both vanish as $n \to \infty$.

Step 1: Select an initial $m = m_o$ and a sequence (L_n) of critical levels converging to infinity at order $o(\sqrt{n})$. Apply the test in Theorem 1. If $|\eta_{m_o}(\tau|\theta)| < L_n$ then go to Step 3, else put $\hat{m} = 2m_o$ and go to step 2.

Step 2: Apply the test in Theorem 1, i.e. if $|\eta_{\hat{m}}(\tau|\theta)| \geq L_n$ then let $\hat{m} = \hat{m} + m_o$ and repeat step 2, else go to step 3.

Step 3: Use the Wald test to determine the maximum number $m^* \leq \hat{m}$ for which the last m_* polynomial parameters are jointly insignificant, with significance level

$$\epsilon_n = 2 \int_{L_n}^{\infty} [e^{-1/2u^2}/\sqrt{2\pi}]du.$$

Put $\hat{m} = \hat{m} - m_*$ and stop.

In the empirical application under review we have chosen $m_o = 50$. Now let $\bar{m}$ be the minimum m for which model (18) with $\theta = \theta_o$ holds, given that θ_o is a linear separator. (Otherwise no such $\bar{m}$ exists.) Then

Theorem 3:

$$\lim_{n \to \infty} P(\hat{m} = \bar{m}) = 1, \quad \text{whenever} \quad L_n/\sqrt{n} \to 0 \quad \text{and} \quad L_n \to \infty \tag{36}$$

This result heavily depends on the choice of the critical level L_n, i.e. (36) requires $L_n = o(\sqrt{n})$, as then both the type I *and* II errors of the test vanish. The proof of this result is not too hard and therefore left to the reader.

In Bierens and Hartog (1988) we have derived L_n on the basis of a Bayesian approach. For $m_o = 50$ and $n = 2,000$ this yields

$$L_n = 4.5597 \tag{37}$$

Moreover, for this L_n,

$$\epsilon_n = 0.51227E\text{-}5, \tag{38}$$

(Cf. Step 3)

7 Estimating and Testing the Regression Function: Empirical Results

We have in first instance estimated the polynomial model (18) for $m = 50$, using the vector of OLS estimates in Table 1 as a linear separator. The estimation results involved are given in Table 2 together with the usual statistics. We note that the t-values involved take into account that the parameter estimates depend on parameter values that were estimated at an earlier stage.

The model specification test proposed in the previous section has been conducted ten times, for $\tau_0 = 0.1$ though 1.0, with the components of θ^* drawn randomly from the uniform (0, 1) distribution. Also we conducted the test with τ_0 drawn randomly from the uniform distribution. The results are presented in Table 3.

Comparing the test statistics in Table 3 with the critical value L_n in (37) we conclude that $m - 1 = 49$ is not too small an order of the polynomial regression model.

Table 2. Polynomial estimation results for $m = 50$

ℓ	$\hat{\gamma}_\ell(\hat{\theta})$	t-values	ℓ	$\hat{\gamma}_\ell(\hat{\theta})$	t-values
1	7.370	1624.	26	.2191E-03	.3880E-01
2	.3173	66.99	27	-.5519E-02	-1.130
3	.2455E-01	5.228	28	.3636E-02	.6109
4	.3320E-01	7.928	29	.1070E-01	1.905
5	-.5162E-02	-1.394	30	.4902E-02	.7498
6	-.7040E-02	-1.895	31	.7128E-02	1.050
7	-.7636E-02	-1.889	32	.3463E-03	.4530E-01
8	-.7487E-02	-1.650	33	-.1100E-01	-2.064
9	-.3508E-02	-.8097	34	.1032E-02	.2342
10	.9963E-02	2.050	35	.1162E-02	.1764
11	.4370E-02	.6409	36	.2036E-02	.2559
12	.3991E-03	.5717E-01	37	-.2507E-02	-.3105
13	-.8836E-02	-1.133	38	-.9043E-02	-1.079
14	-.1258E-01	-2.667	39	-.7627E-02	-.8460
15	-.1043E-01	-2.593	40	-.9572E-02	-1.182
16	-.9375E-02	-1.778	41	-.2851E-02	-.3236
17	-.4998E-02	-.7745	42	-.4391E-03	-.3509E-01
18	-.5717E-02	-.8603	43	-.1229E-02	-.1023
19	.4629E-02	.8251	44	.1031E-01	.7474
20	.2252E-02	.4384	45	.2541E-02	.3506
21	-.1191E-02	-.2481	46	.1194E-02	.1317
22	-.3346E-02	-.6868	47	.6359E-02	.8892
23	-.8177E-03	-.1625	48	-.2340E-02	-.1503
24	.2113E-02	.5187	49	-.5074E-04	-.4821E-02
25	-.6416E-02	-1.210	50	.2410E-02	.3206

residual variance	= .4117E-01		residual s.e.		= .2029
R^2	= .7166		n		= 2000

Table 4 gives the results of the Wald test. The results in Table 4 together with (38) indicate that the last 31 polynomial parameters can be deleted, as the hypothesis that the last $l(=31)$ polynomial parameters are zero cannot be rejected at the ϵ_n-significance level, whereas the hypothesis involved has to be rejected for larger l. Furthermore, these results give empirical evidence that the earnings function is nonlinear, for the test in Table 4 that the last 48 polynomial parameters are zero is in fact a test of the linearity hypothesis. Clearly, this linearity hypothesis is rejected. On the other hand, comparing Tables 1 and 2 we see that the R^2-statistic of the polynomial model is only slightly larger than of the linear model. Thus the non-linearity, though strongly significant, is rather modest.

Table 3. Model specification tests for the polynomial model with $m = 50$

τ	test statistics
.1	2.349
.2	1.819
.3	1.315
.4	.8439
.5	.4096
.6	.1417E-01
.7	-.3424
.8	-.6613
.9	-.9446
1.	-1.195
random	-1.188

Table 4. Test of the null hypothesis that the last l polynomial parameters are zero

l	test stat.(-w)	$P[\chi^2(l) > w]$	l	test stat.(-w)	$P[\chi^2(l) > w]$
50	.3077E+09	0.	25	42.65	.1527E-01
49	.7692E+08	0.	24	37.75	.3678E-01
48	.2440E+07	0.	23	37.66	.2768E-01
47	.7957E+06	0.	22	34.41	.4457E-01
46	.7423E+06	0.	21	25.66	.2196
45	.1412E+06	0.	20	20.51	.4267
44	.1081E+06	0.	19	18.26	.5054
43	.4847E+05	0.	18	17.46	.4919
42	.2507E+05	0.	17	10.19	.8954
41	9809.	0.	16	9.966	.8684
40	3845.	0.	15	9.600	.8441
39	2278.	0.	14	8.475	.8631
38	1527.	0.	13	7.901	.8500
37	1113.	0.	12	6.639	.8805
36	877.0	0.	11	6.121	.8652
35	527.3	0.	10	3.836	.9544
34	416.0	0.	9	3.833	.9220
33	176.8	0.	8	2.845	.9437
32	132.9	.2842E-13	7	2.676	.9133
31	81.63	.1942E-05	6	1.788	.9382
30	81.00	.1417E-05	5	1.679	.8916
29	69.91	.3116E-04	4	1.663	.7974
28	66.79	.5162E-04	3	.1357	.9872
27	64.33	.6943E-04	2	.1105	.9462
26	43.34	.1776E-01	1	.1028	.7485

Table 5. Polynomial estimation results for $m = 19$

ℓ	$\hat{\gamma}_\ell(\hat{\theta})$	t-values	ℓ	$\hat{\gamma}_\ell(\hat{\theta})$	t-values
1	7.370	1608.	11	.4370E-02	.6117
2	.3173	64.74	12	.3991E-03	.5618E-01
3	.2455E-01	5.006	13	-.8836E-02	-1.120
4	.3320E-01	7.364	14	-.1258E-01	-2.516
5	-.5162E-02	-1.313	15	-.1043E-01	-2.326
6	-.7040E-02	-1.822	16	-.9375E-02	-1.663
7	-.7636E-02	-1.836	17	-.4998E-02	-.7474
8	-.7487E-02	-1.569	18	-.5717E-02	-.8343
9	-.3508E-02	-.7332	19	.4629E-02	.7904
10	.9963E-02	1.866			

residual variance	= .0420		residual s.e.	= .2050
R^2	= .7108		n	= 2000

In view of the above test results we decided to cut the order of the polynomial to $m - 1 = 18$. Repeating the polynomial estimation, we now got the results in Table 5.

Comparing the fit of the polynomial model of order 18 with the fit of the linear model in Table 1 we see that the nonlinearity is rather modest. This conclusion is corrobarated by Fig. 2, where the estimated polynomial

$$\hat{\varphi}_m(z) = \sum_{l=0}^{m-1} \hat{\gamma}_l(\hat{\theta})\psi_l(z|\hat{\theta}), \quad z \in [-1, 1], \ m = 19$$

is plotted.

The polynomial appears to be straight in the mid-part. The non-linearity is only apparent for relatively large or low values of the linear response function.

Next we have tested the significance of each of the six explanatory variables in our earnings function, using the result of Theorem 2 with τ running from 0.1 to 1. as well as τ drawn randomly from the uniform $(0, 1)$ distribution. The values of the test statistics $\hat{\eta}_m(\tau|\hat{\theta}, p)$, $p = 1, ..., 6$, $m = 19$, are given in Table 6.

Thus we see from Table 6 that job level, level of education, sex, age are strongly significant in our earnings function, but that company experience is insignificant and the dummy variable with respect to the collective bargain wages is hardly significant at the 5% significance level. Note that using a fixed critical level rather than an increasing critical level is allowed here, as we will not use the test results for reducing the model size further by deleting insignificant explanatory variables.

z	$\varphi(z)$	5.268 (=min y)	———>	8.875 (=max y)
-1.0000	6.474	△		
-.9600	6.552	△		
-.9200	6.768		△	
-.8800	6.792		△	
-.8400	6.786		△	
-.8000	6.819		△	
-.7600	6.875		△	
-.7200	6.925		△	
-.6800	6.964		△	
-.6400	6.998		△	
-.6000	7.035		△	
-.5600	7.077		△	
-.5200	7.119		△	
-.4800	7.155		△	
-.4400	7.184		△	
-.4000	7.208		△	
-.3600	7.231		△	
-.3200	7.257		△	
-.2800	7.285		△	
-.2400	7.315		△	
-.2000	7.343		△	
-.1600	7.368		△	
-.1200	7.391		△	
-.0800	7.415		△	
-.0400	7.442		△	
.0000	7.476		△	
.0400	7.514		△	
.0800	7.555		△	
.1200	7.594		△	
.1600	7.628		△	
.2000	7.658		△	
.2400	7.684		△	
.2800	7.712		△	
.3200	7.743		△	
.3600	7.779		△	
.4000	7.819		△	
.4400	7.862		△	
.4800	7.910		△	
.5200	7.973		△	
.5600	8.058		△	
.6000	8.167		△	
.6400	8.281			∧
.6800	8.355			△
.7200	8.339			△
.7600	8.228			△
.8000	8.123			△
.8400	8.232			△
.8800	8.642			△
.9200	8.587			△
.9600	4.875			
1.0000	-10.74			

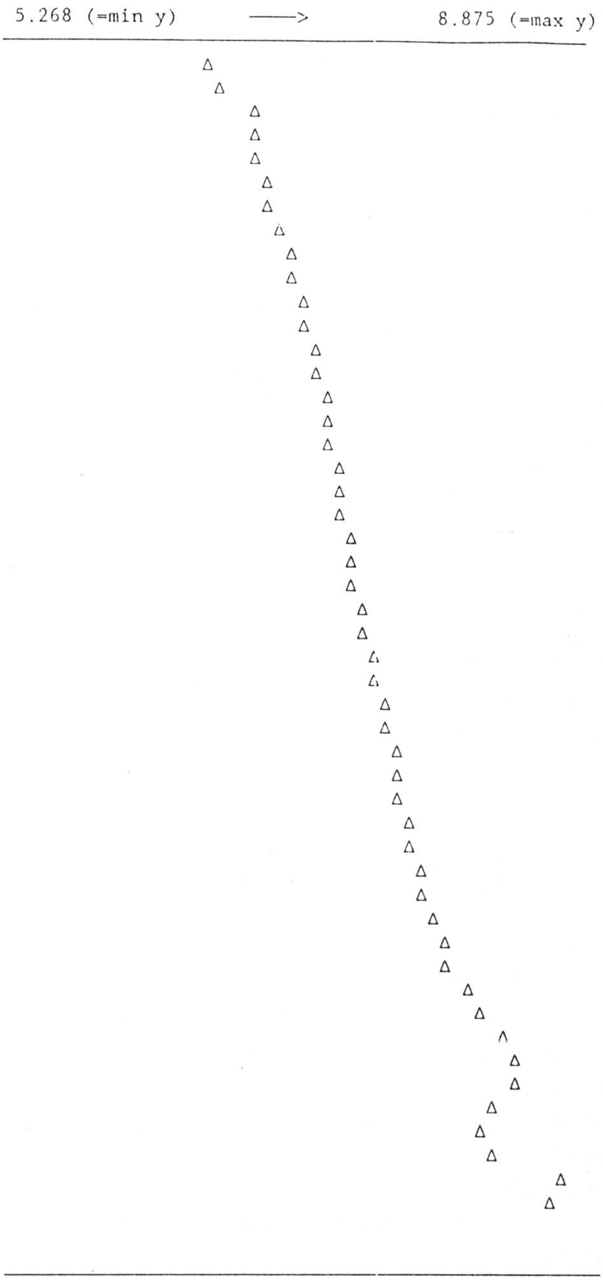

Fig. 2. Plot of the polynomial function on $[-1, 1]$ for $m = 19$

Table 6. Significance tests

r \ variables:	1	2	3	4	5	6
.1	10.13	8.031	9.169	8.727	1.380	2.114
.2	10.06	8.036	9.226	8.682	1.405	2.013
.3	9.980	8.040	9.267	8.634	1.421	1.894
.4	9.906	8.045	9.289	8.585	1.425	1.760
.5	9.831	8.049	9.291	8.534	1.415	1.617
.6	9.757	8.054	9.269	8.480	1.387	1.468
.7	9.683	8.060	9.220	8.425	1.341	1.319
.8	9.610	8.066	9.143	8.367	1.277	1.174
.9	9.536	8.072	9.036	8.306	1.196	1.035
1.	9.463	8.079	8.900	8.244	1.103	.9056
random	9.500	8.076	9.197	8.707	1.392	2.070

8 Interpretation of the Results

So far, the statistical analyses have led to the conclusion that the earnings equation contains significant non-linearities and that a polynomial of order 18 is needed for adequate representation. The deviations are concentrated at the extreme values of the argument z. In the linear earnings function, all variables had significant coefficients, although the significance level for experience class was rather low. In the non-linear specification, experience is insignificant and collective agreement is barely significant. Given the fact that non-linearity of the earnings function cannot be rejected, we should conclude that in the proper functional specification, company experience is not relevant for earnings differentials. This is remarkable in view of the fact that many firms have explicit experience-related pay scales. But apparently, in a proper specification, other variables can reproduce this effect. In particular, it seems that age is the dominant variable here. For the highly institutionalized structure of wage determination in The Netherlands, this result certainly makes sense.

In Tables 7 through 12, the estimated earnings function is used to show the effect of each of the explanatory variables in turn. These effects are calculated as the predicted earnings at the relevant value of the variable under consideration (as given in the first column), averaged out over the other variables as observed in the sample ("mean response"). The third column in each table gives the marginal effect of increasing the value of the relevant variable. For example, in Table 7 the first entry in the third column indicates that between job levels 1 and 2 gross hourly earnings increase by 7.9%. This column immediately shows non-linearities in the earnings function as non-

Table 7. Mean response of job level

job level	response (log)	%change over previous entry	frequency
1	7.142		5.40
2	7.222	7.948	26.90
3	7.298	7.567	36.10
4	7.372	7.471	1.40
5	7.448	7.558	1.45
6	7.526	7.833	14.55
7	7.611	8.500	5.60
8	7.704	9.303	6.50
9	7.808	10.365	2.10

Table 8. Mean response of level of education

education level	response (log)	%change over previous entry	frequency
1	7.226		16.45
2	7.286	5.975	14.45
3	7.345	5.891	30.05
4	7.404	5.958	21.45
5	7.465	6.101	4.95
6	7.529	6.325	8.80
7	7.588	5.939	3.85

Table 9. Mean response of sex

sex	response (log)	%change over previous entry	frequency
1(male)	7.397		80.60
2(female)	7.258	-13.904	19.40

constancy of the marginal earnings effect. Even a cursory inspection of the third column of each of these tables shows that non-linearities are most common. The fourth column gives the relative sample frequences of the values of the variable.

The marginal earnings effect of job level first slightly decreases, and then increases, from just under 8% to over 10% for an additional step on the job level scale. The

Table 10. Mean response of age class

age class	response (log)	%change over previous entry	frequency
1(≤20)	7.202		6.30
2(21-25)	7.248	4.586	14.95
3(26-30)	7.292	4.400	16.20
4(31-35)	7.336	4.371	15.45
5(36-40)	7.380	4.394	12.00
6(41-45)	7.424	4.415	9.80
7(46-50)	7.468	4.408	8.10
8(51-55)	7.512	4.347	7.40
9(56-60)	7.554	4.246	7.30
10(61-65)	7.591	3.646	2.50

Table 11. Mean response of experience class

experience class	response (log)	%change over previous entry	frequency
1(1-5)	7.361		44.85
2(6-10)	7.368	.671	22.80
3(11-15)	7.375	.666	12.05
4(16-20)	7.381	.657	8.55
5(21-25)	7.388	.642	4.55
6(26-30)	7.394	.622	3.90
7(31-35)	7.400	.596	2.15
8(36-40)	7.405	.562	.70
9(41-45)	7.411	.519	.40
10(46-50)	7.415	.466	.05

Table 12. Mean response of wage bargaining

wage bargaining	response (log)	%change over previous entry	frequency
1(collective)	7.375		75.15
2(not collective)	7.342	-3.353	24.85

marginal earnings effect of education hovers around 6%, with a little peak at level 6, higher vocational education. Females, on average earn 14% less than males. The effect of age, starting at 4.6% earnings growth over the first five years, gradually declines to 3.6% over the last five, reproducing the well known shape of age-earnings profiles. The experience effect (years with the present employer) is much smaller than the age effect, declining from 0.67 to 0.47% for five year intervals. For employees whose wages are not set in collective bargaining, the wage on average is 3.4% lower than for those who are covered by such bargaining. This confirms the general notion that unions have a positive effect on the wage rate.

The main motivation for the specification of the earnings function adopted here is the flexibility in allowing for non-linear effects of separate variables and for the interaction effects among the variables. The high order of the polynomial suggests that that these effects may be quite important. The magnitude of such effects can be seen by calculating predicted wages for given values of the explanatory variables. We have made such calculations for each of the six variables and for all pairs of two variables, while averaging out the effect of the remaining variables. To save space, we will not reproduce these tables (they are available from the authors). Instead, we will characterize the magnitude of non-linearities and interaction effects with a few key statistics. Table 13 has been created for this purpose.

In the table, the first column identifies the variable of which the effects are considered. The second column gives the slope estimated in the linear earnings function (cf. Table 1). Hence, according to these results, increased job levels generate an 8.4% wage increase for each additional step, and males earn 13.8% more than females. This latter representation is slightly inaccurate, as the model estimates the effect with a value of sex equal to 1 for males and 2 for females, implying that females earn 13.8% less than males (the coefficient in Table 1 is negative). However, to avoid confusing notation, minus signs are eliminated from Table 13 (this also holds for "collective agreement"). The third column gives results from the polynomial model. Earnings are predicted at successive levels of the explanatory variable (e.g. job level 1, 2, 3, etc.), averaging out the effect of all other variables, and the difference between successive carnings is calculated. The column then presents the range of these differences. Hence, according to the first entry in that column, the marginal earnings effect of an additional step on the job level sclae varies from a minimum of 7.5% to a maximum of 10.4%. Finally, in the remaining six columns such marginal earnings effects of an explanatory variable are calculated separately for all values of one conditioning variable. Hence, if one calculates the marginal earnings of one step on the job level scale for all values of education level separately, the minimum is +4.2% and the maximum is +11.7%.

The relevance of the non-linear earnings function, as compared to a linear specification is clearly brought out, and is seen to be more relevant for some variables than for others. The effect of a collective agreement does not vary much with the other variables, and the 3.6% effect estimated in the linear model is a fairly sharp characterization. The effect of sex varies with job level, between 12 and 17%, but is rather in-

Table 13. Predicted earnings effect (%) of a unit increase in each of the explanatory variables x, for the linear (OLS) earnings function and for the polynomial earnings function, unconditional or conditional on other variables

		polynomial						
			conditional on:					
x a)	lin. OLS	uncon-ditional	1: job level	2: level of education	3: sex	4: age class	5: experien-ce class	6: collect. agreement
1	8.4	7.5–10.4	-	4.2–11.7	7.3–10.6	7.0–14.5	7.4–10.5	7.5–10.0
2	6.2	5.9– 6.3	5.3–8.7b)	-	5.7– 6.5	5.3– 7.4	5.0– 6.5	5.6– 6.3
3	13.8	13.9	11.8–16.7	12.7–13.9	-	12.6–14.5	13.2–13.9	13.5–14.0
4	4.5	3.6– 4.6	3.7– 8.7	3.8– 5.4	3.7– 5.1	-	.0– 4.6	3.1– 4.6
5	.65	.46– .67	.45– .83	.26– .68	.46– .67	-.67– .68	-	.3– .67
6	3.6	3.4	3.2– 4.2	3.0– 3.7	3.3– 3.7	2.4– 3.8	2.5– 3.7	-

a) The numbers of the variables x correspond to the numbers heading the columns
b) A minimum effect of 0.9 occurs at job level 9 for the difference between education levels 6 and 7. This is an exceptional outlyer

Table 14. Marginal earnings effect of job level (%), by level of education

job level (change)	level of education:						
	1	2	3	4	5	6	7
1 → 2	9.115	8.346	7.931	7.291	7.323	7.415	7.288
2 → 3	8.303	7.645	7.241	7.387	7.377	7.278	7.544
3 → 4	7.409	7.271	7.419	7.323	7.321	7.726	8.218
4 → 5	7.337	7.410	7.283	7.423	7.918	8.339	8.670
5 → 6	7.367	7.282	7.577	8.096	8.438	8.904	10.220
6 → 7	7.336	7.763	8.244	8.547	9.262	10.820	11.730
7 → 8	7.954	8.359	8.707	9.750	11.350	11.510	10.700
8 → 9	8.457	8.964	10.340	11.680	11.080	11.190	4.193

dependent of the other variables. The effect of education is similar: varying with job level, but rather uniform across the other variables. The age effect interacts with job level and experience, but not with education, sex or collective agreement. Experience interacts substantially with age class. Job level effects fluctuate most with education and age.

We may conclude first of all that job level is an important variable for understanding earnings differentials. Its contribution is statistically highly significant and it is responsible for substantial interaction effects with other variables. In fact, for inter-action effects it is the single most important variable. Aside from job level effects, the marginal earnings effects of education, sex and collective agreement are fairly uni-form. For the other two variables, age and experience, only the mutual interaction is substantial.

Since one may conclude that the interaction between job level and education is certainly the most important interaction, detailed results are given in Table 14. The table clearly illustrates the non-linearity. The effect of job level is markedly U-shaped at the lowest levels of education, but is tilted at higher education levels. Across levels of education, the marginal effects of job level tend to decrease at the lower job levels, and tend to increase at the higher job levels. Such a pattern is too complicated for an additive, linear specification.

9 Conclusion

This paper has applied a new nonparametric method for estimating and testing a non-linear regression equation with discrete explanatory variables to estimating and testing an earnings function on 2,000 individual observations for The Netherlands. The empirical work stresses the importance of job level for understanding earnings dif-ferentials. The variable makes a statistically significant contribution to earnings vari-ance, and has important interaction effects with other variables, in particular with education. With education as perhaps the most important single grading variable for individuals and job level the single most important grading variable of jobs, the results thus demonstrate that earnings differentials are shaped by the matching process of in-dividuals to jobs. The reward for an individual's characteristics (education, in particular) depends on the assigned job level, and the marginal earnings effect of increasing job levels depends on the individual's characteristics. The implicit prices of these variables are not equalized throughout the labor market.

References

Bartik TJ (1987) The estimation of demand parameters in hedonic models. Journal of Political Economy 95:81–88

Bierens HJ (1982) Consistent model specification tests. Journal of Econometrics 20:105–134

Bierens HJ, Hartog J (1988) Non-linear regression with discrete explanatory variables, with an application to the earnings function. Journal of Econometrics 38:269–299

C.B.S. (1979) Loonstructuuronderzoek 1979. Centraal Bureau voor de Statistiek, 's-Gravenhage

C.B.S. (1980) Statistisch Zakboek 1980. Centraal Bureau voor de Statistiek, 's-Gravenhage

Chung KL (1974) A course in probability theory. Academic Press, New York London

Epple D (1987) Hedonic prices and implicit markets: estimating demand and supply functions for differentiated products. Journal of Political Economy 95:59–80

Forsythe GF (1957) Generation and use of orthogonal polynomials for data-fitting with digital computer. J Soc Industr Appl Math 5:74–87

Hartog J (1981) Personal income distribution: a multicapability theory. Martinus Nijhoff, Boston

Hartog J (1985) Earnings functions: testing for the demand side. Economics Letters 19:281–285

Hartog J (1986a) Earnings functions: beyond human capital. Applied Economics 18:1291–1310

Hartog J (1986b) Allocation and the earnings function. Empirical Economics 11:97–110

Rosen S (1974) Hedonic prices and implicit markets: produduct differentiation in pure competition, Journal of Political Economy 82:34–55

Seber GAF (1977) Linear regression analysis. John Wiley, New York

White H (1980) Using least squares to approximate unknown regression functions. International Economic Review 21:149–170

Software Release Announcement
IAS-SYSTEM & IAS/PC Level IAS-3.7
Econometric and Modelling Software

- IAS/PC Level IAS-3.7 is available now (requires DOS 2.11 or higher and arithmetic coprocessor)

- IAS-SYSTEM Level IAS-3.7 is available on selected main frames and minis (UNIX-machines) and will be implemented on all main stream hardware by April 1989.

- Users with need for a main frame and microcomputer version of the system are pleased that the command structure, features and data file organizations are the same in both systems. IAS/PC can be used independently of the main frame version.

- Features include
  o Data base management
  o Arithmetic and logical processing
  o Estimation of econometric models (some 20 different estimators)
  o Seasonal adjustment
  o Estimation of time series models
  o Model solution, simulation and forecasting
  o Report generation and data display
  o Econometric tests and diagnostic checks (more than 40)
  o Detailed HELP procedure
  o Log files of user input and system output

For more information contact:

Institute for Advanced Studies
Project IAS-SYSTEM
Attn.: Klaus Plasser

Stumpergasse 56
A-1060 Wien, Austria
EUROPE

Tel. +43-1-599-91-126

In North America contact:

GLIMPSE Econometrics
Project IAS-SYSTEM
Attn.: Warren Glimpse

1101 King Street
Suite 601
Alexandria, VA 22314
USA
Tel. (703) 892-8801

Measurement in Economics

Theory and Applications of Economic Indices

Edited by
Wolfgang Eichhorn

1988. 44 figures. XII,
831 pages. Hard cover DM 148,–.
ISBN 3-7908-0387-1

In Cooperation with
W. Erwin Diewert, Susanne Fuchs-Seliger, Helmut Funke, Wilhelm Gehrig, Andreas Pfingsten, Klaus Spremann, Frank Stehling, Joachim Voeller

This book describes the state-of-the-art in measurement in economics. It offers an overview of significant new results on the subject. In 51 reviewed contributions, 62 authors present a broad range of topics on the subject.

The book is divided into nine parts with the headings: Methodology and Methods (4 papers), Prices (9), Efficiency (5), Preferences (7), Quality (2), Inequality (6), Taxation (6), Aggregation (6), and Econometrics (6). The topics range from the 'equation of measurement', a functional equation which plays an important role in the subject, through various approaches to price, efficiency, inequality and tax progression measurement to results on consistency, efficiency and separability in aggregation, productivity measurement, cost functions, allocation inefficiencies, key sector indices, and testing of integrability conditions in econometrics. There are applications to the economies of the U.S.A., Japan and Germany. It contains also papers which deal with preferences, environmental quality and with noxiousness of substances.

Please order through your bookseller or from Physica-Verlag, c/o Springer GmbH & Co., Auslieferungs-Gesellschaft, Haberstr. 7, D-6900 Heidelberg-Rohrbach, FRG